The Journal of an Exile ...

by Thomas Alexander Boswell

Address:
HardPress
8345 NW 66TH ST #2561
MIAMI FL 33166-2626
USA
Email: info@hardpress.net

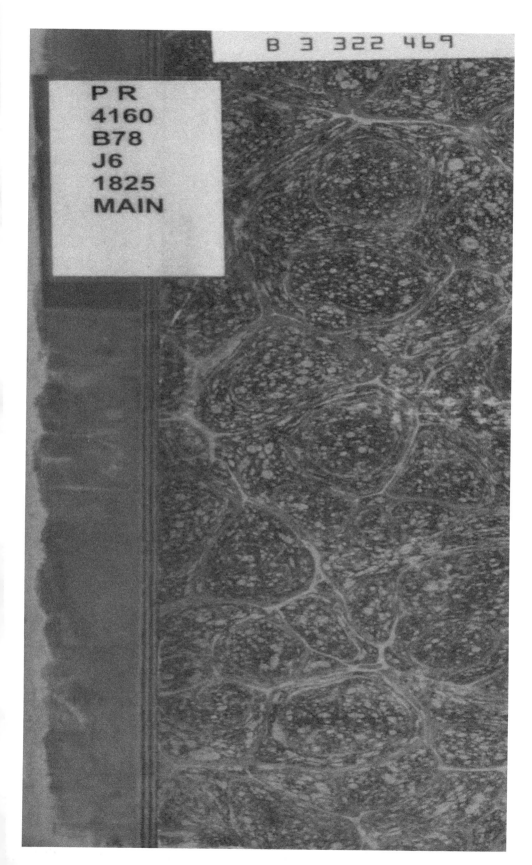

C. Williams Wynn

Williams Wynn

[T A Bonner]

illianus hogan

THE

JOURNAL

OF

AN EXILE.

IN TWO VOLUMES.

VOL. I.

LONDON:

PRINTED FOR SAUNDERS AND OTLEY

BRITISH AND FOREIGN PUBLIC LIBRARY,

CONDUIT-STREET, HANOVER-SQUARE.

1825.

INTRODUCTION.

DURING my residence at Marseilles in th
autumn of 1822, I used often to ramble ou
into the villages which surround that singula
city. Its immediate neighbourhood present
few interesting spots, the suburbs being in
tersected in every direction by stone walls
which enclose the *bastides*, or country-house
of the merchants, and which often prevent on
from gaining some point, apparently near, tha
is thus, perhaps, trebled in its distance. Th
city itself, after one has resided there a shor
time, becomes monotonous and wearisome to th
traveller who possesses no acquaintances with
in it. Its climate, however, is delicious, brigh

skies of eternal blue and a light breeze generally prevailing during the Autumn and Winter for days and weeks together. But these are best enjoyed beyond the city walls, and consequently I used to spend much of my time in wandering over the country, which consists chiefly of mountains, with the exception of the plain on which Marseilles is situated, and which spreads to some distance along the coast. Numerous villages are scattered up and down it, and extend up the mountains, which command a noble view of the sea and surrounding country. I had prolonged my walk one day as far as the small hamlet of St. Joseph, where the ex-director Barras, one of the *exeunt omnes* of the French revolutionary tragedy, had a chateau: this still exists, but belongs to another proprietor. A terrace runs along its front, above a garden filled with flowers; and I wondered how any one, possessed of such a place, could have quitted it for the wars and tempests of political life. A vineyard lay close to the chateau, and, tempted by some mellow grapes which hung clustering among the dark red vine leaves, I entered, and advanced towards the *vignerons*, who were engaged in plucking the fruit. The person who seemed to superintend the others, immediately came up to me, saluted me with much civility, and desired me to help myself unsparingly. He seemed a hearty honest fellow, and with his *vignerons* presently struck up a song in praise of the joys of Autumn, the burthen of which ran thus :

> " Vive la saison de l'Automne,
>   Ami c'est le soir d'un beau jour,
>   Que Bacchus, Amour, et Pomone,
>   Viennent embellir tour-à-tour."

I sat down at the foot of a peach-tree, many of which were planted among the vines, and contemplated the prospect before me. Beneath ne lay a dark wood of pines, mixing their black ops with the fresh verdure of the laurel and wild shrubs which clothed a cluster of broken rocks. To my right lay the rich vineyards, ending along the feet of the brown and arid mountains which reared themselves from the plain, and terminated in vast rugged peaks. From among the rocks and pines which were beneath me, rose up one crag loftier than the rest, upon which was a hermitage cut out of the solid stone. To my left lay the city, looking like a huge quarry, without a spire or turret to relieve the white mass of building. The plain, glittering with its innumerable *bastides*, extended, as I have already mentioned, to some distance, and was then terminated by the same sullen looking mountains that rose to the right : while in front, and stretching far away in blue and sparkling pride, lay that bright sea which bathes so many sacred lands. I sank into a delicious state of dreaming and forgetfulness of all around

me, and remained looking upon those waves whicl
recall so many interesting and impressive event:
to the mind. While buried in the pleasin;
visions which my imagination had been suggest
ing to me, it seemed as if solemn and swee
harmony was gradually stealing around me ; th
sounds increased, and appeared to be no fancifu
dream, for they were evidently approaching. :
had sat so long, that the day was nearly spen1
The sun had sunk behind the islands which li
at some distance from the harbour, and whicl
rose up from the still blue sea in dark relie
against the glowing sky. The breeze, which ha
played over my head among the leaves of th
peach-tree, had subsided ; the air was filled witl
mountain perfume, and the tinkling bells o
the goats, which were returning from pasture
mingled their ringing with the advancin;
voices. The persons from whom they pro
ceeded emerged from the wood, and wouno
round the foot of the eminence upon whicl

I had been sitting. They composed a funeral procession, and I joined them. First came one of the Grey Penitents, carrying a rough cross of dark wood ; a priest followed, preceding the body, which was wrapped in a white sheet, with the pale face uncovered, and reposing on an open bier*, supported by four of the same order of Penitents, who were clothed from head to foot in a long grey robe: their faces were completely concealed by it, there being only sufficient apertures left for seeing and breathing. The procession was closed by a number of male and female peasants, each carrying a small wax-taper in one hand, and a prayer-book in the other. As we advanced towards the church, the priest at intervals murmured a prayer; when he ceased, the followers chanted the *de profundis*, or hymn for the

---

* In the Southern countries of Europe, it is the custom to bury the dead without coffin, and with the features unconcealed ; in Spain, the corpse is generally dressed as a Franciscan friar.

dead ; while the pauses were filled up by th
distant whispering of the sea and the toll o
the passing-bell. We soon reached the ceme
tery : the grave was at the furthest end, look
ing towards the north-west, shaded by a fig
tree, and surrounded by tufts of wild thym
and rosemary. The body was taken from th
bier and lowered into the earth, while th
assistants and myself knelt around, and onc
more chanted the farewell hymn. The sigh
of the corpse was affecting, nay, appalling
One might almost have imagined that som
sleeper had been cautiously taken from hi
pillow, and treacherously hurried into a livin
grave. As we rose up to depart, the sexto
began to perform his office ; the dark moul
gradually mingled itself with the winding
sheet, while the clasped white fingers and tran
quil features appeared here and there throug
the fast-increasing heap. Thus it is that we ar
indeed but dust ; thus do we return to that fron

which we are made: in a few weeks those
eyes that had beamed and wept—those lips that
had charmed in health and life, and prayed in
sickness and agony, would be all black and
crumbling as the earth which covered them.
As we returned, I observed my friend, the
vigneron, among the peasants who had assisted
at the funeral.   He was evidently distressed,
and leading a little boy by the hand, who wept
bitterly.   Having recognized me, however, he
came up to me, and said, " Ah ! Sir, this has been
a sorrowful sight for you, and for us all,—for we
all loved him.   I did not tell you about this
in the morning, for I did not wish to make you
sad, and to send you back to the gay city
with mournful thoughts.   But since you have
seen it, you will be sorry to hear that we
have just buried a young countryman of yours."
" And had he no friend or relation," said I, "to
attend his remains to the grave ?" " None, Sir,
none, but we poor villagers, and we were all his

friends, for he was ours, and may God rest his soul! He came here last autumn, ill and melancholy;—he lived in a small house just above the olive-wood to your right, and there he died, Ave Maria! beloved and regretted by the whole village. After he had been here a little while, he seemed to recover gradually from his sorrow; went often into the city, and sometimes brought back a friend with him, but at times he was still very unhappy. He had taken my little boy here under his care, and was teaching him to write and speak English; but the child used to say, that he had often seen him praying, as if in great pain. But after a letter, which, as his servant told me since, he received from his country, he never went into the city again, and seemed to be quite indifferent to every thing. From that time, Sir, he gradually wasted, but always spoke kindly to all around him, and made many a heart happy by his assistance and advice. He used to wander out

o a rock just below the hermitage you might
have seen yonder, and sit there for hours
looking over the sea; and one night his servant became alarmed at his not returning,
and went to seek him. He found him seated
at the foot of a fig-tree, resting against its
trunk. The servant remonstrated with him
on his exposing himself so to the night air.
His master answered not; alas! Sir, he could
not, — he was dead! His prayer-book was
firmly clasped in his hands; by his side
was a roll of papers; and his face was as
smiling and tranquil as it used to be when he
visited our cottages. In his will, which was
found in his chamber, he bequeathed the money he had, among us peasants, and earnestly
begged that his prayer-book might be buried
as it was found—in his hands. I looked into
the book, Sir, and in the blank leaf was
the portrait of a young lady, with the mild-
est and loveliest of faces; and I thought that

if the poor gentleman had lost the beautiful
lady by death or disappointment, no wonder he
was so sad. His wishes were all fulfilled; and
the roll of papers is in my possession." I felt an
inclination, at the moment, to ask him for them;
but reflecting that, our acquaintance being but
short, he might be unwilling to give them up,
I resolved upon repeating my visit to St. Joseph; and hoped, after a short time, to obtain
them. I then retraced my steps to the city,
musing upon the melancholy fate of my countryman. Before I left Marseilles, I went out
again several times to St. Joseph, and visited
the young man's grave; it was kept in neat
order, and covered with fresh vine-leaves and
flowers. This was my friend the *vigneron's*
doing; and I then saw his little boy come to
throw fresh flowers upon the grave. I carried
with me various things from the city that might
make me welcome at the *vigneron's* cottage, and
became soon upon intimate terms with the family

One day the conversation happened to turn upon the melancholy event to which I had been witness, and I took occasion to express a desire to see the papers. The *vigneron* immediately went up stairs, brought down a considerable bundle, apparently in great confusion, and presented them to me, saying, "You are his countryman, Sir, and can make more use of them than I can. I could not bear to destroy them, and yet the sight of them makes me sad. Take them, and if the poor gentleman has been telling his life in them, I dare say they will be worth your while to read." I received the papers, and, being anxious to examine them, soon returned home. They were written in a very illegible hand, much mutilated and blotted. I succeeded, however, with great difficulty, in putting them into some kind of order, and for convenience sake divided the successive portions into chapters : the examination of them having induced me to think that they would interest others as well as myself. I quitted Marseilles, taking a kinc leave of my friend the *vigneron*, and re mained upon the Continent till very lately.

I now, therefore, submit these papers to the public; and making use of the old adage, *d mortuis nil nisi bonum*, I shall beg them to understand the proverb in a sense that will be felt by many persons,—that the dead leave nothing but what is good.

JOURNAL.

CHAPTER I.

Oct. 27, 1821.

AGAIN am I returned to these well-known
scenes, but, alas ! they are not the same to me
hat they once were : then I had hope and
health, and now both are nearly passed away.
Why am I come here ? and what can change of
place do for me ? And yet these soft breezes and
green olive woods breathe more peace to my

wounded spirit, than the choking fogs and frosts of England.

England! thou art my country, but thou hast nought for me but green fields and trees and strange faces. Thy waters may sparkle, but not for me; thy bright shores may welcome back the traveller, but not me,—for I have no home. I cannot look along a path and say, That leads to my fire-side, and there dwell those that love me dearly. Alas! no. The bark that bore me away, carried with it no prayer for my final return, and the winds that whistled amongst its sails made no heart quail at the thought of my peril. I am alone, an outcast, an exile; and should I talk of hope and joy, which cannot be for him that has none to share them!

Oct. 28th.— I walked into the city to-day. The tumult and activity which reign there, have only increased my depression. I arrived just as they were launching a frigate.

The launch was a noble sight; but the harbour
s so unfit for vessels of this large description
hat they were unable to stop her when in the
vater, and she rushed across with headlong
apidity, upsetting whatever was in her way;
naking the surrounding vessels rock as in a
empest. One man, a waterman, lost his life
midst the waving of hundreds of flags—the
houting of thousands of voices:—his cry, too,
ose up, but it was short, and soon past. Thus
. is, while the multitude are rejoicing and
appy, there are some who are pining un-
narked in misery and anguish.

The yellow fever is at Barcelona. Appre-
ensions are entertained of its communicating
self to this place. Several vessels at the Islands
re infected, and the fever is in the Lazaretto.
iod forbid and avert such a calamity from this
ity! it has already suffered enough from a like
isitation. The precautions are increasing on
very side, and all communication forbidden

with the coast of Spain under pain of death. But the infection may be introduced by smugglers,—horrible idea !

As I was returning home, I overtook a peasant driving some mules laden with chesnuts, which he had been buying at the market. The peasants make great use of this fruit in winter, roasting it, and eating it as bread. As we ascended the long road called the Vista, an interesting scene presented itself. A vast heap of dark clouds were piled up over the sea, and the sun was just setting behind them ;—as it rested for an instant upon their edge, one might have compared it to an immense flaming beacon kindled upon the gloomy Pyrenees, (in the direction of which the sun was sinking,) and warning the homeward bound vessel from the pestilential shore. The road was crowded with peasants, and their mules were straggling along in strange confusion. The man whom I have just mentioned, and who was at some distance behind the rest, wished me a good night, and I entered into conversation with

him. I found his language singularly good
and I almost imagined myself conversing with
one of the *jongleurs,* or inferior poets of Pro
vence. We talked of the beauty of the even
ing and the richness of the view ; " Look," said
he to me, pointing to the dark wood of pines
which extended to the rocks near us, and which
mixed with the laurels, seemed green as summer
woods, "*Ecco la più bella roba di natura.*" And
when I talked to him of his labour and his
vineyard, for I found that he was the proprietor
of one, he told me that he was always stirring
prima che il sole sorta di letto. We continued
our route together, and he conducted me by
another road home, which wound among rocks
covered with pines and wild herbs, upon one of
which was placed a hermitage. As we passed
on, we occasionally caught a glimpse, over the
trees, of the sea flashing like lightning. The
night closed upon us as we reached St. Joseph
and quitting the peasant, I retreated to my soli
tude and my reflections.

*   *   *

Eleven o'clock; the night is lovely; the bright stars are shining upon the dark world beneath, and bidding us hope for a fair morrow.

> " Who ever gazed upon them shining
> Nor turn'd to earth without repining ?"

Whenever I look upon them I feel myself better and happier. They are, perhaps, the habitations of those blessed spirits who have passed through the fire of temptation untainted and unscorched, and who are permitted to offer up their intercession for their weak and sinful kindred upon earth.   *   *   *

The city clocks are striking the hour of midnight. That city, which was so lately filled with tumult and pleasure, and resounded with the hasty tread of business, is now still and slumbering, while I am restless and sleepless; the deep voices of those bells alone, tell that man's habitation is there, and that while he sleeps time wakes. And hark! there is the distant murmuring of the guards, who are stationed to protect us from infection. If those men too slept, that city which now rests in peace and health, might ere long be filled with delirium and despair. But there is One that sleepeth not, and whose eye doth not cease its watching.

*　　*　　*

The light morning breeze is whispering among the pines; and those beautiful lines of Tasso, in which he describes Rinaldo lamenting over the errors of his past life, rise to my recollection

" Così pensando, alle più eccelse cime
　　Ascese; e quivi inchino e riverente
　　Alzò il pensier sovra ogni ciel sublime,
　　E le luci fissò nell' oriente :
　　La prima vita e le mie colpe prime
　　Mira con occhio di pietà clemente,
　　Padre e Signor; e in me tua grazia piovi,
　　Sicchè 'l mio vecchio Adam purghi e rinnovi.

"Così pregava: e gli sorgeva a fronte,
　　Fatta già d' auro, la vermiglia aurora,
　　Che l'elmo e l'arme, e intorno a lui del monte
　　Le verdi cime illuminando indora

E ventilar nel petto e nella fronte
Sentia gli spirti di piacevol ora,
Che sovra il capo suo scotea dal grembo
Della bell' Alba un rugiadoso nembo."

The day begins to dawn; ambition, hope,
and pleasure will soon be awake and in motion.
The busy hum of the city will overpower the
low dashing of the waves, and the dreams and
thoughts of the night will be forgotten by noon.
The East begins to glow, the stars grow fainter,
man begins to be afoot; I hear the distant bells of
the mules, the morning gun is fired, the chain
is raised, the fishermen are crowding out of the
harbour, the peasants are in their fields. The
sun is rising above that bare point of rock that
looks as if it would intercept its light;—now it
looks out upon the plain, and throws a roseate
glow over the thin mists which are spread
round the mountains like a veil,—the plain
looks like a white and restless sea. And canst
thou not impart warmth to me, bright light?

thou givest life and strength and promise to
the vine, the olive, and the springing flower;
and must the morning ever find me sleepless, cold
at heart, and unrefreshed by the dew of hope?

29th. When I returned to my house this
morning, I found my friend, the peasant, with
whom I had walked back yesterday. He had
come to enquire for me, and had brought me
some fine fruit, which he begged I would accept.
His kindness touched me to the heart, as indeed all kindness does now, for I need it. He
told me that the vintage fête was to take
place shortly, and begged that I would honour
it with my attendance. "We are but poor and
ignorant," said he, "but we know how to be kind
as well as the fine Parisians ; and though some
think us brutal, and though our southern blood
may be hot and hasty, yet we can give a
stranger the warmer welcome." I promised to
go to the fête, and he went away.

E ventilar nel petto e nella fronte

Sentia gli spirti di piacevol ora,

Che sovra il capo suo scotea dal grembo

Della bell' Alba un rugiadoso nembo."

The day begins to dawn; ambition, hope, and pleasure will soon be awake and in motion. The busy hum of the city will overpower the low dashing of the waves, and the dreams and thoughts of the night will be forgotten by noon. The East begins to glow, the stars grow fainter, man begins to be afoot; I hear the distant bells of the mules, the morning gun is fired, the chain is raised, the fishermen are crowding out of the harbour, the peasants are in their fields. The sun is rising above that bare point of rock that looks as if it would intercept its light;—now it looks out upon the plain, and throws a roseate glow over the thin mists which are spread round the mountains like a veil,—the plain looks like a white and restless sea. And canst thou not impart warmth to me, bright light?

that givest life and strength and promise to the vine, the olive, and the springing flower, and let the morning ever find me sleepless cold of heart, and unrefreshed by the dews of ...

29th. When I returned to my house this morning, I found my friend, the peasant, with whom I had walked back yesterday. He had come to enquire for me, and had brought me some fine fruit, which he begged I would accept. His kindness touched me to the heart, as in ... feel all kindness does now, for I need it. He told me that the vintage fête was to take place shortly, and begged that I would honour ... with my attendance. "We are but poor and ignorant," said he, "but we know how to be kind as well as the fine Parisians; and though some think us brutal, and though our southern blood may be hot and hasty, yet we can give a stranger the warmer welcome." I promised to go to the fête, and he went away.

he wild herbs
t he has chosen
y calculated for
ould toil and la-
the contempla-
neighbours but
he fig, the olive,
rom the sun; and
and lavender are
From the top of
city, whose cares
look down with
vanities which he

en, and then pro-
Having arrived
took off my hat
o crossed himself
n, and invited me
interior was rude
table, a few chairs,

CHAPTER II.

I PROPOSE walking this morning to the l
mitage, which is in view of my house.   1
hermit, I am told, was once well known
Marseilles, but has long dwelt in his ro
retreat.   *   *   *

                *   *   *

Evening, ten o'clock, I am just returned fr
the hermitage.   The path to it creeps among
wild and wooded cliffs, and, gradually ascendi
loses itself in a thick wood of pines and l
rel, till it reaches the foot of the crag on wh
the hermit lives.   His habitation is hollow
out of the rock, in which are cut some hc
to give light and air.   I looked up, and saw t
peasants kneeling at the entrance.   The heri
was within, praying before a crucifix: and so

rabbits were playing among the wild herb which grew around. The spot he has chose for his retirement is admirably calculated fo such a purpose. No one would toil and la bour up the steep ascent, but the contempla tive and pious; and he has no neighbours bu wild birds and animals. The fig, the olive and almond trees shade him from the sun; anc mountain thyme, rosemary, and lavender ar the flowers of his garden. From the top o the rock he may behold that city, whose care cannot reach him, and may look down witl pity upon those pomps and vanities which he has utterly renounced.

I waited till they had risen, and then pro- ceeded to ascend the rock. Having arrived at the door of the cell, I took off my hat and saluted the hermit, who crossed himself as he returned my salutation, and invited me to enter, which I did. The interior was rude and bare; a small crucifix, a table, a few chairs, and a low bed of straw, forming all its furniture. On the table stood a basket filled with fruit, and beside it a loaf of brown bread. "You are just come in time to partake of my breakfast, Sir," said the old man to me : "these good people never neglect me, be the sun ever so hot, or the tempest ever so loud. God has filled their hearts with the best of riches, charity and kindness." "My father," said the male peasant, who was the husband of the other, "if it had not been for you, we should now be poor and miserable ; my dear Annette might be a beggar, and I still a slave at Algiers." His wife shuddered, and burst into tears. "Enough! enough of this, my children," said the hermit, "I have but done what the good God commands all to do—to succour the afflicted ; and if I have preserved a fellow creature from captivity, I was but the instrument of a higher power. Go in peace, my blessing go with you! and don't forget to pray daily as I have directed you." The peasants kissed the

good man's hands, and silently descended the
rock. A pause of some moments ensued, which
was broken by the hermit's saying, " Come, Sir,
you have had a long walk, some of this ripe
fruit will restore you, for you do not seem able
to bear much fatigue." " Father," said I, " I
have borne and suffered much, and my mind
and body are weakened and shaken, but I may
now perhaps enjoy some peace. The tranquillity and beauty of this place may soothe my
restless thoughts." " Alas! my son," said the old
man, " have you too then, so soon, and so young,
acquired the experience of sorrow ? Would that I
could take your griefs upon myself!—for I am
old, and ready to drop away, and I know what
tears are. But God's will be done! sorrow is
often the means of weaning the heart from many
a vice and vanity, and of making the sufferer fit
for a more peaceful and kinder world. Some day
I will tell you of myself—of my disappointments
and afflictions, but not now. You are weak and

depressed. Cheer up, my son; eat, and be comforted. You cannot yet have been very guilty;
and if your grief be that of disappointed and
withered feelings, and your tears those only
of a broken and affectionate heart, reflect that
soon they will be all wiped away, and pray for
those who may have injured you." "Father,"
said I, " my sorrows have been indeed early, but
not less bitter. Blinded by youthful and mistaken notions, I turned a deaf ear to the voice
of experience; but I am punished: and experience has revenged herself upon my neglect, by
prematurely overshadowing my youth. I sought
for unreal and visionary happiness, and I am
now for ever deprived of all true comfort in this
life. Pardon me, pardon me, my good father;
but your words have awakened thoughts which
turn my blood to fire; which gnaw me for
ever, and which must wear me out. I strove
hard to forget them. I am come here to other
sights and other scenes, and the hope of pass-

ing the rest of my life, at least, in som
tranquillity; but the recollection of those thing
that have driven me from my country is yet to
recent." The good hermit insisted upon m
tasting his fruit; and going out, returned witl
some clear water, from a spring which ra
murmuring down the side of the rock.

If I could ever know peace again, it would b
in a spot like that; and I have not for a lon
time felt so calm as I did when seated at th
hermit's table, and sharing his simple meal
Indeed the tranquil and calm life that
lead here, the warmth and beauty of the cli
mate, and the absence of things and person
which were perpetually bringing bitter thought
to my mind, have begun to soothe and lull m
agony; and the remembrance of other day
may, perhaps, be hushed to temporary sleep.

The sea, which we saw from the cell, wa
sprinkled with vessels, whose white sails wer
swelling in the breeze, and wafting them t

their destined port.   Perhaps, some were going
to England—to that land which contains so
many blessings, though none for me.   Perhaps some one on their decks belonged to that
dear spot where for a few days I forgot my fate.
Perhaps he might see, might speak to that being
whose name is ever mingled with my prayers.
I was roused from these reflections by the old
man, who said, " Look out, Sir, and see what a
glorious day ! let us be grateful for it, and enjoy
it.   There are many sweet paths around my
cell; let us go forth."   We rose, and quitting
the cell, descended the rock by the opposite side
to that by which I had ascended.   When we
had gone some way down, and had entered the
wood, we came suddenly upon a small stone edifice, that looked like a chapel ; it was enclosed
by a railing, and surrounded by a small garden,
containing fresh plants and flowers.   The building was of white marble, quite plain, and crown-
ed by a cross ; under which was an inscription
in Latin, taken from the well-known hymn.

" Tuba mirum spargens sonum
Per sepulchra regionum
Coget omnes ante thronum."

The hermit knelt down before the tomb, fo
such, from the inscription, I now concluded i
to be, and continued in earnest prayer for som
minutes. I also knelt, as a tomb could be n
indifferent object to me. As we rose up, the ol
man slowly shook his head, and crossed himself
and taking hold of my arm, we continued ou
walk through the wood. " Some day," said he
" I will explain to you what you have seen, bu
you are not now in a state of mind to liste
calmly, and derive the profit from my story
wish. Let us walk to the next village, of S1
Cannat. It is now the hour when the peasant
are reposing from labour, and refreshing them
selves ;"—and as the hermit was speaking, th
village church bell tolled the Angelus.* " Yo

* This is the name given to a bell which is tolle

can see the church through the trees," said the hermit; "it is there we are going: and hark, there is some festival, for I hear singing and music." We presently emerged from the wood, and the village of St. Cannat lay straight before us, at a short distance, amidst a rich plain of vineyard. Several peasants seeing us approach, ran to meet us, and seemed delighted in welcoming the good old man. "Good day, good day, my children," said he, "I have brought this young stranger with me to share in your rejoicing, for we heard the sounds of gaiety as we came through the wood." "Yes, father," said a young female peasant, "my dearest brother that we all thought lost and drowned in the sea, came home last night, and we are all so delighted—are we not, Claire?" turning to a

every day at twelve, and during the tolling of which, in the more religious provinces, many of the peasants cross hemselves, and repeat their Ave and their Pater.

pretty young creature who was standing near
her. Claire blushed, and shrunk back among
the other peasants, who smiled and exchanged
significant glances. We all proceeded to the
village, which we found in complete confusion.
The young man whose return had caused all
this joy, was leading his mother, who was quite
blind, along the narrow street which ran up
to a rising ground planted with walnut-trees.
When they had reached it, he placed her carefully in a chair, but did not quit her side. She
still kept his hand firmly clasped in her own,
and seemed determined that the waves should
not recover their rescued prey. The rest of
the village were all assembled on the same spot,
and the hermit going up to the old woman
asked her how she did? " Well, very well,
father, God be praised!" said she; "it is long
since I have felt so happy as I am now. And
yet my heart is not easy. Look at my brave
dutiful boy; alas! I cannot.—Tell me, good

c 5

father, is he not thinner and wanner than he was? They tell me that he is the same, and he chides me for not believing them; but somehow or other a mother's heart—ay, even a blind mother's heart, can never be deceived, and I am sure he has suffered and wasted. Tell me, father, is it not so?" It was indeed. The poor young man seemed only returned to his native vineyards to die among them; and the mother's heart spoke too truly. The good old hermit endeavoured to tranquillize her; and the other peasants had been so delighted and surprised at his unexpected return, that they had not been struck by his wasted appearance. But Claire, I think, had, though she would not perhaps confess it to herself; and the old peasant hearing her voice, called her and bade her sit by her side. "My dear little Claire," said she, "did they say true when they told me that you never smiled after you heard of Auguste's death? or have you quite forgotten my poor boy?" "Oh! my good mother," said Claire blushing and glancing from under her large hat at Auguste, who stood leaning on his mother's chair; "you make me smile *now*, and you are making Auguste smile too;—but yet," said she to herself in a low tone, "that smile is not what it used to be; he certainly is thinner and paler than he used to be;—but no! he is only fatigued.—Come, dear mother, let me take care of you, and Auguste will go and entertain our friend the hermit, and the stranger he has brought with him." "Go, Auguste," said his mother, "bring out some of our best wine; pretty Claire will stay by her mother and yours." The two lovers exchanged glances, and such glances that they made my own heart throb with bitter recollections. The young man invited us to sit down at a large table which was spread under the trees and covered with fruit and pitchers of wine. But his thoughts were not with us : they went with his eyes, which were every moment cast towards his mother and her companion. Claire too appeared to regard the table rather oftener than necessity required. But when I looked again at the young man, my heart bled, to think that his hopes would never be realized. Death was written in his features, and it was a strong instance of the intoxication of joy that none of the other peasants seemed to perceive it ; nay, perhaps he himself knew it not, and was forming sweet projects of bliss and comfort.

In the mean time the party began to give evident proof that wine gladdens the heart. They proposed a song—one of them, who seemed to be considered the Orpheus of the village, struck up some rude couplets, of which the following may give an idea :—

" Let Burgundy * boast of her far-famed vine
  That round Chambertin's trellices clings ;

-----

* The favourite wine of Louis XIV. and Buonaparte.

But while we can make and then drink our own wine
 A fig for the liquor of Kings!
Then drink, boys, a toast—May the vine of Provence
 For ever be fruitful and green,
Vive le roi, vive la gloire, vive l'amour, et la France,
 And Marseilles of all cities the queen!"

A shout of applause followed this exhibition of vocal talent, and the hermit took the opportunity of rising and proposing to me to depart. "Be temperate," said he to them, "and God will crown your labours; but turn not the plentiful blessings he bestows to a vile use." His words had an instantaneous effect upon the peasants, who proposed accompanying us. We wished the old mother good night, and the whole party broke up, Claire and Auguste each leading their charge back to the cottage. Happy Auguste! happy even in death; for thou wilt die in the arms of love and affection, while I   *   *   *

I took leave of the hermit at his cell, and promised to visit him shortly.

CHAPTER III.

My servant has just brought me a letter from England : I have almost ceased to wish for any ; they cannot change or lighten my fate ; and may increase its bitterness, by telling me of things which awaken thoughts that I now try to banish. Matters are in the same state, and my name seems to be forgotten except by the person who writes. Be it so. I have forgotten England, and all its pleasures, for it had none for me ; and why should it waste a thought on me ? Nay ; that being whose eyes, like those of a picture, seem ever looking upon me—she too has probably utterly forgotten me. That idea is, indeed, bitter. My God ! what a mysterious and unaccountable fate is mine ! How have I already suffered ! and what wild and

desperate thoughts have at times taken pos
session of my mind ! But now I begin to fee
calmer, and to interest myself at least for a time
in other things and thoughts.

* * *

Midnight. I have been reading a melancholy
history, ending fatally and darkly.

* * *

I am now somewhat calmer. This journa
too affords me distraction and amusement, and
the bright and shining seas before me commu
nicate some of their peacefulness to my mind.

* * *

30th. The weather seems about to change
the clouds portend rain, and I shall be
prisoner. I cannot always read ; my mind is too
restless : besides, books can tell me nothing tha
I wish to know. Nature is now my only study

* * *

The vigneron's little boy has just been here
with some fruit for me. He is a lively little fel-

ow; he called me *"mi lord Moussou Inglise."*
I asked him if he liked fruit himself; he did not
much care for it, was his reply; he had rather
have a little English book. I asked him what
book he meant, and why English; and he told
me that an English family had lived in the
chateau below the wood, and that he used to
go there to play with a little boy about his own
age, who had a great many pretty books, and
one which was about a little boy that became a
great lord, and rode in a beautiful carriage.
And then he ran on telling me all the good
things he used to eat at the chateau; and I found
the English cakes and pies had quite gained
his heart. "And did you learn any English
there, my fine fellow?" said I. "A little, a very
little, *mi lord Moussou.*" "And would you like
to learn to write and speak it well?" said I.
"Oh that I should," said the little rogue, "for
then I could go to the city and be a clerk and
write at a high desk in a large book." His

earnest artless manner pleased and interested me ; and I catch at any thing that will excite and impel my feelings into other channels. I told him, if he would come to me in the afternoon, I would try to teach him. At this he thanked me, and, running hastily down the hill, fancied himself, no doubt, already writing at the high desk in the large book. Such is ambition : change but a few circumstances, and this boy might be a future hero or statesman.

"Some mute inglorious Hampden," &c.

* * *

The rain begins to fall, the wind is rising, a dark cloud hangs over the sea, which is no longer blue and smiling as yesterday ; a thick mist has shrouded the mountains, and hidden the cross. * * *

Two o'clock. The rain pours down now in torrents along the hollow path which leads down the hill ; the stream which flows at the foot, is black and swollen, and threatens to burst its banks.   *   *   *

It has burst them : the rain rushes down with increased violence, hurrying every thing away with it, as it pours down the ravine. Sure-ly,——but no ;——yes, I was not mistaken,—— God speed me !   *   *   *

I have been returning thanks to God for having made me the instrument of saving the life of a fellow creature. When I broke off my journal so abruptly, the whole road down from my house, a species of deep, hollow, rocky ravine, was nothing but a black torrent, which, rushing into the stream beneath, had swollen it and formed an irresistible mass of water. On a small spot of ground, which had been isolated by the overflowing of the stream, and was completely cut off from the rest of the valley, or glen, I thought I perceived a human figure. I was not mistaken : it made signs for help. There was no time to be lost :

the waters might increase, and the unaided wretch perish! I rushed out, and having, as well as I could, by a circuitous path, reached the brink of the torrent, I saw on the other side my poor little pupil wringing his hands and calling on his father for assistance. There was no way of reaching him except by leaping over the water: which presented a frightful appearance, for one false step must have been fatal, as its rapidity was such that I must have been hurried along and suffocated. There was, however, a broken fragment of rock that was appearing just above the water, and which seemed by some means or other to have been stopped in its descent. It was sufficiently broad to afford a resting-place, and to break the leap; but it might be in such a position in the water as to require only my slight weight to destroy its equilibrium, and send it headlong down the torrent. There was, however, a chance; and without farther hesitation I leaped across the black abyss. I could feel the rock totter as I lighted upon it; and I had just time to leap to the other side, when, as I had feared, it sunk beneath the water, and was probably hurried off. The poor little fellow clung to me, and seemed to think himself saved; but, alas! how were we to return! Another of the streams had burst its bank; I could hear it coming roaring and rushing on behind us. Just at that moment the father and some peasants appeared on the opposite side. They had been in search of the boy, and came furnished with ropes in case he should have been in any dangerous situation. There was, luckily, a large tree close to the torrent, to which I fastened one end of the rope; which the peasant, after two or three ineffectual attempts, threw me. Then fastening the boy by another rope round my body, I gradually, and with great difficulty, slid across; and we reached the other side in safety, while the spot we had just quitted was instantly covered by a large body of water. The scene that ensued I cannot describe. The child ran alternately from me to his father, embracing us both ; while the father, kneeling down, with tears in his eyes and pale as death, thanked God for his child's life. Then coming to me, he kissed my hands, hoped that God would bless me, and give me all I could wish for. Poor man ! had he known the pang he caused me then :—All that I wish for !—O Heaven ! thou knowest what I *have* wished and prayed for, till all hope and desire to wish were passed. All that I wish for !—these words have waked many a slumbering thought. Gentlest, fairest of beings, what have my sinful wishes not been ! I loved thee, though I dared not tell thee so ; yet I lived in a visionary atmosphere of hope, brighter and purer than the foul and dark reality. But the winter of my fate has clouded over that fair sky; and though thy remembrance still clings to my heart, I am now

hopeless and forsaken.   I could have loved thee
as woman would be loved ; I could have enjoyed the world and all its pleasures with thee ;
for I am no misanthrope.   I scorn not the joys
of others.   I despise not the pursuits and occu-
pations of the happy: I do not rail at Providence, and complain that the world is full of
misery and uncomfortableness : no !   To those
whom experience hath taught wisdom when not
too late,—to those who follow the paths of pleasure and ambition with moderation and honour,
and who have never met with any thing to
make life utterly blank and tasteless—the
world presents innumerable objects of healthy
and virtuous exercise.   But it is for blighted
useless hearts like mine, that the sun has no
warmth, and the rain no moisture.   Oh ! if my
fate had changed its course, how happy I might
have been !   But away with such thoughts ;
they only lead me back over paths that I have
already passed with tears and agony.   And yet

the reflection that I have just saved a whole family from agony is sweet and refreshing to me. Since I cannot find happiness for myself, let me endeavour to make others so. Let me look around; perhaps I may yet derive some interest from the various scenes that are passing near me.   *   *   *

Five o'clock. The rain has ceased. The damage it has done is, I fear, great. But the sky is brightening up, the sea begins to sparkle, the curtain is thrown aside from the mountains. The sun is just breaking through that mist which hung round the hermitage, gilding the cross. I will walk down to the vigneron's cottage, and inquire about my little pupil.

   *   *   *

The evening has turned out delicious. The rain, which was so nearly bringing death to two persons, has softened the air. The wild herbs send forth a richer and fresher perfume, and the wood looks green and rejoicing.

   *   *   *

I found the vigneron's family assembled at supper, consisting of his mother, an old woman near eighty, himself, his wife, the little boy, and a girl about nineteen with black sparkling eyes. The grandmother was seated near the open window, around which clung a luxuriant vine. The setting sun shone full into the cottage, across the old woman, shewing the deep furrows of her aged face more distinctly. The rest of the family immediately surrounded me, and invited me to partake of their supper, which I declined. The vigneron told me that the fête was to take place on the next day but one, and entreated me not to forget my promise ; and the little boy exclaimed that he had rather lie a-bed all day and not see the fête, if I was not there, for it would be no fête. I kissed the little fellow, and wishing them good night, continued my walk.

*   *   *

The rain has made great ravages among the vineyards. Many of the vines are completely washed away, and almost all are drooping and mingled together in wild confusion. The fruit so lately ready to furnish its sweet juice, is now nothing but a crushed and watery skin; and instead of rich ruby clusters, nothing is to be seen but broken poles and scattered sticks and stones, and black water. The peasants, to whom a considerable part of the vineyards belong, were all there, looking with anguish on the disappointment of their hopes. They attempted not to clear away the ruin: it was useless, nothing could be done—their vines, at least, were destroyed. But this, fortunately, was only a small part of the vineyards, and which had happened to be just in the direction of the torrent; for higher up, and far away to the right, the prospect was still promising. One of the peasants seeing me looking on the scene before me with sorrow, came up to me, and said, "This is a sad spectacle, Sir; and some of our poor neighbours must be content with scanty food for a long time. The poor old widow, too, what will she do? she has none to comfort or labour for her now, for her unfortunate son cannot." "What widow? what son?" said I. " Why, Sir, it is a sad story, and if you will do me the honour of going with me to my cottage, and tasting my wine, I will tell you all about it." Not caring to return home, or wander farther, I accepted his proposal.

We reached the cottage ; his wife, as the evening was cold, threw some olive and almond wood on the hearth, and we drew round the fire. The wife took up her knitting; a little girl, their child, placed herself in the chimney, within a small nook, and began to torment a cat which had established itself in the same post ; while the peasant, having drunk to my health, commenced his story. He did not give it, however, precisely in the following words, as his narrative was unconnected and broken in upon by various reflections of his own.

CHAPTER IV.

SOME years ago, and before the peace, the population of a sea-port town and the country round, were hurrying to the principal *place*, to a sight which had not been seen there since the days of Robespierre. In the middle of the *place* rose up a scaffolding, upon which was placed the instrument of modern French punishment. Round it stood a numerous party of gensdarmes, both horse and foot; and others were moving about among the immense crowd which was collected, and endeavouring to preserve order, and to keep them back from pressing towards the scaffolding. Various were the conversations which took place among the

persons who were thus assembled, and numerous
the reflections which were made on the object of
their meeting. But they all seemed grave, and
impressed with the ominous appearance of the
scaffolding.

An increasing anxiety of countenance,
and a confused murmur, which now arose,
gave notice that the unfortunate person for
whom these preparations had been made,
was approaching. Preceded by half a dozen
gensdarmes, and supported on either side by
two of the sisters of charity, walked a young
woman, apparently not more than nineteen ; pale
as the white hoods of the sisters, and seeming to
take no note of all that was passing round her.
The procession was flanked by gensdarmes,
who cleared the way up to the scaffolding.
When they arrived at the foot of the steps
leading up to it, the sisters whispered something
into the young woman's ear, who started and

looked up. She could not grow paler, but the expression of her face became that of the utmost terror—passive and powerless. She kept her eyes fixed on the fatal instrument while she was ascending the steps, and seemed to be perfectly unconscious that she was moving at all. The sisters who had supported her, now knelt down with her before the priest, who held up to them a small white crucifix, which he put to the unhappy girl's lips. Still she appeared almost insensible, and evidently could not have risen without the aid of the sisters, who now proceeded to uncover her neck. The change which at this instant took place in the features of the young woman was remarkable ; she clasped her hands over her neck, apparently for the purpose of preserving a black riband which was tied round it ; and her eyes flashed fire and resistance upon those who were near her. The executioner approached, and was proceeding to remove her hands by force, when she darted to the other side of the scaffolding, and uttered one of the most appalling shrieks which ever came from the lips of the agonized or dying. The air was as still as midnight—not a breath was stirring—not a voice heard. The sun was darting his hottest beams upon the multitude; and the sky was as blue as the sea, which appeared through the end of the street leading down from the *place*. The effect of the poor creature's shriek was withering: it resounded over the *place*, and echoed through the adjoining street, like the cry of some spirit lamenting over the desolation of a ruined city. Some sailors, who were just loosening a vessel from the quay, which was about to proceed upon her voyage, dropped the ropes, and hastily ejaculated a *Paternoster;* while the horse of a gensdarme, who was stationed just outside the crowd, and at the top of the street, plunged and started off with his powerless rider, carrying him directly down towards the port. The immense crowd at one and the same moment crossed themselves, and some even dropped upon their knees. In the mean time, the officer on duty near the scaffolding, gave orders that no farther violence should be used for divesting the criminal of her attire, and that the execution should instantly take place. The executioner accordingly secured his victim, and hurried her to the guillotine. In a moment, the quivering head disappeared, but the hands still remained clasped in the same position as before. There was a deep pause; when, suddenly, an indistinct sound arose in another quarter of the town, and presently a horse was heard (so still were the spectators) clattering with the most furious speed towards the *place*. Not above five minutes had elapsed since the fatal axe had descended, when a horseman, scarcely able to retain his seat, pale as death, bareheaded, and his face covered with sweat and dust, rode in among the crowd. His eyes were wildly directed towards the scaffolding, he held up in his hand a sealed packet, and the word 'pardon' passed from mouth to mouth among the crowd, who all made way for him. He still seemed to be ignorant that all was over, for he ceased not to shout as loud as his fatigue and hoarseness would allow him, " Stop ! for the living God's sake, stop !" But when he reached the scaffolding, the whole truth seemed to burst in upon him. The executioner was just removing the headless trunk, and the sisters and priest had approached for the purpose of receiving and burying it. The rider fell instantly from his saddle, the packet escaped from his grasp, and the crowd rushed ungovernably towards the spot. The gensdarmes raised the unfortunate man up; one of them took possession of the packet, and they moved off to the Prefecture, followed by an immense number of persons. When they arrived at that building, the gensdarmes carried their still insensible charge in, and the gates were immediately closed against the multitude. He had, however, been recognised by several persons, who informed the rest that he was the brother of the poor girl, who had been to Paris to obtain her pardon How he had succeeded, and why he had returned too late, was yet to be learned; and it was doubtful if the wretched man himself would ever be able to explain this circumstance. The greatest part of the crowd now began to fall away; a few persons only remained, who were anxious to see him when he came out. They were, however, disappointed; for, after having waited a considerable time, the gates of the Prefecture were opened, some of the gensdarmes came out, and, as they passed, mentioned that the person whom they were expecting, had been taken to the hospital through a door at the other side of the house; as, upon recovering from his insensibility, his behaviour had been so outrageous

as to render it improper for him to be conveyed
through the public streets. The disappointed
people retired ; but the events of that melancholy
day, and the circumstances which had preceded
them, long continued to be the subject of conversation in the town, and were as follows.

About two years before the time at which
the execution described took place, a regiment
of the Imperial guards had been stationed at
Marseilles. They had come by sea from Spain,
and were expecting shortly to join the army
that was then in Saxony. The officers were
most of them young men of noble families ; as
it was Bonaparte's policy, during the latter part
of his reign, to collect around him as much of the
old aristocracy of the country as he could. One
of them, Eugene de Beaumont, was a young man
of an illustrious family of Picardy, and had
already distinguished himself by his humanity
and presence of mind during the retreat from
Russia. But he was unfortunately of the true

modern French school, with no fixed principle:
of religion, doubtful of futurity, and a scoffer
at priests and all the ceremonies of the church
In a city like Marseilles, where the utmos
libertinism and licentiousness prevails, he wa:
not likely to acquire better thoughts or habits
and, consequently, plunged into every dissipatioi
which personal appearance, family, and fortune
could expose him to. But he soon becam
disgusted with the sameness and the coarsenes
of the vice by which he was surrounded ; and
like the palled epicure, sought for novelty ani
untasted pleasures. While he was in this dis
contented state of mind, he happened to wande
one day towards the *cours* or promenade, whicl
leads down from the gate of Aix to the opposit
one of Rome. The day was intensely hot, ani
the shade of the trees, and the perfume of th
flowers which the peasants were offering for sale
lulled him into calmness and a softer mood. H
sat down upon a bench which was placed near

large basket of violets and carnations, and contemplated the scene before him. On either side of the *cours* sat several women raised upon tables; and before them were baskets of beautiful flowers, arranged in various tasteful groups. The orange blossom, the tuberose, and the narcissus, were mixed together in sweet alliance; while here and there a carnation, or fresh rose, threw a glow over the bouquet. Each female had a large parasol fastened behind her chair, which extended itself over the table, looking like a canopy; and upon the ground were placed, all around, boxes containing rose-bushes, lemon and orange-trees. Besides the flowers, there was a great quantity of rich fruits piled up on the tables, and seeming to defy the heat and feverish influence of the sun. There were the apples of Genoa, the oranges of Hyeres, and the Golden Islands; the pomegranates and figs of Gascony, and the plums of Touraine. At some distance from the bench upon which

Eugene was seated, stood a Charlatan with a credulous and admiring crowd around him half quack half conjuror, displaying his magic art with one hand, and sovereign remedies with the other. A little farther stood two dark sun burnt girls, with a cloth spread out on the ground before them, on which was placed a small tin box, a lighted wax taper, and several crosses and rosaries. Numerous groups of peasants were scattered up and down, and some were reclining under the trees. On each side of the promenade, the street, with its shop covered with white awnings, might be seen through the trees; and a long train of mule laden with merchandize, and guided by a few of the wild-looking mountaineers, were passing along, and filling the air with the music of their bells.

Eugene had sat some time; and, tempted by the cool and fresh appearance of some pomegranates which were just opposite to him, had got up to cross the *cours* to purchase some, when his attention was arrested by a group of peasants who were approaching, preceded by a band of music. In advance of the rest, marched one of them, carrying a large loaf, or cake, which was contained within a sort of pavilion adorned with flowers. The rest of the party had all large bouquets in their breasts and hands, and were dressed in their gayest attire ; which to the women is particularly becoming. A large black hat, frequently ornamented with ribands or pieces of silver lace, shades the face; a sort of spencer, drawn into plaits behind, and fitting tight round the waist, covers the upper part of the body ; and a petticoat of some bright colour, with the same coloured stockings and shoes, completes the costume. The men wear a large white hat, a loose green jacket, trowsers and stockings of the same colour, and yellow shoes. On this occasion, then, they were all dressed in the manner

described : and there was one among them whose
dress became her singularly. She was very
dark, her raven hair clustered and clung abou'
her forehead like the rich grape, and almost hic
her black sparkling eyes. Her figure was slight
and there was an air of superiority, and almos
of elegance, in her step. Eugene, whose ey<
never failed to remark beauty, was struck by he'
appearance, and partly from curiosity—partl;
from some motive which he waited not to ex
amine, determined to follow the procession, whicl
advanced towards a church at some distance
When they arrived there, they all proceedec
directly up to the altar, where the priest wa
waiting for them, and which was by the side o
the great altar in a small recess. The assistant:
then took the bread from the peasant, and placec
it near the priest, who commenced the mass
which was accompanied at intervals by th<
organ. Eugene had followed the party closely
and stood leaning against a pillar, looking a

the peasant whose beauty had excited his admiration. The girl seemed intent upon her mass-book; but as the service concluded, in rising, she certainly threw a hasty glance towards the spot where Eugene was standing. This might, however, have been intended for a small painting of a vessel in distress, which hung just above the young officer's head; but it so happened, that the glance fell directly upon Eugene's face, and that their eyes met. The effect of this meeting of eyes needed no explanation, for beauty of form and feature levels every artificial distinction of wealth and rank. These things are too well known, and too often and mournfully proved. The ceremony having concluded, the peasants all quitted the church, followed by Eugene, who had determined not to lose sight of the dark beauty. He watched anxiously to see if she would look back; but he watched in vain; she never once turned her head, but, taking hold of a young man's arm who

was near her, they both walked hastily up toward
the gate of the city, and passing through it, struc
off to the right, along the white stone wall
Eugene followed at a distance, and after havin
toiled across the long burning lane for som
time, they came out upon a meadow, and fol
lowing the dry bed of a stream, began to ascen
by a narrow road which led through the vine
yards. The two peasants had proceeded som
way through the vines, when the female, wh
had quitted her companion's arm, and was some
thing in advance, started back, and shrieke
out. Eugene thinking this afforded him an ex
cellent opportunity for speaking to the peasants
and really alarmed, ran up. Directly across th
path lay a large snake, quite dead, though bu
very lately, and looking as if its folds an
rings would still coil and cling round the unwar
passenger. Eugene and the girl's brother tran
quillized her fears, by removing the monste
from her sight; and the former began to tall

to them of the procession. They seemed very unwilling to enter into conversation with him, as the military were at that time by no means popular in the south. Eugene, however, was not discouraged, but continued to walk by the side of the female, to the evident displeasure of her brother; but this was no new situation to the young officer; and by his affability and engaging manner, he soon disposed the peasants favourably towards him, and Claude, the brother, at last invited him to go to their cottage and rest himself. This offer he was of course not backward to accept; and having walked some way on, they discovered the house, which was just on the edge of the vineyard, without the smallest shade, while nothing was heard all round but the chirping of innumerable grasshoppers. Behind the house, however, as they came nearer, they discovered a large walnut-tree, extending itself over a small spot of ground, in one corner of which were se-

veral flasks of oil, and in another, one of th
singular looking wells used in Provence. A
old woman sat knitting under the tree, an
singing one of the old romantic ballads of Pro
vence, which may be thus paraphrased.

The good old king René * sat down in the sun,
For his blood was fast cooling—his race nearly run ;
And he sat with his nobles and priests on the quay,
And he sigh'd for the youth that was far far away.

" Now tell me, now tell me, ye wardens," he cried,
" Have ye look'd o'er the bright sea so distant and wide ?
" Do your standards wave high in the warm breeze of Spai
" That should bear me my son and my heir home again.'

---

* René was King and Count of Provence, in the 15tl
century ; and there is a part of the quay at Marseilles
where the old king used to sit when the weather wa:
cold, and which is called la Cheminée du Roi René
His son was invited to Spain by the Barcelonese, who
wished to have René for their king ; and the young
prince died there of a contagious fever.

" The warm breeze of Spain is awake on the wave,
" And a vessel speeds hither both lofty and brave;
" Like the sea-bird she skims o'er the billow so fast,
" And the bay's farthest point she hath doubled and past."

" Now haste ye, now haste ye," the good old king said,
" Let my galley be mann'd, with a flag at its head,
" Let the bells ring their welcome, and masses be sung,
" And the city with garlands and branches be hung."

The galley is mann'd with a flag at its head,
And the priests and the nobles, the old king have led,
Down the green slimy steps to his canopied seat,
And the vine leaf and rushes are strew'd at his feet.

The trumpets are sounding, the abbey bells ring,
The people are shouting, and bless the good king;
The cannon are sending their voice o'er the bay,
The rowers are bending—the bark starts away.

" Now tell me, now tell me, my quick little page,
" For my eyes are too dim with my joy and my age;
" Doth your prince on the deck with his nobles now stand?
" Doth he smile at our coming and wave high his hand?"

" A vessel speeds hither, but silent and still
" Is the deck that a bright train of nobles should fill ;
" Though the breeze to our rowers its freshness doth bring
" It bears us no shout for a father and king."

" He hath watch'd for the islands by night and by day,
" And the winds have been hostile, and toilsome the way
" And he sleeps, while his nobles are all waiting near,
" Nor thinks that his king and his father are here."

" A vessel speeds hither so light and so fast,
" But no streamers are waving above the high mast ;
" A vessel speeds hither so swift and so strong,
" But I hear not the mariners' thanksgiving song."

" Now why doth he slumber so fast and so deep ?
" Though ye may, his father may not let him sleep ;
" Go down to his bed, and tell low in his ear,
" That his king and his old doting father are here."

But the ear cannot listen, the heart cannot beat,
Nor the young and the princely now spring to his feet ;
For the hand of contagion hath pass'd o'er his head,
And his sleep hath been long on a funeral bed.

The old woman had continued to sing, without perceiving the approach of her children and Eugene, who stood at some distance, partly concealed from her view by a branch of the tree which hung down before her. As she concluded her song, the female peasant ran up to her, and said, " Dearest mother, how happy I am to find you so cheerful to-day !" " So, so, my girl ! you are returned at last from the city, and where is Claude ? O ! there he is : and who is with him ?" said she to her daughter. " A young officer that we met in the vineyard," replied the latter; " and as the sun was so hot, and the city distant, Claude asked him to rest himself in our cottage till the noon be past." Claude and Eugene now advanced, and the latter, addressing the old peasant, expressed himself to have been much pleased at the song they had been listening to. " It was but a melancholy one," she replied, " but I love it, for it makes me young again, and puts me in

mind of the time when I first heard it. Fift
years ago, Sir, I was young and gay as this gir
here, and that was the day that I heard my poo
beloved husband, God rest him! singing it, wher
he was driving his mules through yon wood
Well! well! time must pass; many a branch
and root hath this old tree put forth since I sa
under its shade first." Claude now proceeded
to tell his mother about the procession to the
church, and his sister Mary's alarm at the
snake; at which the old woman raised he
hands and eyes, and crossed herself. Eugene
and Mary in the mean time were standing i
little way off, looking down upon the plain, and
towards the city, which might be seen at i
distance, with its white walls and long dust
road glaring and glittering in the sun, like i
cemetery in a sandy desert. "They told me,"
said Eugene, "that the Provençal cities were fai
and lovely, and that the world could shew fev
like them. What though their waters be blue

and their harbours covered with masts; who, except the sailor and the merchant, would dwell in such a furnace as the city now presents? Not a cloud hangs above the flat roofs to refresh the flowers which are withering there, and the hot south wind wafts no freshness through its streets. Nay, the pale sun which gilds the minarets of Moscow, and the keen breath of the Russian blast, is less oppressive than these feverish beams."

" Ah ! Sir," said Mary, " you should not abuse our country : as for the city, indeed, you are right; I could not dwell there, every one seems so selfish and grasping; but here, among our green vines we are content if Heaven ripens our fruit.   We have the mountain breeze too, which plays above our heads among the leaves of this tree, and which never visits the gay promenades in the city, but to choke them with dust."

" Ay, here, indeed," said Eugene, " beneath the shade of this tree, I might live and die with some sweet girl of Provence for my companion."

Her face was immediately covered with a deep blush; and at that moment the mother, who had been listening to the numerous greetings and remembrances sent her from the city, came up and invited Eugene to enter the cottage.

Its walls were hung round with pictures of saints; over the chimney was an image of the Virgin holding the infant Jesus in her arms; on each side of the image was a large *bouquet* which seemed to have stood there some time, and the flowers of which were almost dead.

The party who had entered the cottage separated, and the two female peasants set out a table, on which they placed some wine, dried grapes, cheese made from sheep's milk, and bread; while Eugene amused himself with a young tame kid, which had shewed great dislike to the stranger at first, but which soon came frisking about him, and ate out of his hand. Soon, however, he became tired of his new acquaintance, and ran to his mistress, who, Eugene thought, did not caress him the less because he had just been fondled by himself.   Be that as it might, he was fairly established in the cottage, and soon also at the table, round which they all drew.

" Our fare is rude and coarse, Sir," said the old peasant, " but a soldier like you, I dare say, is not very nice or difficult.   We have nothing but our mountain butter, for our sun is too bright for the dainty milk of the cow.   But come, Sir, here is what is well worth that—some of our own wine."—" My good woman," said Eugene, " I have learned to eat whatever is set before me with hospitality and good will ; and, surely, such as we have now is not to be despised.   I have seen the day, when some of this wine would have saved many a man's life, and have sent him home again to his country."—" I have often heard talk," said Claude, " of the Russian campaign ; and to us Provençals the thought of such suffering is dreadful !"—" My blood even now is cold, and my teeth chatter," said Eugene, "at the remembrance of it. My God! what sight and miseries were there!"—"Why, Mary," exclaimed the old woman, "you eat nothing; the very grapes which our good *curé* blessed—you are giving them to your kid." Mary turned away her face and bent it down to the kid, who was fondling at her feet, and picking the grapes from a bunch which she held in her hand. "Come, my child, eat something; you are fatigued, these walks to the city do thee no good." Mary's face was still bent down to the kid, but she was now obliged to turn round and take something on her plate. Eugene glanced at her, and perceived that her cheeks were glowing; and the idea that he had already excited some interest within her was almost confirmed. "You must have seen many a fine country," said Claude to Eugene. "The lot has never fallen upon me to march, and I don't know that I am sorry for it, for the sake of my mother and Mary here; but I like to hear of battles and wonderful escapes."—"Alas! my good fellow," said Eugene, "you are quite right in not regretting your peaceful life; had you seen and suffered all that I have, you would be longing for your native vineyards, and never wish to quit them again." "What, Sir, do the officers then suffer as much as their men?" said Claude; "I always thought that they were safer and less exposed, and that it was the poor men that bore all."—"Nonsense, nonsense, my good fellow. Safer! why, I have seen the Emperor himself enveloped in smoke and fire, while the balls were tearing up the ground beneath his horse's feet; and I have seen him bare-headed and without a cloak, which he had thrown over the dead frozen body of one of his aides-de-camp, riding amidst the pelting of the snow. Why, I have been with king Joachim when our lives were at the mercy of the wolf and the Cossack.

"It was one night just as we commenced our

retreat from Moscow, the flames of which threw
a glare over the wide and pathless waste. Our
men were every moment sinking into the deep
holes, which are often the grave and tomb of
the unwary traveller. As we advanced, the
cold increased, and became so intense, that the
blood would scarcely flow in our veins; the
snow became hard, and whole troops might
be seen stretched out in frightful positions over
its glittering surface. In vain did his Majesty
and myself, who had the honour of being his
aide-de-camp — in vain did we animate and
encourage our men; they were heartless and
reckless of every thing, and they sunk into
that drowsy species of luxury which precedes the
sleep that ends in death. Some were sitting
down, grinning and shrieking with the delirium
caused by hunger, and the agony of some un
healed wound that the wind was searching; while
others were kneeling and praying for death
and bidding farewell to their country. Some

Swiss I heard, who had procured brandy, singing their native mountain air; and probably the next morning they were all dead. Large troops of dogs were howling around; and a black swarm of crows was sailing over our heads, and seemed impatient for their prey. The King and myself rode off to look for some shelter and fuel for the men; and after having wandered about for a considerable time, we could perceive coming over the wide *steppe* a dark mass, and we heard a wild cry, which we instantly concluded to come from the Cossacks. But our horses refused to stir, and stood shivering and shaking with cold. As the cry came near, we could distinguish the wild howling of several wolves, which were galloping over the hard snow straight towards us. We instantly quitted our horses, and fled; and we could hear the poor animals groaning and snorting with pain and fear. The wolves appeared to have reached their prey, and to have stopped; but, suddenly, there arose a

frightful uproar—the hungry animals were dis-
puting the booty; and the grinding of their teeth,
and the wild madness of their yell, were dreadful to hear. We hurried away, this horrible
outcry ringing in our ears; and after some
time, but not till we began to feel benumbed,
we perceived a light at a distance. We hastened
towards it, and found that it came through
the small window of a wooden cottage, and we
could hear the voice of a female singing within
Our situation was perplexing: should we call out
and request admittance into the hut, the person
within would probably refuse it us: and if we
were to enter by force, we might be surprised
by some of the straggling parties of Cossacks
to whom probably the hut belonged. While
we stood in this state of suspense, fancying we
still heard the yelling of the wolves, the sound
of a distant tramping of horses seemed to arise,
and presently a loud hurrah echoed along the
waste. We could perceive the high caps and

long spears of the Cossacks rapidly advancing, and we heard them laughing as they came on. I understood their dialect sufficiently to be aware that we need not expect much mercy from these savage troopers; and we knew that they had threatened to massacre every officer that they might make prisoner. The party was rapidly approaching; and their mirth and exultation seemed to increase. There was just behind the hut, and in a small court or yard, an outhouse, the door of which was open. Within this we immediately retreated, and endeavoured to conceal ourselves in a large heap of straw which lay piled in one corner. We had scarcely begun to move it, when a Cossack, who was sleeping there, awoke; and, taking us for some of his comrades, said a few words to us. They were his last, for the King instantly stabbed him to the heart, and he rolled over among the stubble without a groan. We buried ourselves in the heap as deeply as we could,

and dragged the dead body with us, that n
trace might appear of our being there. W
had but just time to do this, and to draw i
the head of the corpse, when we heard th
Cossacks ride directly up to the door of ou
concealment, and dismount, calling for thei
comrade. Not hearing him answer, some o
them came in, and appeared surprised at no
finding him. But they immediately went ou
again; and we could perceive from the cracklin
and smoke which arose, that they were kindlin
a fire, around which they all, as it seemed, as
sembled. They talked of their day's work, o
the number of heads they had struck off; an
seemed to be displaying the booty which the
had gained among the frozen bodies of our men
They were all sitting just close to the door c
the outhouse, and part of them were in view o
our concealment; for while they were all in
tent upon the examination of their spoil,
ventured to raise my head a little and examin

them.   They consisted of, probably, ten or
twelve persons.   The fire round which they
sat was composed of some of the stunted wood,
which is to be found at intervals upon the vast
steppes, and heaps of it lay there covered with
snow.   The Cossacks with their long beards,
and wrapped in large rough cloaks, were sitting
and lying down close to the fire, and two
or three enormous dogs were devouring the
thigh of a horse that had, perhaps, been
snatched from the wolves.   The flame of the
wood had died away, and the burning logs
were glowing with a still steady light.   On the
ground lay a number of rich military jackets,
which had, probably, been stripped from the
frozen limbs of our comrades.   The Cossacks
were amusing themselves in examining the
various articles which the clothes had contained.
One had a watch with its gold chain, seals,
and rings, which he was surveying with greedy
delight, and which I recognised as having

belonged to one of my dearest friends. Another was turning over the leaves of a mass-book, which was sprinkled with blood, and endeavouring, with horrid grimaces to pronounce some of the prayers in the service for the dead which he had just reached. A third had a small portrait, set round with gold and jewels, which he was tearing from their sockets, while he cast the painted card away, on which were features that had long hung close to some faithful heart, had been pressed to his freezing lips, and whose original was, perhaps, then smiling far away amidst luxury and warmth."

Eugene here paused, and looked round upon the peasants, who were listening with intense curiosity. Mary had her eyes fixed upon the young officer's face, which she immediately cast down in confusion, and began breaking some bread which lay near, into innumerable crumbs and shreds. The old peasant looked at her son, and then at the image of the

Virgin, and seemed to be thanking her saints for preserving him to her. Claude filled a large glass of wine, and drank to king Joachim's health, saying, " I may say, Sir, that his Majesty would have been content to be called plain Joachim all his life could he have been in his warm bed at Paris."—" Ay ! you are right, my man," said Eugene ; " we should both have been content with a bed of snow, cold and hard as it was, to have been among our own men." "Well," said the mother, " do let us hear how you escaped from these cruel pirates ; the Blessed Virgin protected you, or you must have perished."

" As to that," said Eugene, " if the Cossacks had not fallen asleep, I believe the Virgin's protection would have done us little good. But, however, sleep they did ; and every thing around was now still, with the exception of the hard breathing of the men, and the occasional snorting and pawing of their horses, which were fastened at some distance. 'Now

then,' whispered I to the King, 'now is the
time for us to make an effort to escape. I
your Majesty will disengage yourself with a
little noise as possible from the straw, we may
yet baffle these bloodhounds.'   '*Par dieu*,'
muttered he, 'we are but fools to have brough'
ourselves into this scrape; what will the Em
peror be thinking ?   If we get out of it safe, 1
expect to be stamped and frowned at * for the

---

* Buonaparte was accustomed to treat the tributary
sovereigns with great haughtiness ; and even his best half
Maria Louisa, seemed to feel sometimes that if she
were Empress of France, there was yet an Emperor
On one occasion she had sprained her foot, and when
they were walking in the garden at Fontainebleau sh
stopped to rest herself. Buonaparte, who was out o
humour that day, and wished to hurry on, desired sh
would rise and proceed ; and upon her saying that he
foot gave her such pain that she could not, Buonaparte
who was not very considerate of pain, exclaimed, "*A*
lons, allons, Madame, il n'y a personne qui ose desobéi
à mes ordres."

next week.' This short dialogue passed between us while we were gradually creeping out from our concealment; and we then stole gently to the door. The Cossacks were stretched out among their booty, each with his long spear by his side, and his head resting upon a log of wood; while the deep-red glare of the fire threw a swarthy hue over their ferocious countenances. One of them lay directly across the door; and he had placed his spear in such a position against it, that it was impossible for either of us to pass through without throwing it down. It must, therefore, be removed, and the utmost caution was necessary, as the handle was resting close to his arm. Having, however, a steady hand, a qualification which was of no slight value here, and being nearest the door, I took hold of the lance and softly removed it, drawing it within the door. But whether I or some dream had disturbed the sleeping Cossack, he suddenly raised his arm,

and turned himself over on his side. We stood
in the most dreadful suspense for a few instants
expecting every moment that he would star
up, and his Majesty had even raised his swor
to destroy him, when we heard him draw
long sigh and continue to breathe hard and
regularly, without again stirring. We then
cautiously stepped over him, and moved through
the rest of the sleepers without any of them
being disturbed. But when we had passed
them and their large dogs, which, probably
from the excessive cold, and their voraciou
supper, slept more soundly than usual, we could
perceive another of the Cossacks standing clos
to the horses, which were fastened along the
side of the wall that ran parallel to the house
The night was quite dark, and one of the dense
fogs so frequent in Russia, was fast coming on
The Cossack began to walk up and down be
fore the horses, occasionally striking the end
of his spear upon the ground and stamping

with his feet as they became numbed by the cold. His Majesty and myself had crouched down behind a large pile of the wood which was scattered about the yard; and there we anxiously watched the motions of the sentinel and the sleepers. The fog, however, now became so thick that the former could not be seen, and the latter could be just distinguished through the red mist that hung round them. Determined to take advantage of the darkness, we cautiously crept out, and along the wall, and presently found ourselves close to the horses. These animals were fastened by rings to the wall, along which ran a set of mangers, and which was covered by a projecting roof. There was a space of twenty yards between them and the Cossack, who kept close to the hut, which sheltered him from the cold. He now suddenly stopped short, and seemed to be listening. We listened too, in hopes that some of our columns might be marching that way—but all was

still, and the Cossack continued his round. :
ought to mention that we heard the same femal
voice singing within the hut; and through ai
aperture opposite to us we could just dis
cern by the dim light of a lamp which hun₁
down from its roof, a woman sitting by the sid₁
of a bed, on which was extended the dead bod}
of one of the same horde.

"The woman was singing in a low melan
choly voice, and the sentinel occasionally accom
panied her in an under-tone. In the mear
time King Joachim and myself were cowering
down close to the horses behind another of th₁
large piles of wood which lay near them, anc
anxiously watching some opportunity to extricate
ourselves from our perilous situation. The only
way that presented itself was by creeping under
the bellies of the horses, which extended beyond
the space occupied by the Cossack in his
march; while the fog was so thick, that if we
could reach the farthest horse unheard, we might

hen escape unpursued, and by chance fall in
vith some of our posts. Accordingly we both
passed under the belly of the first horse, and so
on till we came to the last. They had all
uckily remained perfectly quiet till we came
o the last; and he, whether younger or more
estive than the rest, or seized with some sudden
panic, snorted and struck his hoof upon the
teel cuirass of his Majesty, which sent forth a
oud clang. The Cossack heard it, rushed
owards the horse, but we were on our feet and
inhurt. He could just perceive us through the
og, and uttering a loud hurrah, fired a pistol
it us. We stayed not, as you may suppose, to
eturn his fire, but hurried off. We could hear
he rest of the party in motion, and the deep
rowling of their dogs, and we gave up ourselves
or lost; when, to our great joy, we heard close
o us one of our trumpets, and a party of
cavalry that had been in search of us, rode up.
The officer who commanded them, informed us

that the Emperor was near, and expecting us
But we determined upon having some of the
fuel and warm cloaks we had left behind, and
immediately returned to the hut. Our friends
the Cossacks, however, had heard the trumpet as
well as ourselves, and had made the best of
their way off; the expiring fire being the only
trace left of them. The soldiers were proceeding to break down the hut for fuel, and to turn
the poor woman with the body adrift upon the
snow; but I prevented them; and his Majesty
was pleased to approve of my interference. We
then rode off, his Majesty and myself mounting
two of the cuirassiers horses, who got up behind
two others, and we presently arrived at the
Emperor's bivouac; whom we found walking
about in great agitation, and taking, as usual,
immense quantities of snuff. "How, gentlemen," said he, "where have you been
amusing yourselves? *Parbleu*, we have enough
to do without being obliged to attend to the
duty of our officers." The King explained

to his Majesty the situation in which we had
been placed, by endeavouring to do, what we
conceived, an essential pàrt of our duty. The
Emperor laughed heartily at our danger; but
turning suddenly to the band, which on the
King's arrival had struck up *Où peut-on être
mieux qu'au sein de sa famille?* he said
sharply, ' *Vous feriez mieux de jouer Veillons
au salut de l'Empire.*' Thus you see that we
had all our share of peril and suffering ; but
Vive l'Empereur! I hope soon to be chasing the
Austrian white coats among the Bohemian
mountains, and to taste some of their emperor's
Hungary wine."

"But," said Mary, blushing slightly, "you
must not learn to forget our wine of Provence,
though it be not so sweet or so rare as the
wines you have been accustomed to, Sir."
Eugene exclaimed vehemently, that "he had
rather drink that which was before them, than
the richest wines that were made from the

grapes of Champagne or Burgundy. I shal
learn to make love and fight better after livin;
upon the same fruit that made your old trouba
dours so gallant," said he. "Say you so, Sir ?"
said the old peasant, "*par la Sainte Baume,* :
warrant you are already good enough at either
A young cavalier like you has not doffed hi
cap to a lady's balcon in vain." Mary smilec
archly as she glanced at Eugene; who seemed
as he returned her look, to be fast putting int«
practice the virtue of the Provençal wine
Rising suddenly, however, and going up to th«
wide chimney, he began to pluck some of th«
flowers from off the *bouquet*, and scatter them
about the floor of the cottage. The old womar
observed him, and, instantly stretching forth her
hands, desired him in an earnest and peremptory
tone to desist. "Those flowers," said she, "are
our preservers from sickness and misfor.
tune: they were gathered while the dew yet
hung upon them last St. John's morning, and

blessed by our holy priest. Mary, gather up those withered leaves, as you would be happy and fortunate. I ask your pardon, Sir, but I am old and must soon leave these children; and I have long known that they who scorn and cast away St. John's blessed flowers, are in danger of being rejected by the good God." Mary gathered up the scattered fragments, and placed them in her bosom; while Eugene exclaimed, that "had he known the flowers were indeed so precious, he would have shuddered at harming them." "Come, come," said Claude, "make yourself easy, Sir; my dear mother has never failed sending us, since we were children, to gather flowers on St. John's morning; and always thinks some mischief must befall us, if those *bouquets* are not in their old place and untouched. But I am sure you meant not to vex or harm us, Sir." Eugene's conscience here whispered something to him, by no means of a satisfactory nature; but he immediately

replied, "Mean it, my good fellow! why, though
we cannot boast of our flowers and vines ir
Picardy, yet we too cherish those we love. My
own mother, when I quitted her to join the
army, hung round my neck the dry leaves of a
rose that had been consecrated by a blessed re
lique; and I have it now where she placed it
As the young man spoke thus, the tears started
into his eyes at the remembrance of his mother
and he turned away, and stooping down stroked
the head of the kid which was playing with the
tassel of his boot. Mary had stood silent be
hind her mother's chair, distressed at her ab
ruptness to Eugene, and interested and affected
by the genuine emotion which he betrayed
The old peasant, however, had been quite
pacified by the mention of the holy rose, and
said, "We Provençals are hasty, Sir, for our sur
is hot and our blood warm; but our anger i
soon past, like our winters; and I trust I have
not offended you." "Offended me, my good

mother !" said the officer ! " it is I that am the
offender—to have caused you all this agitation
in return for your kind welcome; there is only
one here, I am afraid," patting the kid, "that
would receive me again with welcome.   But I
must be going, the sun is set, and my presence
will soon be required at the barracks."   " We
are friends then," said all the peasants at once,
" and we shall see you again."   " Good, artless people !   Oh !   surely," said Eugene, "if
you will promise as hearty a reception as I have
had to-day.   But I must not stay, for I think
I hear the *retraite*."   In fact, the drums and
trumpets of the garrison were sounding that
part of military discipline; and as the sound
echoed up to the spot on which the cottage
stood, it formed a remarkable contrast with
the stillness of the vineyards and dark mountains which were spreading above the city.   The
young officer left the cottage, and hastened his
steps down the hill; and as he once turned his

head to look to the spot he had just quitted,
he perceived the black hat with its white
ribands, hastily drawn within an open window
of the cottage. He reached the *cours* just as
the last trumpets were sounding. The lamps
were all glittering among the trees, the flower-
women had their little candles beaming through
the plants and nosegays, and the promenade was
crowded with gay idlers. But Eugene hastened
on to the fort St. Nicholas, where his regiment
was quartered, and immediately retreating to
his room, shut himself in, and began to reason
with himself on the absurdity and wickedness
of the feeling the day's adventure had excited within him. For he was no heartless
seducer. He had lost his mother when very
young—he had no other near female relation,
and had never enjoyed those intimacies and intercourse with the virtuous part of the sex, that
preserve young men from their two besetting
sins—extreme bashfulness or confirmed liber-

tinism.   He had entered the army when a
mere boy ; had led, till now, a soldier's life,
and, like all those of that profession, was fond
of adventure and enterprise.   But amidst all
his dissipation, he had preserved a certain
delicacy of feeling that delighted in nature
and simplicity, and that shrunk from deliberately
planning the ruin of an innocent girl.   True,
he had followed the peasants, had lingered
long at the cottage, and entirely for the sake
of the pretty Mary ; but it was rather the
freshness and novelty of the circumstance that
had led him there, than any dark and wary
plan of deceit.   The artless and honest manners of the family had pleased and interested
him ; and the simple graces of the fair Provençal had touched him nearer than he could
have supposed possible.   Was he then, the admiration of the bright beauties of Paris, after
passing amidst their witcheries unwounded and
indifferent—was he to feel love for the first time

for a peasant? Love! the idea was ridiculous
and he determined to forget his day's adventure altogether. But the young man was ignorant of the hold which previous habits of idleness and dissipation have upon the mind. He
was not aware either that unaffected native
beauty, though clothed in rustic habits, and
with no instruction but that of its own uncorrupted feelings, may often twine itsel
more closely round the heart than all the bril-
liancy and gloss of nobler maidens. His feelings had been excited by his previous listlessnes
and *ennui ;* and as the sun shone in upon him the
next morning, he awoke and walked out upon
the ramparts of the fort to look towards the
peaceful vineyards. The morning was bright
and fresh. The blue waters of the sea which
bathe the walls of the fort were crisping and
rustling with the rising breeze ; and a vessel that
had just finished its quarantine, was slowly
riding into the harbour. The quays were be-

ginning to be peopled with the various crowds which business, amusement, or curiosity, daily collect there ; and a few light boats, covered with awnings, were moving among the thick lines of vessels, and bearing provisions to the awakened and busy sailors. Eugene looked on the scene before him, and then turned away with that sort of dissatisfaction with which he who has no employment or pursuit, beholds others engaged in the full career of interest and business. His thought wandered to Mary and the cottage ; and his eyes rested upon the fig trees which grew just above it. His past and feverish years rose up before him, and a pang of repentance and wish for some tie of affection and love were mingled in the deep sigh that he uttered. "Were I but a peasant," said he—"had I for ever dwelt beneath those mountains, and never heard other music than the bells of my goats and the village song, I might now be content and uncorrupted."

I shall not follow the young officer in the various visits which I was told he made to the cottage. He had gradually accustomed himself to stroll there daily, and there he lingered till nightfall. He had gained the old peasant's heart by a present of a rich gilded painting of her patron St. Magdelaine, and Mary's heart too he had gained by his stories of war and danger; and she would often sigh to herself, and wish that she were other than a poor simple peasant; and then look at Eugene and sigh again. Claude too was delighted with the young officer, and almost wished to be a soldier that he might march with him. They would tend the vines together, when the strong *mistral* had loosened and thrown down the poles: and they talked of the approaching vintage. Eugene expressed his hopes that he might still dance at it, and, as he repeated this in the cottage, he took care to whisper aside to Mary " *et avec toi.*" Mary would blush and smile and say to him,

"Oh! Sir, our dances are so rude and wild that you will scorn them." "Oh no!" would Eugene reply, " I have long learnt to admire all your native sports, nay I have seen the gay Provençal danced amidst the glittering lustres and canopies of Paris, while the rich and the noble looked on and admired."

Here followed the peasant's detail of the gradual increase of Eugene's influence at the cottage, during which three or four weeks flew rapidly on, bringing at length an order to his regiment, which was quartered, as stated, in the fort of St. Nicholas. On the morning of the day referred to, that regiment was drawn out upon the narrow square within the gate of the fort. A despatch had been received from the Prince of Neufchatel, informing the Commandant of the city, that the Emperor had given orders for the regiment of guards to be replaced by other troops, and that the former should immediately begin their

march for Dresden, where the army then was.
Three days were allowed for them to prepare
for their departure. The dispatch was read
aloud by the commanding officer to the men,
who received it with shouts of *Vive l'Empereur*
and as the parade broke up, they might be
seen embracing one another and repeating their
acclamations. The barracks soon resounded
with the note of preparation. Many a dialogue
passed among the busy soldiery ; and one among
the rest, an old *Sapeur*, with a beard as long as
a Jewish patriarch's, mounted upon a table and
shouted out the well-known military song, " *Le
tambour bat il faut partir*," which was taken
up by the rest and echoed through the open
gratings of the fort over the sea.

In the mean time the officers had assembled
in a circle upon the rampart, and were discussing the probable situation of the army.
Most of them were laughing, and in high

spirits at their approaching departure ; and they all dropped off to make their preparations, leaving Eugene standing alone. He was astonished at the sort of discontent which he felt at the very thing he had so long been anxious for, and found that his thoughts were more among the green vineyards about him than on the distant plains of Saxony. " I will see her this evening," said he ; "it is perhaps well for her, for me, that this is so ; but yet I must know if she will grieve at my going." He passed the few hours which remained before evening in irritation and impatience ; and soon as the busy hum of the port had subsided, and his particular duty been performed, he hastened through the crowded *cours*, and passing rapidly along the vineyard, soon arrived near the cottage. As he advanced, he heard a voice, which he recognised as Mary's, singing one of those romances which abound in Provence, and which appeared to relate to some fair lady and her crusading troubadour, alluding to some customs and places which I may probably hereafter make myself acquainted with. The romance I discovered lately in a collection of these compositions, and translate it as follows:

" St. Victor's shrine with gold is crown'd,
 It's tapers burning bright ;
St. Victor's monks are kneeling round,
 And pray for Bertha's knight.
Her bare white feet stand on the stones
 Where kings and nobles rot ;
Her lips have kiss'd St. Victor's bones,
 Yet Bertrand cometh not.

" St. Victor's rock looks brown and bare
 Amid the burning sky ;
And Bertha now is kneeling there
 So distant and so high.

No gentle breeze or fountain sweet
 Plays round the holy grot,
And bleeding are those tender feet,
 Yet Bertrand cometh not.

" Through yonder painted lattice beams
 A light that may not sleep :
In yonder turret Bertha dreams,
 And starts to watch and weep.
A hasty step is hurrying near,
 It mounts the winding stair ;
And kisses charm the falling tear,
 For Bertrand now is there."

As she concluded the last words of the song, Eugene, who had advanced silently and unperceived, echoed them from behind the walnut-tree under which Mary was sitting.

" O how you frightened me !" cried the peasant : " what ! have you been listening to my poor song too, Sir ?"

" That I have," said the officer ; " and the

fair Bertha herself could not have sung it more sweetly. Would that my absence could cause so much grief and lamentation to any one !"

"Oh Sir," replied Mary, " we have all some one that loves us, and whose heart is lighter at our approach. Even when I go to the city there below, I am so happy to get back to our cottage, and my dear mother is so pleased to see me, as she sits singing under this tree."

" But all must love thee, Mary, thou art so kind and gentle. As for me, I am a wandering soldier, and have no kindred but a father, whose heart is too full of ambition to feel much tenderness for me. Mary, dear Mary, I am going far from these vineyards; in three days I shall be marching whither you see those clouds driving along in the southern wind. We are summoned to the army, and my peaceful life is at an end. Will you think of me sometimes ?" The poor girl was pale and trembling: of the nature of her feelings for the young officer she was quite ignorant ; but the idea of his departure had affected her deeply. She felt that she was about to lose something to which she was accustomed, and on which her thoughts and eyes had longed to rest. She made no immediate reply to Eugene's question ; and when he repeated it, she burst into tears.

"My dearest girl," said he, throwing himself down before her, "why do you weep? what have I said or done to distress you?—or is it because I go that you shed those precious tears? Tell me, is it so?"

Mary's tears now fell the faster as she replied, "Why, oh why, Sir, will you talk thus to a poor girl like me? You came to our cottage, and we welcomed you ; we were all happy when you were with us, and shall grieve to see you go:—but why do you talk to me, as if I were a noble lady and fit to be your wife? Go, Sir ; I will pray for you to our

holy Saints, and may they preserve you from
danger in battle !"

" And can you then easily bear the idea
that you may never see me again ?—that he
you now see before you, may be, ere long
stretched out far away beneath the dark cold
sky of the north ! Will you not at least say
that you will always think of me ?"

" Think of you, Sir ! why should you wish
it ?"

" Why should I ?"

" I know too well already the vexation such
thoughts have given me."

" And is it so?" exclaimed Eugene ; " have
you then done so already, dear Mary ? Would
to God that I could stay with thee for ever
and thus be certain of being always present
to thy thoughts and sighs;—but it may not be.

" Look," said Mary, still weeping, "look at
that hermitage which is clinging to yon green
crag: when you are gone, I will go thither

daily and pray with the holy hermit for your safety."

"And will you pray also for my safe return to thee, dear girl?"

"You are very curious," said she, endeavouring to smile, but the attempt was useless, and she hid her face in her hands.

"Shall we not walk?" said Eugene. "See how lovely the green wood looks waving in the evening breeze. And where is thy mother, and Claude?" "They are gone down to the church, whose cross you see there among the leaves of those fig-trees. It was on this very night, two years ago, that my poor father died ; and they are gone to the mass that is said yearly for the repose of his soul." As she spoke, the bell from the church tolled the evening office. Mary crossed herself, and, taking a rosary from her bosom, kissed it fervently. Eugene threw an envious glance upon the holy beads, and said, "And am I then to have no token of remembrance from thee, that I may press to my lips as fondly as you have kissed your beads?"

"Alas! I have no rich rings or jewels which would be worthy of you, Sir. We peasants have no wealth but our flowers and vines."

"And those flowers are rich and precious,' said Eugene; "for they are the pure sweets of Nature; but come, give me some of those blessed violets that I scattered so rashly about the cottage. Come in and pluck them with your own dear hand." They entered the cottage, the stillness of which was only broken by the uniform ticking of a clock that stood near the window. Mary drew the withered leaves from amidst one of the *bouquets*, which were still standing by the side of the image of the Virgin, and cutting some of her shining ringlets, she wrapped them round the flowers; and giving them to Eugene said, "I fear you will say I am too bold, and think lightly of me; but indeed I never gave such things before; and as you are going so far away, I would not wish you to forget us and our cottage entirely." Eugene kissed them as he took them from her hand, and they drew near the open window. The days had shortened sensibly since Eugene's first visit to the cottage; and the moon was throwing her full light upon the country beneath. The Lazaretto might be seen extending its white walls along the shore to the right of the harbour; while to the left the rocky coast was stretching away in dark shade till it terminated in a bold promontory. The long road which leads up from the city was white and still; the distant sound of the wheels of some traveller that was returning home, alone disturbed its silence. As they looked out upon the night, Eugene pointed to that part of the mountain where the road, winding among the dark pines, was lost from view.

"Beyond that point," said he, "lies many a fairer clime and softer scene than that which

is now spread before us. Hast thou neve
sighed for the gay sights and sounds of Paris?

"Oh! never, never," said Mary; "no sound
would be sweet, or sights gay to me, if far from
my home. My old mother's song as she sit
knitting, is more precious to me than all th
rich music of our city festivals. And Paris is s
far, so very far,—why I could not return befor
midnight; and then what would my mothe
do?"

Eugene smiled to himself at the sweet girl'
simplicity. "And do you love none but you
mother, Mary?"

"Oh yes, my dear Claude, and little Fan
chon," taking the kid with its ringing bell
into her arms.

"And none else. Will you not love me too
Oh! say that you will, that you do, and w
must, we surely shall meet again!"

Mary said nothing, but smiled, and as sh
pointed to the violets, blushed and looke

down.   Eugene was delighted, and she looked
so soft and innocent that he suddenly threw his
arms round her waist, and imprinted an ardent
kiss upon her lips.   She shrunk not from his
embrace ;   her   heart   was   innocent,   and   she
might   never   see   the   darling   object   of   her
thoughts   again.   But   she   was   foolish   and
imprudent ;   that   kiss   had   kindled   other
thoughts   and   other   feelings   than   her   pure
tranquil life could ever have known, and which
are not soon quelled.   The young and handsome
officer   still   encircled   her   waist ;   and,   while he
whispered   his   promises,   sorrows,   and   love,   as
his cheek lay close to hers, she sunk into his
arms,   and   for   the   first   time   gently   murmured
" Dear Eugene ! "

Oh !   where   was   the   mother   then—where
was   the   brother,   that   loved   her   with   a   love
far   stronger   and   better   than   his   who   was   now
breathing poison into her heart ?   Alas !   they
were kneeling before the altar, and praying for

the repose of the dead; while the peace of the living was for ever lost!

The clock ticked on; the kid slept quietly among the soft bed of vine-leaves, the moon shone full in upon the pictured saints, and all was still; but Mary was never to know rest again! Time would in future be to her long and dreary; the sports of her kid would no more delight her, and the saints would seem to frown upon her. Voices and steps were heard approaching; the old peasant, led by Claude, came along the path, peaceful and happy at having performed their annual duty. They entered the cottage. The guilty and the weak were there. But the mother knew not of that guilt and weakness. Her face, as the moon fell upon it, was calm and smiling; and she welcomed Eugene as she had ever done. His confusion she perceived not, but something struck her in Mary's manner as unusual. Some uneasy thoughts came across her mind, which

were not tranquillized by seeing Claude stand
gloomily aloof. Eugene, however, hastily told
them of his approaching departure, and they
all appeared uneasy and perplexed. At that
moment the trumpets of the guards were heard
sounding the *retraite*, and mingling their martial
echoes with the drowsy hum of the mosquitoes
that were flitting around; and Eugene took a
hurried leave of the peasants, and retired to
his barracks conscience-stricken, humbled, and
repenting.

There was one he left behind that slept not
that night. The old peasant's alarm had subsided, and she rested; but Mary sat upon the
bed with her hands pressed to her head and her
heart, dark and cheerless. The morning came,
the sun shone in, but her eyes were hot and
aching, and her limbs stiff. Her mother was
again anxious, and suspected that perhaps Eugene's departure might have made her sad, and
that so fair and brave a youth had touched

her heart. And this thought was strengthened when Eugene towards evening entered the cottage. Mary's dark eye brightened, her step was lighter, and she smiled again, though not as she was used. They talked of Eugene's departure. But there was an air of restraint over them all. Suspicion had been roused and crime consummated, and their peaceful and trusting intercourse was at an end.

The time which intervened before the day fixed for the departure of the regiment passed away. The last evening had arrived, and Mary was looking anxiously down the path for Eugene. She saw him slowly advancing up the hill, and she retreated within the cottage, as her brother was among the vines just below the house. Alas! she had begun to learn concealment. Eugene arrived, but he was not welcomed as before; the mother had at last perceived the danger of his visits, and she was vexed and hurt at her daughter's evident distress.

"I am come to bid you farewell," said the officer; "to-morrow, ere the sun be risen, we march; but I shall never forget you all."

"Say not so, Sir," said the mother, "you only mock us. Is it likely that a young noble like you, when you are in the bright palaces and gardens of Paris, will think of our rude home and manners? You are brave and handsome, and many a fair face will smile upon you: but beware, beware, young man, of turning those smiles to tears. A woman's heart is soon softened, and soon broken."

Mary drew back, and, quitting the cottage, stood under the walnut-tree looking towards the long road. Eugene's heart smote him as he looked at the old woman, whose anxious eye had followed her daughter; and he felt that his heart would be heavy as he marched to battle.

It was time for him to leave them. Claude had come in from his labour, but his suspicions had been roused by the circumstances which he had observed when he returned with his mother from the church, and he had become sullen and almost quarrelsome. Mary's feelings may be conceived, but not described : virtuous and gentle, one fatal moment had made her weak and guilty; and the man for whom she had felt that weakness and incurred that guilt was about to leave her, perhaps for ever. She dared not speak to him of all that her heart was bursting to say; but she could not restrain her tears, which now fell freely. The mother and Claude, however, appeared softened when Eugene prepared to depart : their acquaintance had been one of those which a young man of gentle and romantic disposition may frequently form with the honest peasants of a country; and they could not behold him leave them and know that he was going to danger, and possible death, without feeling some real pain. But they were at the same time relieved from their fears by his departure, and consequently their manner towards him softened and became what it used to be.

" Mary, come in," said the mother; " our young officer is going to leave us; come in and let us give him some of our wine of Provence for the last time."

" Oh not for the last time," said Mary, unable to restrain her emotion, " not for the last time;" and alarmed at having shewn such agitation, she added, " he is going to battle, and we must not talk of last times."

Claude said nothing for some minutes, and seemed hurt at his sister's evident distress; but suddenly taking the young officer's hand, he said, " Fare ye well, Sir, fare ye well; you are rich and noble, and may be no stranger to women's tears, since you have seen many a foreign land: but go, Sir, my sister is dearer to me than all the wealth which yon city contains, and you have tarried but too long already. Our prayers shall go with you, for I

think you good, and incapable of wishing to
make my mother, myself, and poor Mary
wretched." And as he spoke these words, he
threw his arms round his sister's neck, and
endeavoured to comfort her.

The old woman sat thunderstruck at the
scene which was passing around her: her eyes
turned first to her daughter, and then to Eugene, who was standing before her in real distress and confusion. She raised her hands,
and pointing to the cross which might just be
seen mingling with the broad leaves of the fig-
tree, said to the young man.—

"That white cross is not more pure and
innocent than my Mary: look at her, Sir,
and tell me if you have ever seen a fairer or
a better girl among all the beautiful ladies
that wait upon our Empress; and till you
came, she was always gay and cheerful; and
if she wept, it was but at the moaning of
her kid, and her tears were soon past. But now

she stands there as I never saw her before, and her heart has been sad and her tongue silent for these three days. I blame not you, Sir ; you are young, and pause not to think that your soft words and eyes may be dangerous to a poor simple girl. Come hither, Mary," and she put her daughter's hand into Eugene's : " Had ye both been peasants, my blessing would have rested on you, and yon church might have received you; but it is otherwise. Since my Mary has loved you, young man, I must too, and have done so; but now say farewell to her, and thank your God that you leave her innocent !"

The guilty pair stood before the old woman with misery and remorse in their hearts : " Farewell," said Eugene, " farewell, dear friends. My God! how bitter it is to leave those to whom we are endeared by habit and affection." And then, as if struck by some sudden feeling, he added, " Yes, affection ; for I love this

sweet girl, and would forget ambition and pride,
and return to remain for ever with you. If I
fall,"—and Mary shuddered and almost sank to
the ground at her mother's feet,—"if I fall, my
head must rest far from here ; but if I am spared
I will return to my mother, my brother, and my
wife." As he spoke thus, he flung his arms
round Mary, and taking from his neck a black
riband to which hung a small portrait of a lady,
"This was my mother," said he, "by those
blessed features which have never yet quitted me,
I promise to return to you all. I have met with
kindness and affection, that have refreshed my
heart as the rain does your parched vines; and I
prize this innocent girl's love more than the
smiles of noble dames. Take it," said he,
giving the picture to Mary, "take it, and preserve it, as you value your happiness and mine.
Within its frame are the leaves of the blessed
rose—blessed to me, since they were my mother's
last gift."

Mary took the picture, and kissed the smiling features, saying, as she looked at Eugene, they were your mother's.

"Be it so," said the old woman : " if God and our Holy Virgin so direct it.   If I have wronged and hurt you, forgive me, dear young man, and may God bless you both, my children !" She bent forward, and kissed Eugene's forehead. While Claude threw his arm round his neck and called him brother.

But the time was fast speeding on, the evening star had risen above the glowing horizon, and the trumpets were about to sound from the city for the last time.   The old woman rose, and bringing out a mass-book from a small room beyond, she knelt down at the open window, and pointing to the star, said, "Every evening when that blessed light appears, we will pray for you, and chant our country hymn. Pray with us now, and Heaven will send you back safe and unhurt !"

Eugene knelt down—alas! he seldom prayed, but he was softened, harassed, and filled with pity and shame. They prayed. Mary, whose hand was still clasped in Eugene's, raised her timid voice, and chaunted one of those hymns with which the peasants celebrate the fête of *la belle Etoile*. Eugene was affected to tears by the scene, but the hymn sank mournfully to his heart, and it seemed more like the requiem of the dead than the sweet and cheerful supplication for the living. Suddenly the trumpets of the guards were heard mingling their lengthened notes with the soft hymn, and Eugene started up. "I must be gone," said he; those trumpets call me to other scenes, but one fond thought will ever mingle with my toil and danger, and make me forget both."

"O forget not danger," said Mary, throwing her arms round him, "remember, remember me, and let not the fierce Cossack rob thee of my precious violets."

"Farewell, farewell," said the officer, " ere those masts which crowd the harbour have reached their distant ports, I may be here again. Our eagles will soon drive back the carrion birds of Russia; and our Empress's father will not long march against his Imperial son-in-law. Once more, farewell "—and kissing Mary for the last time, he hurried out of the cottage.

The hearts he left there were sad; but one was indeed full of bitterness. She had not the consciousness of innocence to support her during the dreadful period that must pass before her lover's return. And if he should never come—if he should fall—for that he might deceive her, she never thought; she was too artless and sincere herself. Time passed on. She daily went to the hermitage, from whence the distant plains might be seen, and there she prayed, and looked towards the north. But she soon felt other and new horrors, and her state of mind became dread-

ful. Her mother, poor unsuspecting woman! endeavoured to soothe her, and talked of Eugene's
speedy return. Her brother insisted upon her
going with him to see the new-year gaieties
of the city; but her heart sickened at the sight
of the fort where Eugene had been quartered.
She refused to quit the cottage; or if she did,
it was but to toil up to the hermitage.

Months passed before intelligence had arrived
of the army, when a letter entrusted to some person who had brought despatches to the city
was forwarded to the cottage. They opened it,
it was from Eugene; but the hand that had
traced it was now nothing but dust. That letter
he had written when he was dying of the wounds
he had received at the battle of Laon; and contained the blessed violets, and the still dearer
ringlets. They will strip me," wrote he, " and
bury me with the rest in a soldier's grave, and this
precious treasure will be lost. I have kept them
near my heart, till that heart has almost ceased to

beat, and now I send them to you that no other hand may touch them. The concluding lines of his letter could scarcely be distinguished: they were unsteady, and nothing but the words *forgive*, *protect*, and *comfort*, could be made out. Mary fell senseless to the earth. Her worst fears were confirmed; disgrace, irremediable disgrace and desolation, were now her portion. When she recovered, and her situation gradually returned to her recollection, she had well nigh broke forth into a wild and dreadful confession of her condition. But she looked at her mother, who was sitting powerless in a chair at some distance, and determined to be silent. She might die, she might never reach the period she so much dreaded; and that distress at least would be spared her poor mother. But the shock which the letter had caused to her had hastened that fatal period; and ere the following morning she had been seized, as she went at night-fall towards the hermitage, with the pangs of labour; and when she was found by some peasants, the work of despair and deli rium had been accomplished;—the once inno cent and tender girl sat beside her dead infant!

She had contrived to conceal her pregnanc; entirely from all observation, and the afflicted peasants could scarcely believe their eyes when they discovered her. But soon the intelligence spread, the police were informed of the dreadfu circumstance, and a *procès-verbal* was drawn u] of it. Mary, the once loved Mary, passed along that *cours*, where but a few months before she had walked amid the happy peasants a happy as themselves, and now moved slowly be tween the military escort, chained, and plunged in misery. Her mother could not accompany her, she was incapable of moving from her bed but her brother walked by her side, and sup ported and screened her from the gazing crowd. But at the prison gate he was pre vented from accompanying her farther; and the

G 5

poor girl, who had never passed a night from her mother's side before, now lay upon straw in a dark and solitary cell.

The day for her trial arrived. She was brought in between two gensdarmes; her brother stood at some distance, pale, the tears running down his cheeks as he looked at her, and the spectators were apparently deeply affected at the melancholy situation in which the poor unhappy girl was placed. The story was known, but in the then unsettled state of public affairs, no attempts had been made for her pardon; and when the evidence had been gone through, so clear and undoubted was the case, that the advocate declined addressing the court, and the judges immediately pronounced the fatal sentence. Mary heard it, but cared not. She could not live. She was not what she had been. She felt that her peace, her innocent delight in nature, in her home, and her village pleasures, were gone for ever; and the thought of her mother had scarcely power now to increase her utter desolation. The sentence was to be put into execution in twelve days' time; and as she was led back to the prison, many a young female shuddered, and crossed herself. But Claude has spoken to her, has whispered hope to her, and told her that he had heard of Eugene's father being now at Paris, and that all the savings of many years should be used for his present purpose.

He stayed not a moment; but leaving his mother under the care of a young female peasant with whom he often had danced at the vintage *fêtes*, he joined the courier which was just leaving Marseilles, and in four days reached Paris. He found out Eugene's father, who was in deep mourning for his son, and who was likewise depressed at the situation of the Government. But Eugene had written to him before his death, told him his story, and entreated him to protect Mary ; and the father had determined upon sending a person to make inquiries about the poor girl. His agitation was great, therefore, when Claude related to him all the circumstances that had taken place. His interest with some persons high in office was still considerable; and, before the clocks of Paris struck eight that evening, Claude was on his way back to Marseilles with a pardon for his sister.

He travelled on in the most dreadful impatience; every hour that he heard strike made him shudder, and by the tenth day he had reached the banks of the Isere. It afterwards appeared from the reports of persons along the road, and from his own wild ravings, that when he reached that mountain stream it was black and swollen, its waters had been increased by continual and heavy rains; and when he reached the river, the boat had been carried away, the ropes broken, and the banks washed down; while pieces of floating timber and boards of houses, and even animals, were hurrying along

in the whirling current. There did he stay the
rest of that afternoon, and a great part of the
next day, in madness and distracted fear; and
he could almost fancy he heard the hammers
of the workmen that were erecting the scaffolding. At last toward the evening of the second
day, a passage was effected, and he hurried on.
When he arrived, on the morning of the twelfth
day, at a village about ten miles distant from
the town where the execution was to take
place, the clock struck nine. He quitted the
carriage, and mounting a horse hurried along
the stony road, and reached the heights above
the town. He could not help pausing a moment before descending, and looking towards it
to see if it was in unusual motion. But it
seemed still as the deep blue sea which was
sleeping beneath the hot sun, and his heart beat
more freely. How he arrived, and all the suc-
ceeding circumstances, were at first related.

The poor old mother could not bear to

remain in her former residence. The walnut-
tree no longer shaded her as she used to sit
spinning and expecting her daughter's return.
She quitted it, and came to live close to the
church.

Poor Claude has never recovered the dreadful
shock he received. He is a madman, a wild and
terrible one, and a *vigneron* told me a story
of him which had made my blood curdle. He
was at first confined in an old building not far
from the village church, which has since been
removed : and one night as a peasant was returning home through the cemetery, he thought,
as he passed among the grave-stones, that he heard
a noise at some little distance. He was not
deceived, for immediately some one uttered a
loud yell, and a figure ran towards the terrified
peasant, rattling some chains which were in his
hands, and grinning and howling in the most
horrible manner. The peasant had just time
to put out the lamp he carried, and creep

through a gate, along a low wall which in
closed the cemetery ; while he heard the enraged
madman, for it was poor Claude who had escaped
from his confinement, rushing among the graves
and dashing his chains upon the stones.

"I had just opened my window," said the
vigneron, "to look at the night to see if our
vintage was likely to prosper, when I heard one
of the most dreadful cries that man can hear
It was like the yelling of some tormented spirit
in purgatory; and I hastily shut the window
and, kissing my wife and child, who slept
soundly, said my prayers and went to bed; but
that cry still rang in my ears, and I dreaded
some visitation upon the city. But the next
morning the news of the madman's escape
was told me, and that the peasant was very
ill of his fright. My God! what dreadful
things happen in the world; the madman was
secured, and he is now confined in the city."

Such was the conclusion of this melancholy story. Mysterious Providence! A poor harmless girl, that never would have injured the smallest reptile, became, by the course of these events, a murderess and a convict. And the peace of that cottage which the soldier had partaken of and enjoyed, was by him turned into desolation, death, and delirium. When we look upon the stream of life, as it flows on sometimes in uniformity and gentleness, and at others like the wild and rushing torrent, fertilising and refreshing the lands of some, while it swallows up the flocks and smiling gardens of others, who can refrain from feeling perplexity and doubt? Who has not sometimes, amidst his miseries and misfortunes, looked round upon the very different situation of others, and wondered and almost repined? Who has not at some time or other felt within his heart a consciousness that he was formed for higher and better situations than that in which he is placed? But when all hope, all prospect of a change are passed, and we are influenced by the same noble and generous impulses, it is then that we turn to the highest and best of places, it is then that we feel indeed that there is a Providence. Though the outward world be dark and cheerless, though the storms of life surround us, yet we have within our hearts the pure stream of mercy from on high, comforting, and soothing our spirits like the spring that gushes from the rocks on the shore of the raging ocean. And because we see inequalities and apparent contradictions and confusion, are we therefore to doubt the existence of a protecting and balancing hand? Do we not feel within our own hearts the history of the system of the great Creator? Do we not feel the powers of virtue and vice each acting in their separate way, but both conducing to some wise purpose? The virtue that makes the better and higher feelings of our nature more green and fruitful, renders us happy and contented. While the devastation and ruin which our vicious propensities may have caused, have only swept away many a noxious vapour, and left our souls clear and calm. And if we see in others vice so far prevail as to choke up the course and influence of virtue, are we therefore to pronounce rashly that this is unjust, and unworthy of an impartial being? How do we know but that the vice which we lament, may be the means of good and blessing, as the treachery of Judas, and the weakness of the Roman governor acted together in the great plan of our redemption? When I see some shallow worldling, whose paltry aspirations have been baffled, and whose life has been one of sense and selfishness, repine at his lot, and arraign the ways of Providence, I look upon him with dread and pity. The tempest that may dissipate the noxious vapours from his mind is yet to come, and long and bitterly may he suffer before it works its destined end. The fool hath said in his heart "There is no God," or what comes to the same thing—has dared to re-pine at, and accuse his works and will.

CHAPTER V.

I WAS yesterday at the vintage fête. But the story I so recently heard, and the destruction caused by the late rains, dwelt too strongly on my mind to allow it to derive much pleasure from the really cheerful scene. The form of the hapless Mary seemed to wander before me, and the cry of her poor brother rang in my ears. The *vignerons*, however, who had lost their vines in the storm, seemed to forget their misfortunes amid the mirth of the other peasants, who were all assembled upon the small *place* in front of the church, from which the procession, with its rude Saints and banners, and preceded by the priest, advanced and marched thrice round. In the midst of the *Saints* was carried a figure covered with grapes and vine-leaves, and seated upon a tun to represent Bacchus; the pagan superstitions being thus united, as they frequently are in Provence, with the ceremonies of the Roman Catholic religion.

The descendants from the Phocæans cannot forget their classical origin; and the bust of Homer which they have set up in one of the streets of the city, looks down upon the children of those who rejected him, and recalls the recollection of the fate which so many illustrious spirits have met with. Homer, Camoens, Tasso, Dante, Chatterton, Burns, all died in exile, or hopeless poverty. Homer wandering blind and homeless; Camoens dying as he had lived—poor and neglected; Tasso pining away the brightest years of his life in darkness, captivity, and hopeless love; Dante the fierce, the vindictive Dante, banished by the country, which, like Coriolanus, he scorned; Chatterton perishing in a common workhouse; and lastly, the Scottish poet, he who wrote the " Cotter's Saturday Night," left to wear his ardent soul away in the drudgery of detecting petty frauds and measuring brandy. O ye who now rule the hearts of mankind with your verse and words, be not too elated with their incense and acclamations; but in the midst of luxury and the honours which an obedient world showers upon you, think sometimes of the dark bed of Chatterton— the solitary cell of Tasso, and be humble.

November 1. This day was one of gloom and solemnity in the city. I walked there in the morning. The shops were all shut, the bells of all the churches were ringing the funeral chime, and flags upon the vessels in the harbour were half-mast high. It was *le jour des Morts,* the day of the dead, when the living cease from their labours to pray for the repose of the millions of souls that are passed away. The churches were all hung with black, and the people were kneeling around the confessionals, whispering their guilt and repentance to the unseen con-

fessor ; while the still silence was only broken
by the ringing of a small bell, which announced
the different periods of the service.   But soon
the whole multitude joined in that solemn and
thrilling hymn, which is more particularly
striking to the traveller, meeting, as he does,
with extracts from it, inscribed upon crosses
amid the dangers of his Alpine wanderings.
There is something singularly affecting to me in
this ceremony.   Young and old, rich and poor,
are all mingled together as they pray for their
buried kindred ; thus pointing out to the contemplative mind an emblem of the future mingling of their dust.   In the catholic churches
there are no invidious pews with their rich crimson linings, and no stately powdered footman
bearing the gilded prayer-book, marches before
the haughty master as he passes up the aisle
to his privileged seat.   Each person comes
silently in, and making the sign of the cross
upon his forehead, quietly takes a chair in the
position where he can best see the altar.   True,

ome small mite is paid for this, but the chair
s not a necessary part of the attendance at mass;
or the poor and devout peasant, to whom, per-
aps, that mite is an object, stands beside the
vife of the rich merchant, and is content to
kneel upon the hard pavement. But I am far
rom approving of many other parts of the
catholic service as I shall have occasion to men-
ion hereafter.

I remained during the day in the city: the
gravity and composed appearance of every thing
suited my feelings. *Fêtes* and noisy rejoicings
destroy me; they irritate and make me feel displeased with myself for not being able to share
n the cheerfulness of others. But it must be
unshrinking resignation indeed, that can learn
o derive consolation at all times, either from the
smiles or tears of others. When the friend to
whom I have poured out all the misery of my
soul, has told me that there were many others
more wretched than myself, and that this should

comfort me, I have smiled and wondered at such doctrine. What! shall I, who know what it is to look round upon life, and not see one green spot to refresh my eyes, whose days are full of disappointment and grief, shall I comfort myself with the idea that others are wearing away their lives in the same situation? If my heart be humane, such thoughts can only add to my sorrow; besides that they deprive me of the meagre satisfaction of the unhappy, the belief that they are struggling with unusual afflictions. Away with that poisonous and blighting maxim of the French philosopher and duke, that we rejoice even in the misfortunes of our best friends: he that does so, never had any friends, and never will.

I strolled in the evening into one of the public *cafés.* The variety of persons one sees there, makes me forget other thoughts for a time. When I entered it, I perceived two Turks sitting on one side with their cigars and their coffee before them; a few Englishmen were lounging

bout, and the noise of the billiard-table was
eard from an adjoining room. I had scarcely
at down and called for some coffee, when some
ther turbaned personages came in and placed
hemselves on the opposite side of the room to
hat on which the Turks were seated. There
was an evident difference in the appearance of
he two parties. The Turks, with their over-
anging eyebrows and shaggy beards, looked
iercely at the group which was opposite to
hem. This latter consisted of an elderly man,
wo younger, and a boy of about fourteen, who
ppeared very much inclined to ridicule the
Turks. The costume of these last differed from
hat of their neighbours. They were Greeks,
with clear oval countenances, and a brighter and
arker eye than the Turks could boast of. The
wo parties stared at each other with that sort of
xpression of countenance with which two bulls
ay be supposed to regard one another, when
eparated in their furious strife. Here were the

two bitterest enemies which can perhaps exist
the insurgent and his tyrant, sitting quietly with
in the same room. While the troops of eithe
party were at that moment engaged in war eve
to the knife, they were sitting at their little mar
ble tables beneath the soft light of the lamp, anc
listening to a German girl who was playing upo
the harp in the midst of the *café*. But, as]
have already said, the Greek boy appeared very
much disposed to commence an attack upon the
Turks ; and had they not been more peaceably
disposed, a scene of confusion might have en
sued. They, however, got up and quitted the
café. The Greeks remained ; they were from
Smyrna, spoke a little French, and told me that
they had made their escape from that place, anc
were going to the Morea. May they be successful in their righteous cause !

I entered into conversation with a young
Englishman who is residing here, and whc
pleased me much. His manners are simple and

etiring, his dress plain, and almost shabby; but I could perceive that he was looked upon with respect and regard by the rest of his countrymen who were there. He has been a considerable traveller, but chiefly on foot. "I am not rich," said he to me, "but I am of an ardent, inquisitive disposition, and prefer living here upon hard fare, and denying myself the gaieties and luxuries of the city, that I may reserve my money to enable me to see other countries. I am in a short time going to Italy by way of Nice." His way of thinking and independence of mind coincided so much with my own temper, that we soon became upon good terms; and as I am endeavouring to procure myself all the distraction I can, I asked him to come up to my house the following morning, which he promised to do. The gay, dissipated idlers of this large city do not suit me. If I have any society, it must be that of the quiet and the reflecting.

November 2.   This day has been spent by me

with my new acquaintance the English pedestrian.
He came up early in the morning, before the heat
of the sun had become oppressive, and breakfasted
with me. His conversation is animated and ima
ginative, and his situation, I suspect, unfortunate
another reason for our intimacy. We strolled ou
after breakfast into the wood. "What a contrast,"
he exclaimed, "what a contrast does our situa
tion now present to that of our friends," and
he sighed, "in England! They are gathering
round the crackling fire in their carpeted rooms
with the doors and windows closed against ever
blast, while we are breathing this mild and per
fumed air. But yet all the beauty and warmth
of these skies are not worth the dark fog which
as it hangs over the street, makes the dear and
cheerful fire-side more precious."—"Such may b
your feelings," I replied, "but such cannot b
mine. You, after having stored your mind
with the various knowledge to be acquired in
travelling, will return to display it to your won

dering family, and tell of your perils and pleasures to some fond heart that wishes for your return. But I have now nothing in common with my country ; my health is ruined, my happiness gone, and these breezes and the humming of these bees will help me to dream away the rest of my life. Were I to tell you all I have suffered, all I have lost, you would acknowledge that the softer sounds and beauties of Nature can alone now comfort me. It would seem impertinent and weak in me if I were so soon to tell you of all this ; and yet I have no one to whom I can talk of those things that are nearest my heart, and thus somewhat relieve it."
' I too have known sorrow," replied my friend, " but, thank God, it will now soon cease. I have been a wanderer ; but by the end of the year I hope once more to see the white cliffs of Dover. I was careless and extravagant ; my father was the reverse : I had large debts, my father refused to pay them, and I fled : he has,

however, at last relented, and I shall soon be freed from all my difficulties. I have lived in different parts of the Continent; I have toiled up mountains, and along burning plains, and consequently I have met with adventures. The day is too hot to walk; if you choose we will sit down under this fig tree, and, as we watch the course of yonder vessel, I will relate to you a singular circumstance which happened to me some years ago." I thanked him; we sat down, and he commenced as follows.

CHAPTER VI.

" I HAD been passing the winter of 1814, and
part of 1815, at Aix ; but as the spring was fast
advancing, and the heat began to be oppressive, I determined upon quitting that place
for Grenoble, where I had resolved to reside
during the summer. Accordingly, one morning
at the beginning of March, a little before sunrise, I quitted Aix with my knapsack at my
back. There are many of our countrymen
who would scorn to load themselves with this
badge of poverty, but I have always found
it the most independent and agreeable plan. I
strolled along the banks of the Durance, that
winds along between high rugged rocks, with
here and there a scattered vineyard and half-
ruined tower perched upon a broken crag, the

former habitation of some princely troubadour
Not a house of any kind was in sight ; all wa:
wild, but beautiful, and such a scene as th(
imagination might have peopled with those
bright beauties and eloquent poets that once
held at Aix their Courts of Love. I passed on
by Manosque, which rises at the end of the
valley in a pyramid of vines and olives, and
whose houses are built up among the rich
gardens to the top of the rock. When I had
passed this place, a wide plain extended itself
before me. The Durance, inclosed within its
stoney channel, still kept along the side of the
road, but was no longer hemmed in by the
narrow defile we had passed. It might be seen
coming down like a silvery snake winding
through the fields from the lower Alps, where it
takes its rise, and which glittered in the sun
along the distant horizon. I continued my
route, occasionally joined by the kind peasants,
in whose cottages I often found welcome and

refreshment ; and passing by the bleak and gloomy Sisteron, and over some of the most desolate mountains I had ever beheld, I arrived on the third day at Gap, a small town at the foot of the Higher Alps. These mountains give their name to the department which is a part of the ancient province of Dauphiné, and which they divide into two unequal portions. As I entered the town, the weather, that had been hitherto still and warm, now seemed about to change ; and I was vexed at this, as I had not intended to sleep at Gap, which presented nothing to interest me, but to continue my route over the mountains to a small solitary inn which had been described to me as likely, from its situation, to delight me much. The storm, however, if storm were indeed impending, kept off, and I determined to go on. I began to ascend the high rock, at the foot of which Gap stands, and which stands as an outpost of the wild chain that extends away towards Piedmont. After

reaching its summit, and travelling along it fo
a short time, the road as suddenly and steepl
descends into a deep valley, on one side of which
appeared almost close to the road, the towering
chain of the Alps, pointing their white peaks t
the sky, and looking like a long line of silen
shrouded spirits. A rapid torrent rolled close t
the road, and the parapet which had been for
merly erected to preserve the traveller from mis
taking his way, had fallen in, and afforded no se
curity, should night overtake the stranger in thi
part of the country. After following the cours
of this torrent for some hours, I began toward
sunset to ascend the principal chain of th
mountains, having crossed the torrent by a rud
wooden bridge that trembled as I passed it.
continued gradually to make my way up th
steep winding road, enjoying the magnificen
view that opened itself upon me, of a vast val
ley, with the old town of Les Diguieres lying
beneath on one side, and a labyrinth of broker

rocks and precipices on the other; while the bright snowy pinnacles of the more distant Alps were peering one above the other, as if impatient to burst from their ranks. The weather, however, began now to look very threatening, and the storm gave strong signs that its hesitation was at an end. The wind rose, the sun looked red and misty as it was preparing to set amidst that vapoury haze that announces an approaching tempest, and dark masses of cloud spread themselves slowly around, gathering above the sharp peaks, glimpses of which appeared occasionally through them, like the scraggy skeleton hand of a spectre thrust out from its shroud. I had often been told of the danger of a storm among these mountains, as the only road across them runs along the very brink of an immeasurable precipice, and the wind is sometimes so strong as it sweeps through the gorges, as to bear off with it the powerless passenger, and even sometimes mules. I pressed on, however,

hoping that I might reach the inn before the
storm burst ; but my hopes were disappointed,
for a tremendous peal of thunder, which broke
over me, and echoed far away among the desolate recesses by which I was surrounded, gave
notice that the tumult was beginning. And no
sooner had it begun, than it raged with the
greatest violence, very unlike those storms which
prevail in plains. There the rain and wind come
on by degrees, and retire as gradually. But at
the signal given by this terrible piece of artillery,
the whole rage of the winds burst forth. They
roared about like a tempestuous sea, and almost took away my breath. To add to my perplexity, the snow began to fall ; and the wind,
seizing and whirling it in all directions, filled
the air with such mist and confusion, that I was
every moment afraid of stepping down into the
horrible gulf beneath. The lightning, as it
flashed over the abyss, shewed me the waters
of the torrent boiling and glittering along ; but

though it looked like a rushing river, I could
hear no sound but the howling of the wind. I
shrunk under the shelter of a projecting part of
the mountain which pressed close to the road;
and there I remained, expecting every instant
to be swept off by the *tourmente*, or smothered
by the snow, and looking anxiously enough,
you may suppose, at one of those crosses that
are erected to commemorate some fatal accident or
crime, and which was directly before me. I was
soon, however, relieved from my dismay, for the
duration of the tempest was short in proportion to
its fury, and I had presently the pleasure to hear
the wind sink, and to find that the snow ceased.
The clouds, however, still continued to hang,
like reconnoitring parties, in different quarters of
the sky, and I hastened on through the new fallen
snow towards the inn. In about ten minutes I
reached the house, which stood quite isolated,
close to the foot of the impending rock. The
road there was a little wider than in the other

parts ; and advantage had been taken of this circumstance for building the inn. I entered, and found the innkeeper sitting near a large iron stove that was in the middle of the apartment, and two gensdarmes were at some distance smoking their cigars, who were stationed there for the proper *surveillance* of the road. Of course, a suspicious-looking knapsack traveller like myself was immediately requested to display his passport. " *Monsieur aura la complaisance de montrer ses papiers.*" Now, I keep a journal of my travels by way of amusement, and the term *papers,* was so general and sweeping, that I began to think it included my diary, which I certainly was determined to resist the inspection of. But recollecting that the same word also included certificates of being a good mechanic, a servant, &c. and not having such, it was of course only necessary to produce my passport. The gensdarme to whom I presented it, as he opened its torn folds, said, " *Monsieur a bien vu des pays.*" I admitted that I had been a tolerable traveller, but in no country so agreeably as France, I added. The innkeeper and both the gensdarmes made me a low bow, and the one to whom I had given my papers, as he turned them, made me a still lower ; which I attributed to my being described as *gentilhomme ;* and as my journey was to be a short one, I was dressed quite well enough to support that title. I then ordered my supper and some wine, and drinking to the health of Louis XVIII., I invited the gensdarmes and the innkeeper to assist me in my bottle. At my mention of the King's name, I had observed that they all three glanced at one another, and the innkeeper said to me, " *Monsieur* apparently comes from Provence,—is there any thing new there ?" and the gensdarmes bent towards me, as if anxiously expecting my reply. Now the truth was, that just when I left Aix, a dark confused report had been spread of some disturbances at Frejus or

Cannes, two small ports upon the Mediterranean. But I had neither time nor inclination to investigate the truth of it, and I had taken good care to say nothing upon the subject as I came along, well knowing, as I did, the French police. I replied, therefore, that "I really was not aware of any thing new, and that, besides, I never troubled myself with politics." The others, whether equally cautious or ignorant as myself, said nothing more, and our conversation turned upon the storm by which I had been overtaken. I mentioned the awkward situation that I had been in, and made inquiries respecting the cross I had seen erected upon the road. One of the gensdarmes told me that it had been put there in memory of a dreadful event that had taken place upon the spot. "I have been some years stationed in this part of the country," said he, "and never saw such a horrible sight. It is now about four years that I was standing one morning in the month of August at the door of this inn. A carriage coming from Grenoble, drove up, in which were M. de Vitrolles and his two daughters, relations to the *Prefet* of Gap. *Ma foi!* they were young and pretty creatures, and I assisted them out of their carriage. They all came in and refreshed themselves. M. de Vitrolles asked me if the roads were safe. ' You have nothing to fear,' said I, ' but the snow and the *tourmente*; and if there were any rascals among the passes, I am sure they would never think of being uncivil to two such *gentilles demoiselles* as these,' and I made a low bow to them. *Pardi,* they smiled and looked as pleased, and M. de Vitrolles seemed quite enchanted with my politeness." Here the gensdarme, who seemed as great a coxcomb as it was possible for a gensdarme to be, brushed up his whiskers and drew his hands through his hair. "Well!" he continued, "when they had finished their soup and their wine, of which I had my share, in a bumper to the young ladies' health, M. de Vitrolles ordered the postillion to mount his horse, and he handed one of his daughters into the carriage, while I had the honour of handing the other, who seemed *en verité* taken with my manner. So off they set, laughing and calling to the postillion to make as much haste as he could with safety, as they were anxious to reach Gap in time for the ball that was to be given in honour of the Emperor, that is to say, Bonaparte's fête ;" and the gensdarme here moved back his chair, and looked as if he had committed some blunder. I was, however, quite unable to see why he should have thus taken himself up, as it was very natural for him to have made use of the expression he was first going to use. He recovered himself, however, and continued his narrative. " Well, they drove off, Sir, as I told you ; but they had not been gone above five or six minutes, and had just turned the projecting part of the mountain, when I heard a desperate shriek and the barking of my dog here," pointing to a large rough dog that lay at his feet. "I rushed out and ran to the spot, and, my God! when I got there, what a sight it was. The carriage, just at that instant, swung over the precipice, and went whirling away, bang, bang against the rocks, with the horses kicking in the air, and the poor creatures that had been in it, dropping like flakes of snow down into the torrent. The postilion had been thrown off and lay in the road; and as I continued to look down after the carriage, I saw something white among a heap of bushes that grew half way down the precipice. I thought it was a patch of snow at first, but presently it seemed to move; and lying down on my belly, and putting my ear close over the brink, I certainly heard a kind of shrieking:—but what could I do? it was impossible to reach the poor girl that was clinging there; and presently all was over, for I saw the whole bush give way and go plunging down with a quantity of dust and a large piece of rock. I went down into the valley, and got assistance. When we reached the spot where they had fallen, we found the horses all dead and battered, the carriage in shivers; but, to our terror and astonishment, the poor gentleman and one of his daughters were still alive. It would have been better for them, though, to have been killed upon the spot; for they died all the same, after lingering two days in dreadful agony. They were all three carried to Gap, and buried there; and soon after, the cross you saw was put up."

I thanked the gensdarme for his story, and ordered another bottle of wine for him and his comrade; but as I was fatigued with my long march, and the danger I had been in, I retired directly to my room. The wind had again risen, and moaned along the passage that led to my apartment, the door of which had no lock or fastening to it, and against which I placed a large chair. I undressed myself, and got into

bed, but I could not sleep : some nameless feeling kept me feverish and restless. The moon at
intervals shone into my room, and fell upon the
gigantic figures of a piece of tapestry which hung
over the decayed walls of my room, and which
had probably been torn from the rich chambers of the castle of Les Diguieres, which lay in
the valley beneath, and had belonged to the
famous Constable of that name, to whom Louis
XIII. assigned the reputation ' *d'avoir toujours
été vainqueur, et de n'avoir jamais été vaincu.*'
They were swinging about in the wind, which
penetrated through the thin walls, and seemed to
be brandishing their spears and shields. I tried
to compose myself ; nothing would do. I tossed
from side to side, sat up, shook my pillow, and
put into practice all those manœuvres that a
nervous and fidgety man thinks likely to render
him more comfortable. But all was vain ; so I
got up. and opening my window, looked out
upon the night. The moon was struggling like

a gallant ship with a rolling sea of clouds; and
here and there a few stars appeared like the scattered vessels of a fleet. The precipice was before
me, dark, deep, and yawning; while far away
on the other side, and occasionally lighted up by
a sudden burst of the moon, lay heaps of brown
and broken rocks, looking like the ruins of a vast
city. I stood listening to the groaning of the
wind, and fancied I could hear now and then the
howling of wolves. But my attention was suddenly attracted to another sound, that seemed to
come from the direction in which I had that day
passed. I even thought that I could distinguish the noise of wheels; and yet it was not
likely that any carriage would be travelling at
that late hour, except perhaps the courier.
There was certainly, however, a low murmuring sound, scarcely to be distinguished from
the wind, yet still audible. It gradually increased; and whatever it was that caused it,
the object seemed to be fast approaching. I

could soon distinctly hear the hollow rolling of
wheels, and the heavy tramp of apparently a
considerable body of men, whose number was
at least sufficient to make themselves heard, as
they marched over the light snow that still lay
slightly on the road.   The other persons in the
inn had, it appeared, been roused by this unexpected occurrence ; for I heard them in motion
below, and I saw one of the gensdarmes come
out and stand before the door of the house
listening to the noise.   Presently a horseman
turned a projecting point of rock, and rode rapidly up to the inn.   The gensdarme immediately advanced towards him, and the horseman,
stooping down over his horse's neck, said something to him in so low a tone that I lost it.   He
then dismounted, and, giving his horse to the
gensdarme, came into the house.   I had not
time to speculate or conjecture who or what this
man was ; for at that moment a considerable
party of men advanced along the road, pre-

ceded by a few horsemen. As they came near, I could perceive that they were a military detachment; but their appearance struck me as singular, and not at all like that of the troops I had seen at Aix or Marseilles. The soldiers, however, and their officers, came directly up, and halted beneath my window. They consisted of about five or six horsemen, and from forty to fifty foot-soldiers. The horsemen were but indifferently mounted, their horses were wretched-looking animals; and two that were harnessed to a small piece of ordnance, seemed as if they were very unused to their present appendage. The infantry were noble-looking veterans, but had a fatigued and harassed appearance; and there was an air of hurry and confusion in their manner, that seemed more adapted to a party of troops in full retreat in a hostile country, than to a French regiment quietly changing its quarters. Some of the horsemen were dismounted, and paid particular attention to one whom I concluded to be the commanding officer. This latter was a short man, with a plain cocked hat. He came into the inn, followed by two of the dismounted horsemen ; two or three of the other horsemen rode hastily on; and the soldiers, as they rested on their arms, kept up a murmuring conversation among themselves. Suddenly the door of my room was pushed open, down tumbled the large chair, and my friend the gensdarme, with his sword drawn, walked in, and requested that I would dress myself directly and follow him. The request was made in that sort of way that admits of little hesitation : so, hurrying on my clothes, I accompanied my friend along the passage, and down the narrow stairs, wondering what all this could mean.

When we got into the kitchen, the short offi-cer was standing directly in front of me, with his hands behind him, near the stove; and under his great coat, which was thrown back, his uniform appeared, of a dark-green colour. Two other

officers in rich uniforms stood by him, the innkeeper in a corner of the room, and the other
gensdarme erect against the open door of the inn
with his sword drawn. I was proceeding to ex-
press-my surprise at having been thus disturbed
in my sleep, and had prepared a very eloquent
and conciliatory compliment to the general civility of the French military, when the short officer
fixed his eye steadily upon me, and said rather
in a sharp tone,—"*Eh bien ! M. l'Anglois, vous
voyagez donc comme cela tout seul à pied ? D'où
venez vous ?*" The abruptness and haughtiness of
the question irritated me; and I replied, that I
had already shewn my passport to the gensdarmes,
and that I considered myself to have been very
unnecessarily interrupted in my repose, to answer
useless interrogatories. The other two officers
looked at each other and smiled, and the short one
said,—"*Doucement, doucement, M. le Voyageur:*
I am the Emperor." I was thunderstruck, and
the whole singularity of my position burst upon

ne. Here, then, was the explanation of those dark rumours which I had heard before quitting Aix. Yet in spite of the unpleasant circumstances in which this might involve me, I felt a certain satisfaction at the opportunity thus afforded me, of seeing that remarkable man. I remained silent, and undecided if I should apologize for my incivility, when he continued, saying " *Vous venez de Marseille apparamment,* how many troops are there in that city? Was there any disturbance there when you left it?" I stated, that I had just come from Aix.— B. " *Etes vous militaire?*" " No," I replied, " I am in the law." " *Bah! Avocat!*" said Bonaparte, taking a long pinch of snuff. " Have you been at Paris lately?" " Yes, Sire:" I did not choose to mince the matter, and call him General there. B. " *Vous avez vu le Roi?*"— " Yes, Sire." " What do you think of him?" The question puzzled me, but I luckily found words to reply, that it was difficult to form any opinion of a king who had reigned so short a time.—" *Bon! vous avez raison, M. l'Avocat*; but he is not fit for France. I am going to replace her in the splendid position which belongs to her. *Mais soyez tranquille*, you will not be molested. England has always been my enemy; I hope that in future we shall be friends, and we will make Europe happy. Your Parliament will be well pleased to see me again on the throne of France;" and he added, "I have many partisans in your Parliament." This question I certainly was not prepared to discuss, so I let it pass: had I been a member of that illustrious assembly, I might, perhaps, have opposed it. He then pointed to his grenadiers, who were seen through the open door: "*C'est une partie de ma garde*,—I am going to cross the whole of France with those forty men. Grenoble is already mine, and by to-morrow *le drapeau tricolor* will float upon the steeples of Lyons." I ventured to remark their fine appearance. "*Oui, c'est le reste de ma vieille garde;* with thirty thousand men like those I could beat all the Allied Powers. *Mais allons, Bertrand,*" turning to one of the officers, "*depêchons nous — Drouot, donnez l'ordre,* let us go and see what Labedoyere has been doing for us."——The word of command was immediately given: the grenadiers shouldered their arms and marched, while the Emperor mounted his horse, and slightly touching his hat, rode off, followed by his generals.

I was not disposed, as you may well imagine, to return to bed that night. My examination had too much discomposed me, although I had turned out a very harmless character. The next morning I continued my route, and reached Grenoble. When I arrived there, I found the town in great confusion. Bonaparte was still there; and, as I passed along the streets, I was enveloped in a crowd of persons who were carrying the gates of a part of the city upon their

shoulders; and which, I was afterwards informed, they had presented to Bonaparte,
saying, " Napoleon, we could not give you
the keys of your good city of Grenoble, but
here are the gates." The general commanding there had, it seems, made away with
the keys. Here my friend having concluded
his story, we separated, and I returned home,
after having exchanged promises to meet
again shortly.

CHAPTER VII.

NOVEMBER 30.—I have been for some time past low and depressed. I have written nothing here, and have never once gone down to the city since the day of All Saints. My mind has been engaged in its own thoughts and reflections, and has been unwilling to look abroad. There is a season approaching which I used once to welcome with innocent and expecting joy. I remember, when I was a child, how delightful the gradual advance of Christmas used to seem to me. The serenades of the parish wakes, the gay shops with their windows heaped with citrons and raisins, and the preparatory collections of the joyous holly with its deep-red berries, used to make me leap and dance with anticipation, as I walked with my nurse along

the street. Then at home : the plan that
listened to for the Christmas dinner—the part
to be invited—the enumeration of the present
from the country, and of the Christmas-boxes t
be given. I think I see my father now—(afte
we had lost my mother)—consulting with my sis
ter, who is now no more, upon the viands tha
were to be collected for the approaching feast
And when the long-looked-for day did arrive, 1
was awake and restless long before morning, witl
the anticipation of that beautiful and cheerfu
salutation, " A merry Christmas," of the annua
new shilling, of the droning sound of the carols
of the new suit of clothes, of the gaily deckec
church, of the dinner and the dessert ; and ther
the kisses of the kind ladies, of their little book:
and boxes of sweetmeats, and finally, of the
triumphant entry of the galanty show ! Blessed.
happy season ! when all these simple joys coulc
please, when I knew not distrust nor sorrow, bui
looked forward to one long and bright Christ

I 5

mas. How different is my present state! I
have learnt the history of life, that history so
full of revolutions and wonders. And yet the
style of its great Author may be traced through-
out its pages; and when we close it, we ought
to rise wiser and better from its perusal. There
are many, who, disgusted too soon with its dry
preface and unadorned commencement, shut the
book in silence and aversion, and cast it, like
a noxious weed, away. There are others who
hastily pass over its graver and more instructive
subjects, and speed on to its flowery passages,
without retaining or remembering one useful
lesson contained within it. But there are others
who come to its examination with seriousness and
impartiality; who, aware of its difficulty and
pleased at the instructive contrasts it presents,
pass from word to word, and from page to page,
with cautious application, and, combining the
whole into one system of information and knowledge, are thus prepared to instruct others in the

various mischiefs which they have remarked prevailing during the successive reigns of the passions, and can look back upon the time they
have thus spent as neither wasted nor improperly
employed. Such men are, indeed, happy; for
their happiness is that of reason and experience,
and not the unreal and vapoury light which proceeds from the unwholesome exhalations of an
uncultivated soil. I could have been such, I
feel that I could, but my fate has been otherwise directed. * * *

  * * *

December 2.—I walked to Marseilles yesterday morning. I was anxious to make some inquiries respecting the progress of the yellow
fever at Barcelona. The fearful scourge is still
raging in that city; thousands are dying daily.
When one stands upon that beautiful terrace
which extends from one side of the harbour
along the coast as far as the old church, which
has been built upon the ruins of a Temple of

Diana,—when one looks over the fair waters which flow by the infected shores of Spain, the imagination wonders how the fresh waves could ever bear upon their living crests the fatal and pestiferous vessel. It would seem that the influence of those winds that blow from Palestine should dispel the blight and corruption of these infectious plagues, which, like the original sin of our nature, deform and pollute the lovely shores of the Mediterranean. Was it not enough that the dark rocks of Africa should send forth the pestilence and the pirate? Must the Atlantic too—the mountainous Atlantic, waft destruction into Europe? Why did not the Pagan God close with his gigantic columns the treacherous strait which connects these seas with the great ocean? The vessel, the single vessel, which was bearing death and agony into a busy city, passed unheeded along; and as it anchored in the unsuspicious harbour, the delighted and smiling kindred of the mariners ran to its deck, to clasp pestilence and inhale contaminated breath.

*   *   *

The intelligence which has reached Marseilles is indeed melancholy. But I have been told of an affecting instance of heroism and devotedness : two of the Sisters of Charity have left Paris, in order to go to the suffering Barcelonese, and succour the sick. Such are the fruits of that blessed religion which preserves the unshrinking believer from the mouth of the lion and the sevenfold heat of the furnace ! What system of morality or philosophy would command us to act thus, or even support us under such a trying task when commenced ? Morality will teach us to live honestly and honourably ; Philosophy will enable us to bear the evils of life with calmness ; but will either of them say to us, " Go and search out the unhappy and the sick : thou hast done thy duty in society as others, and as thou oughtest, thou hast supported thy

misfortunes with patience, since what would it
avail thee to do otherwise? but there is still a
higher duty to be performed. Thou must not
only be passive in thy virtues, but active. Go
to that city which lies in tears and misery; go,
and by thy humble exertions alleviate its distress. 'Thou shalt not be afraid of the pestilence that walketh in darkness, nor for the sickness that destroyeth in the noon day.' And
though nothing but pain and incessant labour
await thee, though thou mayest die in the ful-
filment of the duties I command thee to perform; yet be assured, that nothing which is done
from firm and ardent conviction of its being
required by the humane and charitable precepts
of the Christian religion, can be done uselessly. Go—thou wilt feel, amidst all the horrors which will soon be before thee, a consciousness that thou art doing what thou couldest not
do of thyself alone."   *   *   *

Barcelona appears, indeed, to be in a dreadful

state of confusion. The horrors of anarchy and revolution are added to its other sufferings. Spain is a prey to one of those eruptions which are sometimes the means of clearing a distempered country of its humours and corruptions; but which, if unskilfully managed, or too hastily checked, are only the sources of incurable disease and evil. She cannot, I fear, derive any benefit from this crisis in her nature, as her mighty neighbour has done. There is an original weakness, a sort of unnaturally long childishness about her, that checks and paralyses the developement of her moral powers. The indolent bigotry of the people, and the suspicious tyranny of the sovereign, have both contributed to retain her in long and ignorant tutelage. And now that she has attempted to take her place amid the nations of Europe, who have attained their full strength, either internal disunion, or foreign interference, will send her back to the nursery, there to play with her beads and her guitars.   *   *   *

As I stood upon the quay with my friend the young pedestrian, whom I met, the *Mistral*, or north-west wind, was blowing violently into the harbour. The sky was black, the sea white and stormy, and a few small fishing-boats in the offing were hurrying along towards the harbour. Presently, a shot was fired from the fort above; and while we were wondering what this could mean, we saw the boats that had come close up to the mouth of the port accosted by a boat containing the officers of health. We were shortly after informed, that these boats came from the coast of Spain, and that they had been driven in by the violence of the weather. Of course, the crowd upon the quay was thrown into considerable agitation, but they were soon somewhat tranquillized, by observing, that the boats were stationed just under the guns of the fort, and watched by several boats filled with armed men. I trust, therefore, no mischief will ensue from this unlucky occurrence.

The accounts from the Lazarette in this city, are more satisfactory and encouraging; the cases of disease which existed there, are fast decreasing. What a striking reflection it is, that this building should be so near these populous streets; and what gratitude ought not their inhabitants to feel for those, whose vigilance and unceasing care prevent the infection from spreading beyond the walls of its prison! The regulations respecting the system of quarantine are interesting, and, I may say, impressive. There are always stationed at Pomegue, one of the islands which lie in the bay, and where all vessels are compelled to stop, boats which belong to the Board of Health. As soon as any ship has cast anchor at the island, one of these boats approaches it, and the captain of the ship getting into his own boat, is towed by the other up to that part of the Lazarette which looks upon the sea. As soon as they have arrived there, one of the officers of health presents himself in a balcony in front of the lodge that overlooks the coast, and holds up one of the Gospels, framed and covered with a glass. The captain extending a long rod, touches it, and swears by the holy Crucifix to speak the truth. He is then asked from whence he comes, the nature of his cargo, the number of his crew, the communication he may have had with other vessels, and, finally, the number of his passengers, and their quality. The captain then presents his bill of health at the end of the rod, which the attendants receive with pincers, dipped into vinegar, and spread out upon a plank before the officer. According to the orders which this latter may give, the captain regulates his proceedings, and either places his vessel near the chain of the port, or returns to Pomegue and awaits farther instructions.

These depend upon the circumstances. The

Consuls of the respective ports, from which the vessels come, are obliged to deliver to their captains bills of health, of which there are four kinds. The first is, the unstained, indicating that the crew are in perfect health. The next is, the possibly suspicious, the vessel having come from a suspected port. The third is, the positively suspected, as coming from a country which is infected, or which has had communication with others that are so. And the last is, the awful one, that the plague is on board. It is therefore the state of these bills which determines the duration of the quarantine, and which varies according to the nature of the case. Sometimes twenty-five, twenty-eight, thirty days are considered necessary or sufficient; but in the case of positive infection, forty days are required, and five weeks purification of the vessel afterwards. This last consists of washing it, or plunging all its tackle into the sea, and a strict examination of its cargo. Should any one fall sick on board, he is immediately carried to the Lazarette; should he die, the cause of his death is ascertained, and he is directly buried. The internal regulations of the Lazarette are not less peculiar. It is placed under the exclusive direction of the Board of Health; the captain is generally a merchant who has travelled to the Levant, and unmarried. He must sleep in the Lazarette. He has the management of the whole of the interior police. He accompanies the officers of health in their visits to the different chambers; he punishes, and is responsible for faults; and he draws up the wills of the dying, which have the same force as if they had been prepared by a notary. The persons who are performing quarantine within the building, are allowed to walk in different quarters, as the case may be. But they are all watched and attended by guards, who at night are locked up with them. When any one falls sick, a physician is sent to him, who remains at the door of his apartment, and having ordered proper medicines, departs. Should there be no hope of saving the unfortunate person's life, the captain presents himself at the door of the room, and the dying wretch dictates his will to him.— Should he ask for a priest, one is sent to him ; but he places himself in a corner of the apartment, from whence he hears the confession, and bestows his absolution and blessing. The host and extreme unction are never administered to the sick here. When the priest goes out, he is obliged to swear upon the cross that he has not touched the sick person. When the latter is dead, he is buried in quick lime ; every thing which belonged to him is burnt, the walls of his room are cleaned and whitened, and his death carefully concealed from the other persons within the Lazarette.

Such is the constitution of this remarkable establishment. It has afforded shelter and relief to numerous vessels which had been rejected by other ports; and in the year 1801 the whole French army which returned from Egypt was at once admitted within its walls, which circumstance may give an idea of its extent. Its situation is very favourable to the attainment of the object for which it was built, being placed on a rising ground to the right of the harbour, and exposed to the full force of the mighty *Mistral.* I shall walk up to it one of these days.

CHAPTER VIII.

I WENT with my friend to the same *café* which I have before mentioned. There is something certainly quite peculiar in these places in this city. Persons of all nations are mingled together within them. There were the Algerine and the Turk of Constantinople seated at one table, with their heads bent down upon their breasts, and dozing in listlessness and indolence. Farther on sat a knot of German students, who have come here in order to embark for Greece, and enjoying the only refreshment their finances admit of—*eau sucrée*. At the table opposite to me were two emigrants—one from Spain, flying from the Constitutionalists, and the other from Piedmont, being himself one of this very description of persons. Leaning upon the *comp-*

toir, and talking to the presiding genius, was a young English officer all fresh from Florence, with his travelling cap of straw, and his eyes repeating the lessons they had been taught upon the banks of the Arno, to the fair Provençal, whose husband stood by black and scowling, looking as if his hot southern blood would not allow him to be as complaisant as Sterne's glove-merchant. Some English captains of merchant-men were collected together in a small room, into which I could just see through a glass door, and had got their grog, their pipe, and their song as merrily as in the parlour of the Gun at Wapping. In another cabinet at the other side of the *comptoir* were a number of young *commis*, or clerks to merchants, playing at billiards, and singing, in confusion worse confounded, all sorts of songs, both military, amatory, and political. Of the latter, I could just catch this burthen, which probably alluded to the missionaries :

" Soufflons ! soufflons ! soufflons !
    Eteignons la lumière,
    Et soufflons le feu."

Then, in the midst of the *café*, and just under
the lamp, stood a blind German harper, attended by his daughter, who sang occasionally ; and
who, at the request of an American captain sitting near me, struck up " Yankee Doodle," which
he had somewhere learned, and which had
attracted some of the Yankee sailors about the
door.   And of all these persons, I was, perhaps,
the only one that looked on without sharing in
their mirth, or even tranquillity.   For nothing
seemed to disturb the opium stillness of the
Turks.   I could fancy that I saw them sitting
before their doors at Constantinople, after having
well drugged themselves with the Lethean po-
tion, looking over the bright Bosphorus, and
buried in their noxious dream.   So might I sit
beneath the shade of my wood, and gaze upon

s glorious a sea; but then, the dream—where vould the dream be? Opium, too, would give it ne; but how would it leave me? More wretchd, more desponding than before. I have often elt a strong temptation to try this antidote to)itter thought; but dread the tyranny which, tealing on with petty pace, it would soon exert)ver me.

December 8. I have quite neglected my little)upil of late. He was with me this morning, affectionate little fellow! I had been reading an Italian and favourite author, and had cast myself .pon my knees in agony, as I finished the following passage: " Cos' è la vita per me? Il tempo mi divorò i momenti felici: io non la conosco se non nel sentimento del dolore! ed ora anche l' illuzione mi abbandona. Io medito sul passato, io m'affisso su i dì che verranno, e non veggio che pianto. Questi anni che appena giungono a segnare la mia giovenezza, come passarono lenti fra i timori, le speranze, i desiderj, gl' inganni, la

noja ! e s' io cerco la eredità che mi hanno lasci-
ato, non mi trovoche la rimembranza di poch:
piaceri che non sono più, d' un mare di sciagure
che atterrano il mio coraggio **** La sola morte.
a cui è commesso il sacro cangiamento delle cose,
mi offre pace !" The little boy had entered the
room unperceived by me, and crept up to my
side. Suddenly, as I wept, he threw his arms
round my neck, crying, " My dear Monsieur,
what have you lost? or why do you cry ?—don't
cry; you know you saved me from being drowned, and you must be happy." Alas ! what had I
not lost, and what would I not have given to be
as innocent and happy as that child ! I would
have given fame, wealth, and title, all the years
that man may live, for one short month of that
love and harmony, which I could so well
enjoy. Nay, I would even be content to linger
out the rest of my life upon a bed of sickness,
to be tended and soothed by one voice and hand !
my fever would scorch me less, my eyes would

not ache and throb, if they could be fixed upon one gentle well-remembered face, that now seems, as I press its image to my lips, to smile upon me. Here are, indeed, "lips parted by sugared-breath," and I could almost say, the picture thought. The little boy now sprang up and cried, " *Mais, mon Dieu!* I have forgot my commission. My pretty little sister is going to the church with Adolphe to-morrow, and you must come and see us all. She will look so pretty, and we shall be so happy, and so will you, and so shall I : I'm to have my new jacket ; and Adolphe has promised to take me to the city: oh ! how I love Adolphe. Won't you come ?" I promised that I would go. "But *allons !*" said I, " we must begin our lesson ;" and he began to murmur and stammer his broken English, all the time looking up in my face, and seeming to be aware of the curious mistakes he was making. Those who have been met by the little ragged children who haunt the valleys and descents of France, recollect the amusement they have received from listening to their jargon, half pathetic, half ludicrous, as they dance and tumble and sing, while they force upon the traveller their *bouquets*.

December 4. I went this morning to the marriage: I found the *vigneron's* cottage in considerable confusion. The bridegroom was not arrived. But the pretty bride was seated in the room which I entered, surrounded by some of her young friends, and dressed in her gayest colours. She had a portrait of her future husband hanging round her neck, and her hair was adorned with flowers. The old grandmother seemed to be quite young again : she was posting about from the kitchen and back again, with that sort of restlessness that old people display when they see any thing which they do not thoroughly comprehend. My little pupil was running round her, and displaying his finery. Presently we heard music ; and the bridegroom, accompanied by some of the peasants, entered the cottage, and advanced up to his intended. *Allons, allons à l'église,*" shouted my friend the *vigneron;* and we all set off to the little church. When the ceremony had concluded, we all returned to the cottage. Tables were there spread out upon the place before the house, and we sat down to dinner, which was soon over, for the peasants were anxious to begin their dance. Accordingly they soon commenced, and a very pleasing sight it was. They formed themselves into a long chain, or rather several chains, for there were two or three parties ; and as they all wound among each other, their bright dresses made them look like so many twining garlands. Many of them had small bells fastened to their knees, and these joining their tinkling to the noise of the fiddles, produced a very pleasing effect. The old grandmother sat at the door of the cottage, beating time with her shaking head, and endeavouring to retain prisoner her little grandson, who had been expelled from the chain for his unruly style of dancing.

After the first dance was concluded, the bride came up to me, and asked me to dance the Provençal, another sort of figure, with her, I suppose out of compliment to the stranger. I smiled, and almost laughed at the idea. But a bitter recollection, as usual, suddenly shot across me. The last time that I was asked to dance was, I remember, at a public ball, in my own country. I sat silent and musing near some of my friends, who knew my melancholy mood; but happening to raise my head, I saw before me one of the sweetest faces that the eye could wish to rest upon, or the memory cherish. She was dancing in all the free delight of her first ball; and her fair clear skin, and deep blue eyes, were flushed and sparkling with pleasure and animation. I knew not who she was,—I enquired not,—what was it to me? Yet

I continued to look at her as she moved lightly
and gracefully along ; and there was something
in her features, that made me think of rest and
domestic comfort and virtue,— all ! all lost for
ever lost to me ! The delicious music of the quad-
rilles which floated around me, and the perfume
of the flowers that decked the room, thrilled
through my veins ; bringing to my recollection
those lines which describe the agonizing impression produced upon some persons by such odours.

> " As when roses steal
> In balmy perfume o'er Circassian air,
> So soft, so wildly sweet, they almost wake despair."

A friend, who observed me sitting silent and
serious, came up to me, and proposed to me to
dance.   I looked at the lovely creature that was
passing before me, and hesitated ; but the recollection of what I was, and what I would be,
darted through my soul, and I shrunk back in

scorn and contempt of my own weakness. Was
a desolate unworthy being, like myself, to
presume to touch the hands of that pure and
innocent beauty? Could I forget, while I held
her hand clasped in mine as we swept through
the airy circle,—could I forget that a deep gulph
was fixed between me and nature?—that my
heart might beat, but only to torment me? No,
the memory of my bonds, of my nothingness,
would have paralysed all my motions; I should
have thought of the days when I was as innocent and artless as this fair girl; when I might
have, but for the unaccountable darkness and
waywardness of my mind, entered upon life as
happily, and not have been, as I then was, an
useless, degraded, and miserable man! I felt
like the fallen spirit. I trod upon the burning
marle, and looked up to the crystal gates of
Heaven in hopeless regret. There is not upon
earth a keener agony than to feel what none
can guess; to be considered calm and contented,

while the coals of fire are smoking within our bosom. It is like that terrible trance which is said to overtake some persons, rendering them incapable of speaking or moving, yet leaving them the faculty of hearing ; and, thus in intense and palsied pain, of listening to the preparations for their funeral, the plans which are formed of pleasure and amusement, the world speeding on in its active busy course, while they are considered dead, cold, and nought ! I have somewhere met with an idea that would teach us to believe in the existence of a terrible penance, which we are compelled to perform here for our misdeeds in some past state ; that we are doomed to see all around us happy, every one engaged in healthy toil and occupation, surrounded by friends, and blessed by the enjoyment of home and its holy influence ; while the pilgrim-spirit is working out its pardon in darkness and tears, unsought and unloved. The feelings which at times beset

me are, indeed, worthy of such a doctrine.
The whole world around me seems full of pleasure and rational objects of ambition, while I
cannot join in their pursuit.   What had I done
that I should, so young, and, I think, so harmless, cast away all that can render this sufficiently difficult life still more so? What had I
done? I was proud, self-sufficient, and a visionary; my plans and prospects were as
wild and unstable as the moving sand, and
my penance is long and bitter.   And yet, let me
reflect once more upon what I might have still become, amid the temptations, the gloomy, ghastly
temptations, that gathered round me.   At times,
the idea of self-destruction has passed before
me, and flashed over my agitated mind, like the
forked lightning that shows to the harassed mariner the black coast frowning amid breakers and
sand-banks, which may either shelter or destroy
his ship for ever.   But, then, the horrible uncertainty, the possibility of our lying in a conscious

istening trance, of hearing the mirth and shouts
that fill the street, whose lamps reflect their light
through the church-yard gates upon our tombs;
or of being plunged in thick-ribbed ice; or *feel-*
ing the worm that dieth not, and the fire that is
never quenched, gnawing and consuming our
vitals!   Often, as I have wandered at night
through the bright streets of London, the sight of
one of those church-yards, those white and silent
cities, which stand out before the passenger,
has made me shudder.   I have turned, looking
in through the bars of their gates, upon the wide
and wan assemblage of stones, that seemed to be
gathered together in mockery of the long and
brilliant streets that surround them.   And, while
I have thus remained, a carriage, with its glittering lamps and prancing horses and sparkling
inmates, has dashed past me; the kindred, perhaps, of some of the denizens of this second capital. Capital! ay, and a mighty one it is! You
may build and heap chamber upon chamber—you

may spread your boasted streets and squares,
busy, ant-like man ! but death is a better work-
man, his tools are sharper, and his arms stronger ;
ere you have finished one paltry house, he will
have erected many a splendid storied edifice.
How would the population of all the cities that
now exist appear, if the inhabitants of death's
city were to confront them?—Like the contempti-
ble dust we shake from our feet before the immeasurable sands of the Great Desert. Then,
as I stood, would come by the wandering musi-
cians, with their instruments and songs ; and
the organ's lengthened and drowsy notes would
bring back the days to me, when I used to
hear those sounds as I sat upon my sister's
knee, whose grave was visible through the gate
of the church-yard. And all that I had ever
hoped, and felt, and done, and suffered, has
swept over my soul, and I have prayed for peace,
and pardon, and strength. And they have
been granted me,—at least, the latter ; else I

should have sunk into the abyss that yawned for me.

O ye who have held the even tenor of your way in calmness and peace, think not such thoughts the romantic raving rhapsodies of folly!—alas! I have done with romance; I feel too truly what I write. If to be possessed of a heart capable of virtues, and alive to all the true sources of natural happiness, and then to have all this counteracted by some early fatal blight, and to be cast into outer darkness, be afflicting and wounding to that heart, then is my language no rhapsody. It is the language of misery, of hopeless misery! I have sat near the only being that I ever truly loved, with those feelings that render our nature pure and exalted; I have sat near her, and have not dared to speak to her. I have seen others fluttering about her, while I, who would have given my life for one soft and kind glance of those blue eyes, trembled to look at them.

Yet, when I did venture,—my God! the recollection makes my heart, even now, burn,—methought there was at times a slight blush, a hasty averted cheek, that would have told me that I was guessed; and I remember, after the last agonizing night I passed in her company, composing these lines when I retired to my room.

When the lips have said farewell,
　　When the eyes have look'd their last,
When we *feel*—but dare not tell,
　　That our only joys are past ;

When we gaze upon the face
　　That we ne'er may see again ;
When in it we strive to trace
　　That we have not loved in vain ;

Should the cheek be still as glowing,
　　Should the eye be still as bright,
Should the thought that *we* are going
　　Quench not all its cheerful light :

JOURNAL

'Then farewell to memory's pleasure !
  Farewell all that might have cheer'd !—
Thus we lose each fancied treasure
  Which our woes had so endear'd.—

But should grief, though still and noiseless,
  Blanch the brow and dim the eye ;
Should the heart, that must be voiceless,
  Check in vain the struggling sigh :

'Tis this that gilds our lonely way
  Through many a path beset with sorrow ;
'Tis this which cheers us on to-day,
  And bids us hope and live to-morrow ;—

While all around but mocks our sight,
  And every day unmark'd departs,
'Tis this which sheds a holy light
  O'er the dear world within our hearts.

For oft mid sounds of joy and mirth
  Our wither'd prospects rise before us,
And ask us why we cling to earth,
  Since nought can now to peace restore us

OF AN EXILE.

Mid scenes of happy love, alone,
  Our hearts adore their mystic power;
But all their sweetness fades unknown,
  As round the grave fades many a flower.

Yet one dear thought, like music stealing,
  That soothes the madman's brain to rest,
Breathes freshness o'er our waste of feeling,
  And whispers, that our love was guessed!

CHAPTER IX.

I STOOD to-day with my friend the pedestrian upon the ruins of the Abbey of St. Victor, which are upon an eminence overlooking the harbour and the busy quays. Just beneath me was the yard for building ships, and the noise of innumerable hammers rang in my ears, which were employed in making a frigate for the Tunisian pirates. Around me were the remnants of the Abbey, seeming to look down in grief at the treacherous preparations. When it had stood in all its strength and sanctity, the holy monks, as they passed through the gate of Paradise, which was the name given to the entrance of the house, on account of its superior piety, could have little suspected that this unusual din would have echoed through their ruined cham-

bers. The prophecy of the Cordelier Hug《
respecting the refectory of the Abbey, was ever
more fully accomplished than he expected; since
not only did it become the stable of a king, a:
he had predicted, but the clattering of the infidel frigate's works resounded into its grass-growr
soil, and over the graves of those who had perhap:
preached the crusade. Time! time! thou mighty
master of contrast, what mayest thou not have
done here ere another century be past?

Of all the hurrying thousands that were engaged below me in these money-making specu-
lations, how many would be alive? Of all the
ships that crowded the harbour, and were receiving or delivering their various cargoes, how
many, ere a few years were past, might be lying
full five fathom deep, with all their crews? And
I, that stood thus reflecting upon these things,
where should I be? what should I not have
learnt? I might be smiling at the shallow me-
ditations that then perplexed me; I might be

surveying the past, the present, and future, with a spirit's eye, and have forgotten that I had ever lived amid time and space.

*   *   *

My friend and I remained looking upon the active scene. Directly opposite to us was the *Consigne,* or office of health, near which floated several boats belonging to the vessels which were in quarantine, and who were receiving their provisions through the iron gratings of the little room, in which the officer of health makes his appearance, and presides at their distribution. No person can now quit the harbour even in a small boat, without express permission from the Board of Health; and the Catalan fishermen are all obliged to come up to the office the moment they enter the port, to give a strict account, upon the crucifix, of their proceedings at sea. Some of them were just sailing in and up to the *Consigne.* Further on, upon the quay, stood the beautiful *Hôtel de Ville,* the work of Puget, who was a sculptor, painter, and architect. The open space before it was thronged with merchants and brokers of all nations, awaiting the opening of 'Change. " Parthians, and Medes, and Elamites, and strangers of Rome, Jews and Proselytes, Cretes and Arabians,"—they were all mingled together for the same end. There they were, bartering and exchanging the produce of the soft climes of the South for the ruder productions of Northern regions: the rich juice of the olive might be given for the dark Norwegian pine; and those glowing fruits of vegetable gold that had glittered upon the shores of their native seas, would be sent to the fogs and mists of London, in traffic for some of its more solid merchandise.

As we continued to look down upon the quay, some of the German students I have before alluded to, made their appearance among the crowd, looking like a party of wandering Huns, with their fur caps, bearded faces, and long

white hair.   Two or three police agents were
lurking at some distance from them, and seemed
watching their motions.   " Look at those bar-
barians !" said my companion to me, " for what
other name can we give them, in spite of their
enthusiasm in the cause which they are come here
to support ?   The least glance of astonishment
at their singular dress is enough to excite their
instant wrath.   I remember once to have been
very nearly engaged in a serious dispute with a
brother student of theirs at Heidelberg, where
one of their academical detachments is quartered.
We were sitting in the same room, and were the
only persons there, and the fellow would insist
that I understood German sufficiently well to
converse with him, but that I would not do so
from pride.   They have, however, conducted
themselves quietly enough here, *grace à la police*,
that, like the ever-wakeful Cerberus, bears and
sees all.   Its vigilance is really surprising ; and
ι circumstance happened to me which will show

you the exact information that it receives of every body's motions. I was returning from Cette, a small port in Languedoc, to Lyons. In the public carriage I found a very agreeable Frenchman ; and as our journey was a long one, we became intimate. He was lively, sang numerous songs, and the journey seemed by no means tedious. We made two or three excursions together upon the road, and, as he said that he was going to reside at Lyons, I congratulated myself upon having formed an acquaintance with so agreeable a person. For in this country these intimacies are very frequent among travellers, who remain together sometimes a week or ten days. We arrived at Lyons, proceeded to the same inn, and were sitting over our dessert after dinner. All of a sudden the door was thrown open, and three or four gensdarmes walked in : ' *Le voilà*,' said they all, and I turned as pale as death, I am sure, for they said, 'O Sir; don't be alarmed ; our business is with this gentleman ;' and turning

to my companion, I perceived him pale and
trembling.   The gensdarmes carried him off.   I
made enquiries in the inn about this extraordinary circumstance, but they could tell me
nothing ; so away I went to the Commissary of
Police.   The moment the man saw me, he said,
' Oh, I know what you want ; but make yourself
easy, we know very well how you became acquainted with that man ;' and then he recounted
to me all we had done on our way to Lyons.
' But you will never see him again.   He had
been transported for some political offence, and
since he has chosen to return before his time,
we have sent him to the gallies.'

   " I remember, too, that at the *Restaurateur's*
at Paris, where I used to dine, there came a
gentleman very smartly dressed, with the cross
of the Legion of Honour.   He used to fare
most sumptuously, and all the waiters paid him
uncommon attention.   I concluded him to be a
person of great rank ; and so indeed he was ; for

I was afterwards told that he was supported by the Government, and that he dined about in this way as a spy upon the proceedings of other persons; at least, so it was strongly suspected."

*   *   *

I went to-day to look at the chateau which stands below my house, and which belonged formerly to the director Barras : it is deserted; for the republican, if alive, is now in exile. It excites impressive reflections to see so many of the persons that were concerned in the terrible scenes of the Revolution, now almost all either in banishment, or in untimely graves. And he, too, the modern Cæsar, the *vir ambitionis vi commutatus et commotus,* who would have exhausted worlds, and then invented new—he, too, is gone to his scanty sepulchre! Born on a barren and rude rock, he has died upon one. After having wielded the thunders of war, and ruled almost the whole world, he dwindled away into a captive, railing at his keeper, like the rich and titled gamester in his cell. He set his power upon the hazard of a cast, and lost it ! and mortification and

> " The fiery spirit working forth its way,
>   Wasted the puny body to decay."

I have been shown a portrait of Madame de Maintenon. This is another instance of the tide in the affairs of men, which may lead on to fortune, if taken. Her history is singular. Passing her earliest infancy in a dungeon, where she even then gave indications of her wit and spirit, by replying to a taunt of the gaoler's daughter as to her being poor, " *Oui, c'est vrai, mais je suis demoiselle, et tu ne l'es pas*." Becoming afterwards the wife of a worn-out libertine, whose pains and infirmities she soothed, and attracted as much society to his house by her powers of conversation, as her husband by his humour. And finally dying the widow of the proudest monarch of Europe, to whose children she had been governess. So completely did she

fascinate the attention of those who listened to
her, that upon one occasion the servant is reported to have whispered to her, " Another
story, Madame, for there is no roast to-day."
Madame de Maintenon amused herself by writing poetry occasionally ; and I lately met with
the following specimen of her powers of composition, written in the character of a gaoleress.

" Ah ! l'ingrat, le maudit metier
   Que le metier de Géolière ;
   Il faut être barbare et fière,
   Il faut enrager un pauvre prisonnier ;
   Ah ! ce n'est pas là ma manière.

" Ceux que je prends dans mes liens
   D'eux-mème sont venus s'y rendre ;
   Je n'ai pas cherché les moyens
   De leur plaire, ou de les surprendre.
   Prison ou liberté je leur donne à choisir,
   Et je puis dire sans être vaine,
   Je prends mes captifs sans plaisir,
   Et je sais les garder sans peine."

December 28th.   We have had for these four
days the most tempestuous weather. On the
day preceding Christmas-day, I walked to Marseilles in the morning, intending to return at
night.   I had, at first, determined upon not
quitting my house till all the *fêtes* and rejoicings
incident to this season were past, as all these
things recall other and happier days to me.   But
my friend, the young English pedestrian, having
come up here, prevailed upon me to accompany
him back to the city.   His society is very agreeable to me, just suiting the tone of my mind.
We rambled out to the other side of the city towards a chateau called Borelli, which is beautifully situated, and its marble statues and terrace
are bathed by the waters of the sea.   This chateau derives its Italian name, I was told, from a
Count Borelli, a Genoese nobleman, who married
the heiress of the property.   There are a few
pictures within it, particularly one representing
the Chevalier Rose superintending the burial of

the dead, during the great plague which raged at Marseilles. We strolled about the gardens, and dined in a small inn, from whence we had a beautiful prospect of the sea, the vineyards, and the lofty rock called Marseille Boyré, upon which is the famous grotto called *la baume de Rolland*. On the coast, a little beyond the chateau, are the ruins of an old house, with a large fig-tree growing among its broken walls; close by it were stationed a party of the troops employed in guarding against any infringement of the quarantine regulations; and at some distance, sheltered by a small point of rock, lay a few of the suspicious vessels. Further off, were the three islands, which lie like blockading vessels in view of the harbour, called, If, Pomegue, and Ratoneau. In the first is the famous castle d'If, which was formerly used as a prison of state. Pomegue lies at a greater distance, and it is there that the vessels which come from the Levant perform quarantine. Ratoneau is bare and deserted. Its castle was built in the time of Francis I. (who paid several visits to Marseilles) to protect the harbour from the attacks of the Spaniards. Francis, shortly after his accession to the throne, came here, and was received in a most sumptuous manner. Among the curious shows which had been provided to entertain him, was a battle, in which the combatants pelted each other with oranges; and the gallant King, says the old Chronicle, being always fond of reaping glory, having taken a buckler and joined in the onset, "*fit de fort beaux coups, après avant reçu quelques-uns à la teste et à le corps.*" In 1597 a small fort was built, which was garrisoned by a party of invalids. A curious circumstance is told of one of these soldiers. He was the corporal, and commanded a party consisting of four men. He took it into his head that he was the King or Lord of the Isle, the monarch of all he surveyed, " from the centre all round to the sea." His garrison had gone one day to fetch provisions, and on their return were wonderfully surprised to be received in a hostile manner by the governor, who threatened to fire upon them if they approached. The man remained unmolested in his new dominions for a short time; but at last, having become extremely troublesome to the fishermen, whom he compelled, with the gun of the fort, to bring him provisions, two stout men approached the island, with a white flag, and requested refuge in his Majesty's states from persecution. The King of Ratoneau, like his brother Persian, received the unfortunate exiles who had relied upon his magnanimity. He was, besides, well pleased to have some one to partake in the fatigue of the government of so large an empire. They were admitted; but the treacherous and sacrilegious intruders laid immediate hands upon his sacred majesty, and carried him to an hospital for the deranged, where he died.

As we returned from our excursion, the weather, which had been for some time past invariably calm and bright, seemed to be changing. The waves began to murmur in that sort of low prophetic tone that frequently precedes a tempest, and the clouds were darkening and gathering above the city. There is a tall white column erected in a conspicuous part of the city, in memory of those persons who perished through their exertions in the plague; and this was now rearing itself against the dark and threatening background of cloud, like the *pillar* of salt which suddenly shot up and sparkled amid the blackness and desolation of the perishing and disobedient cities.

I accompanied my friend to the *café*, which I have before mentioned; and we took some refreshment. My old friends, the Turks, were there, and the usual complement of singing clerks and captains.

I soon left the *café*, and walked out upon the quay, which was close by. It was Christmas-eve. The churches were all bright with the preparations for the midnight-mass ; but the quays were deserted, except by the *Douaniers*, or custom-house officers, who were pacing along in front of the vessels. The tempest had now set in ; the masts were all rocking, and their ropes creaking ; while the wind howled through the long street of *la Canebière*, which leads up from the port, like the roaring sea itself. Further down towards the mouth of the harbour, were part of the vessels in quarantine, rolling and heaving upon their anchors, as if they were about to slip them, and hurry among the other ships. I mounted the *Place de la Tourette*, which extends along to the right as far as an ancient church, which I have before alluded to ; and from thence I could hear the storm raging among the rocks and caverns which line the coast ; and I could just distinguish two or three vessels, which were performing quarantine at one of the islands, labouring and striving against

L 5

the vast rolling billows.   The clouds were driving along like a flying army ; while, just in one quarter of the heavens, I could at intervals discover a solitary star, that seemed as if it were endeavouring to chase away the darkness and dreariness of the scene.

It was Christmas-eve.—Good God ! Here was, indeed, a type of my life before me. How many times upon this anniversary had the quiet waters slept beneath the bright and starry sky.   Perhaps, for many years before, the night preceding the holy festival of our church had been soft and undisturbed by aught but the hymn of the Catalan, as he was returning from fishing ; or the dance and song of the joyous citizens, who might have been assembled where I then stood ; while some vessel, that had just returned from its distant voyage across the Atlantic, might have been gently dropping into harbour with its streamers, and shouts of *Noel ! Noel !*   But now all was different.   The waters were black as the heavens above them. The fishermen were safely housed in their cabins, and shuddering, or repeating their Ave, as they listened to the wild uproar. The place where I stood was dark, cold, and desolate; and the morning would, perhaps, rise upon a sad scene of ruin and wreck.

And such it is with me! The winds which whistled by me, came from the north: they had passed over England, where my prospects were once as happy and smiling as the day which had preceded the storm, and from which I was now for ever severed by the unkind breakers of misfortune. Even then, were those I still loved, and with whom I could have lived in friendship and pleasure under other circumstances, gathering round the cheerful hearth, amidst affection and comfort; stirring the fire, and drawing the curtains closer as the tempest increased, and wearing away the social evening in domestic and peaceful amusements. And so was I once; but then I was a child : as a man, I was not destined to be happy ; the storm that was to break over me, even in my infancy, might have been heard muttering in the distance.   Yet it might have passed away, I might have weathered it; others have done so, and swept triumphantly into port ; but my pilot was less cautious, and my vessel carried too much sail.

Descending from the *Tourette*, I returned along the quay.   The midnight-mass had commenced.   At one end of the harbour, and at the entrance of a small street, I could see the glittering windows of a church.   The wind, as it occasionally blew aside the crimson curtain which hung down before the open door, showed me the altar, with its tapers, and flowers, and silver crucifix.   Presently I could hear the loud tones of the organ, mingling itself with the voices of the choristers ; and as I advanced nearer, all this was again hushed by the sound of the little tinkling bell, which announced the elevation of the Host. The church was crowded to excess, and around the door knelt a great number of persons, bending their foreheads to the earth, as the priest held aloft the holy image. All was still, save the howling of the wind, and the rushing and raging of the sea; while a rich cloud of incense spread itself through the church, and floated out upon the prostrate throng. Suddenly the organ burst majestically forth into the triumphal *Te Deum*, and the loud and harmonious chorus echoed down from the gallery. The mass shortly after concluded. I remained wandering about till daybreak. It was then past four, and I felt no inclination for sleep.

* * *

The storm has done its bidding :—a gallant vessel has been wrecked, and the whole coast is covered with floating spars, and logs of wood, and all the miserable remnants of what yesterday was walking " the waters like a thing of life."

* * *

It appears that the vessel which has terminated its voyage thus fatally, was an American, from Campêche, laden with the wood of that name, which is used for dyeing, and which is scattered all along the coast. She was performing quarantine, but anchored in an unsafe position, too near some rocks, which ate into her cables, and, during the worst fury of the tempest, she drove upon that part of the coast in the direction of the Chateau Borelli, which is there steep and rugged. The mast was within a leap of the rock, which the crew succeeded in gaining, except one man, and he, too, the pilot, who had but entered the vessel a day or two before, and whose foot slipping as he was preparing to take the leap, he fell headlong into the boiling gulph below. The crew remained huddled together upon a narrow ridge of the cliff, which rose up straight and steep above them ; while the vast breakers threw their spray and surf upon them in disappointed malice. They called for help, but the wind roared too loudly, and drowned their feeble voices. When the day broke, however, the shivering and trembling men were removed, and safely conveyed to the Lazaretto. Such a circumstance has not occurred to the vessels in quarantine, I was told, for many years.

* * *

Christmas-day was passed amidst the usual festivities which then take place in these countries. But many of the old Provençal customs have been discontinued, which are alone interesting to the observer of human nature; for, in spite of the general gaiety of French *fêtes*, I think that the celebration of Christmas-day in England is the most affecting and beautiful festival that can be witnessed. There is no pomp of incense and richly-robed priest; the churches are not loaded with silks and tapestries,—all is plain and unassuming; the simple and fresh holly, ranged in regular lines along the aisle,— the tasteful and arduous task of the more than

usually attentive pew-openers ;——the happy ser-
vants trooping-in in their new clothes, and with
the just received Christmas-box ; the impressive
prayers and collects uttered and understood by
the whole congregation ; the Christmas-hymn
sung with additional spirit and melody by the
neat charity-children, in their fair white caps and
bright green gowns ; and the appropriate sermon,
the remembering of whose text is to be the test
and trial of many an anxious child, awaiting, in
hope delayed, the mysterious and long-promised
gift.   And then, when the religious service of
the day is concluded, when long separated
friends and kin are met round the amply covered
board, the street resounding with music and
song, in single and impressive contrast to the
usual . termination of a holy day in England.
Here one *fête* telleth another : all is glitter, and
banner, and show,——which may heat the imagination, which may dazzle the ignorant, but cannot
touch the quiet and lasting feelings of the heart.

January 2.—As I had not seen the good her
mit for a considerable time, I yesterday went u
to his cell.   I found him sitting at the entrance
reading.   He had not perceived my approach
so intent was he upon his book.   I stood stil
for a moment to look at him.   His face migh
have served as a model for Rembrandt, shadow;
and contemplative, such as that of the Philoso
pher in meditation, which has always struck m
as one of the finest compositions of that painter
The rustling of a wild rabbit among the herbs
which had been alarmed at my approach, made
him raise his head; and he then saw me.   " Ah
my son," said he, " I have long looked for thee
and wondered at thy delay.   Have the pleasure:
and festivities of the city made thee forget thy
sorrows and me ?"   " Oh no! good father," I
replied, " I had not forgotten you ; but I have
been endeavouring to look abroad from my own
reflections, and observe what passes in the city
Its *fêtes* and amusements have no charms fo

ne; but they afford me food for thoughts and observations, which distract, in some degree, my attention from myself." "Alas! my son," said the hermit, "that city, which now is the source of some relief to you, would only revive in me the remembrance of the horrors and distresses I have seen and felt there. Great God! when I look down upon it now, and see it full of busy and happy beings, hurrying through the crowded streets, and celebrating the opening year; when I cast my eyes upon the long road, and behold it covered with merchandize, and travellers hastening towards its walls,—I think of the time when that road was unoccupied, save by troops of soldiers, who were encamped around, and cutting off all communication with that miserable city. I see again the streets filled with far different sights than those which throng them now; and my own sufferings and losses seem fresh and recent." And he bent his head upon his breast, and wept. I was much affected by his distress, and remained silent. "If you are come to me for comfort, young man," he continued, "my instruction and advice cannot teach you such resignation as the history of the events which have occurred to me. The day is warm and bright; sit down here beside me upon this smooth rock, and I will relate to you my sorrows. The fig-trees will shade you; and should the noon-day sun reach us, I have good store of fruits to refresh us, in my cell."—I sat down upon the rock, from whence I could see the city, and part of the Lazaretto, to which latter some boats were seen hastily moving, as if from the infected ships.

CHAPTER X.

AGE and misfortune, began the hermit, make sad changes in man. Once I was strong, and full of hope and ambition ; but time has told me many a tale of experience and disappointment. I was the son of a merchant of Marseilles ; my father had long carried on a successful trade with the Levant, and realized a considerable property. He had married early in life the daughter of a Spanish merchant, who had resided some time at Marseilles, and who was a native of Cadiz. He was still living when I was born, and my father's correspondent in that city. I was an only child, and fortune and every prospect of happiness seemed mine. I had from infancy been attached to the daughter of a friend of my father ; we had grown up together; and it was settled that, upon my return from Cadiz, where my father had occasion to send me to transact some business, we should be married. I quitted Marseilles in the month of February, and reached Cadiz in safety. The business which I had come upon detained me there till the commencement of May, and was beginning to make my preparations for returning home. A vessel belonging to my father was expected shortly to arrive, and I was to return with her. She did arrive, and brought me letters. My family and my beloved Aimée were all well; but my father mentioned that some alarm had been excited at Marseilles, on account of a vessel having lately arrived from Syria, and which was supposed to be infected with the plague. But, he added, that the reports of the physicians, who had attended and examined the few persons who were ill on board, were favourable, and that the terror was subsiding. I could not help feeling a little uneasiness and agitation at this intelligence, and was very anxious that the vessel should complete her cargo, that we might sail immediately. At length that moment arrived ; and as we made but little way, I used impatiently to pace the deck daily, and almost nightly, watching for the Mountain of St. Victor, which first presents itself to the homeward-bound vessel. Our voyage was tedious ; the weather was beautifully bright and clear, but the winds were too gentle and soft for my wishes. The deep-blue waters were like those of some inland lake, and the sea-birds floated and almost slept upon their smooth surface. I beguiled the time as well as I could, by reading and conversing with the Captain, who was an old experienced sailor, and told me many a tale of peril as I paced the deck with him, when the sun had gone down. I am old and forgetful now, and all the pleasure I experienced in listening to them is almost effaced from my memory ; yet I can still recollect the awe and interest with which I heard him tell of

the time when he had been wrecked; and I
will endeavour to relate what he said, in his own
words, which made great impression upon me at
the time. It was in the Bay of Biscay, as he
told me, not far from the mouth of the Gironde,
which runs down from Bourdeaux. "For some
days the weather had been as still and smiling
as it is now," said he, "and the bay was looking
as innocent as if it knew nothing of the bones
and treasures that it had swallowed up. The
pilot-boats were flitting about with their dingy
sails, and watching for their work. But sailors
are not to be deceived by the treachery of the
winds and waves; and there was a little oval
cloud hovering in the west that we had often
seen, and knew well what it meant; so I ordered
every thing." continued the Captain, "to be
kept close and steady, and as night came on, I
had almost all our sail taken in. I knew that
we were not far from the mouth of the Gironde
and we were looking out for the light on the

Tower of Cordouan. A bright star was just rising, and we at first mistook it for the beacon; but as it gradually lifted itself into the sky, we laughed at ourselves for ignorant landsmen. At last, however, I spied the little flame twinkling and glimmering through the darkness, and glad enough we all were to see it. Just then a light breeze got up from the westward, and I had the rest of our sail taken in, that we might lie-to for the night. We had scarcely made fast our ropes, and got all safe, when the wind freshened, and in seven or eight minutes was blowing a hurricane. You have never been in the Bay," said the Captain to me, " so you can't tell what a place it is: currents, and rocks, and sands, and a sea as high as the mast of one of our ships at Toulon! The night was as black as ink, and we went flying along straight towards the land. which I knew must be about three leagues off. All of a sudden the man at the helm uttered a terrible shout, and there came driving past us a large hull, keel uppermost. So much for the poor souls within her," added the Captain; " they should have taken-in their sail in time. But it was a terrible sight; my men all crossed themselves; and I made a vow to our Lady, that if I got my ship safe into port, I would hang up a model of her in the old church of St. Andrew at Bourdeaux, and repeat ten *aves* a-day for a week." Here, said the Hermit, I remember he was interrupted in his account by a cry from the man at the helm, of Look out a-head there! and, turning round, we saw a large ship bearing down upon us. She came up, and hailed us. It was a frigate, engaged in cruising, as the Algerines were supposed to be abroad. The Captain mentioned whither we were bound, and we were allowed to pass on. He then continued, as nearly as I can recollect, in the following words: " We drove on, our sails all in shreds and tatters, one of our masts split in two, and the waves sweeping about the

deck like hungry wolves. Presently we heard
them roaring and boiling upon a ridge of rocks
which stretch along at some distance from the
shore, and we could just see their white heads
breaking about ; but a tremendous billow threw
us over them, and we breathed again. It would
not do, though ; for we soon heard our keel
grounding and grating among the sands," said
he, " like the growling of a sea-monster. My
men directly hauled over the boat, and all, except another man and myself, leaped in ; but
they had not got, I am sure, five yards from
the ship, when I heard a deadly yell, and the
boat came floating past with a poor creature
clinging to it, who was swept off in a moment by
the breaking of a huge wave. The man and
myself," he continued, " passed a horrid night ;
but luckily the ship stuck so fast in the sands,
that she remained steady ; and having lashed
ourselves to the stern-posts, we got through till
morning. The tide seemed to be falling, and
I began to be alarmed lest it should loosen, and

carry us out to sea. But, *grace à Dieu!* in about five hours time it left us nearly dry, and we both waded ashore. One of our kegs of brandy had been washed up; and my man,' said the Captain very truly, "like a wicked ungrateful heretic as he was, fell to drinking it, instead of going down upon his knees and re turning thanks to the Virgin; but he had his reward, for he drank so much that he died upon the spot. I got assistance from the people of the country, and saved some of my cargo; but my ship, poor thing! was soon knocked all to pieces But here I am," concluded the Captain, "having made many more voyages since that; and by to-morrow morning I hope we shall see St Victor's crag peeping up to welcome us back."

In this at least he was right, for towards day break the next morning the long line of rocky coast, which forms the bay of Marseilles, opened upon us, and St. Victor's rock appeared above all in the distance. The sailors saluted it with the usual cries of " *La Victoria! la Victoria! lou deloubrou de la Victoria!*" and we sailed slowly up to the Island of Pomegue, where every vessel is compelled to bring-to. Our bill of health was in a perfect state, and I anticipated no delay, as we came from a port which was not suspected of being infected with any contagious disease. But it appeared that the recent alarm had made the officers of health more than usually cautious; for we were ordered to remain at Pomegue till further orders. My impatience was at its height, and if I had dared, or if it had been possible, I should have instantly left the ship, and gone on shore; but, by so doing, I should have rendered myself liable to be fired upon. I remained therefore, daily looking towards the city, some of whose white houses, and the old fort above the harbour, I could distinguish, and wishing myself with my Aimée on the banks of the quiet Huveaune, where my father had a chateau. The heat was excessive, and our vessel lay exposed to the burning rays of the sun, which glared upon the dry and barren rock where we were anchored. Four days passed over; and at length the Captain received permission to place himself at the entrance of the harbour, where he was to remain for two subsequent days. As we took our station, I looked round upon the quay, and saw my father and mother, with Aimée, standing near the fort of Saint Nicholas, part of which, as you may have observed, still exists. The ramparts of the fort were covered with soldiers, who were watching us and another vessel that was making her way out of the harbour. You are not aware, perhaps, that this fort was built by Louis the Fourteenth, at the suggestion of Cardinal de Mazarin, to curb the restless disposition of us Provençals; and that he is said to have remarked upon the occasion, that he would have his *bastide* too at Marseilles.

My father and mother, and, alas! dear Aimée, waved their hands; and I murmured at the precautions which detained me from them, and which I considered unnecessary. At last, however, our quarantine concluded; and early on the third morning I hurried into one of the small boats that ply in the harbour, and in a few minutes was clasped in my father's and mother's arms. I then hurried off to Aimée, whom I found at her father's; and sweet and joyful was our meeting. "I am come at last," said I, " my soft bride; the sleepy envious winds have made me cast many a longing look towards the glowing clouds that I knew were hanging over my native city; but, dear Aimée, have you thought of me, and prayed for me in my absence?"

" Prayed for you, Henri?" said she; " every morning and night, as the matin and vesper bells have tolled. I have gone to the old cathedral, and knelt before Saint Nicholas, the patron saint of mariners; and I have made a vow too, dear Henri, that if you came back safe, I would go up in the noon-day sun to our ladies' fort on the rock, and hang up thy picture on the white walls. And when we were alarmed about the plague, your father and mother would not write till all immediate danger was over; lest, should we have been visited by it, you should have returned; and I am sure I had rather have died, too, than have wished you to come." I threw my arms round her, and we felt that innocent and unspeakable happiness which two persons, who have been separated for the first time since their infancy, feel when they meet again. Her father came in, and welcomed me with tenderness; and I proposed to him to fix the day for our marriage.

" Oh!" said he, " you must talk to Aimée about that;" but Aimée had disappeared, and I went in search of her. I found her in a small garden that looked on the country, which she had filled with carnations and jasmin, which were shaded by some almond-trees.

" Aimée," said I, " do you love your flowers better than Henri, then, that you have left him for them? Sure, your love is not like yon pale jasmin that stands cold and white beside those blushing roses? Come, my well-beloved, let us talk of our marriage. The dark beauties of Spain have had no power to cloud the light that thy soft blue eyes have shed upon my heart. We have loved one another since we were children, and let us soon vow at the altar that our love shall cleave to us till we die."

" O let me attend to my flowers," said Aimée, " they are all parched and drooping: I declare I have quite neglected them of late, to think of you."

" But now that I am come," said I, " you will neglect me for your flowers! Oh, Aimée, I am sure I have thought daily and hourly of you when I was on the shores of Andalusia, and I have counted the minutes and hours that must elapse before I could call you wife; and now you affect indifference, and seem to be ignorant of my wishes."

" Oh, no, dearest Henri!" said she, taking my hands, " forgive the passing pleasure which I took in teazing you. I have loved you when we used to ramble among the olives, on the banks of the Huveaune, and gather wild shrubs and flowers — I have loved you all my days; and when you will, I am ready to promise to love you as a wife for ever."—Such words as these may seem strange for an old withered man like myself, but then I was young and straight, and these white straggling hairs that streak my forehead were then dark and glossy, and pleasing to the eye of woman. Every word, every minute of that happy time, is present to my mind, as the departing sailor sees the quay crowded with his friends, though the coast be like a speck upon the sea. Well, my son, we were married;—alas! alas! well do I recollect that day;—and as I clasped my tender Aimée in my arms, I thought that my life was to be one of bliss and domestic comfort; and such did I taste during the first week of our union. But soon a fresh alarm began to arise in the city. The circumstances

which had first excited uneasiness respecting the
plague, it appeared, were these:

Intelligence had reached Marseilles, in the
month of April, that the greatest part of the
Syrian cities, and those of Palestine, were
afflicted with the plague. Some time in the same
month a vessel had arrived at Pomegue, which
came from Tripoli; its bill, or certificate, of
health was unsatisfactory and soiled, because
it had left that port about the thirty-first of January, and after the plague had shown itself in
the place from whence it came. The captain
stated, that he had put into Leghorn, and that
he had there lost, by sickness, six of his crew;
but the report of the physicians of that town
stated, that these men had died of malignant fevers, arising from bad nourishment. A few days,
however, after the arrival of the vessel at Pomegue, one of the crew died; and on the following day his body was removed from the ship, and
examined;—the principal surgeons of the city,
by their report, declared that they had not disco-

vered any symptoms of contagious disease, and
this tranquillized the general alarm. The Board
of Health then proceeded to make fresh regula
tions respecting the quarantine, which was fixed
to be for forty days. Towards the end of the
same month, three other vessels arrived at the
islands : one from Seide, which harbour it had
left since the plague had shown itself there ; ano
ther from the same place ; and the third from
Alexandria. They were ordered to perform stric
quarantine. The terror which the arrival of the
first vessel had excited had now subsided, and
it was just at this period that I returned to Mar
seilles. The circumstances which then occurred
I have told you ; and Aimée and I were just think
ing of visiting our favourite walks on the banks
of the Huveaune, and passing some delicious
weeks there, when it was reported in the city that
one of the guards, which were stationed on board
the vessels performing quarantine to prevent
any infraction of the sanitary laws, had died ;
but it was also said, that the surgeons had

examined his body, and had made the same satisfactory report as before. Still a second occurrence of this nature left an uneasy impression upon the mind; but when the passengers of these very ships had finished their quarantine, and were allowed to communicate with their friends, we began again to recover from our dread. Suddenly, however, a report was again spread that another of the crew, and a porter, who had been employed in removing the cargo, had fallen ill. The day after, the report was confirmed; with the addition, that two more men on board another vessel had likewise been taken ill. Two days after, my father, who was one of the Syndics of the town, received intelligence that all the four had died; but this circumstance was concealed from the people in general. The surgeons again, upon an examination of the bodies, made precisely the same report as before. The Board of Health, however, notwithstanding these several reports, determined upon separating the suspicious vessels from the rest, and sent them to perform their quarantine at a remote island. My father received constant intelligence from the Board of Health of all that was passing, but carefully concealed it from my mother; and, in acquainting me with the circumstances, recommended my observing the same precaution to my wife. Poor Aimée! she was surprised at my frequent conferences with my father, and used to chide me so fondly and so sweetly, saying, " That I was keeping some secret from her, and that I was cruel to irritate the chief failing of her sex by such mystery.' But we were unwilling to communicate to those so dear to us, the restless uneasiness my father and myself both felt ; and as I kissed her, I told her that we were preparing a festival for her —Alas! I little thought what that festival would be.

A few days after the death of the last persons, two others fell ill, and died. The surgeons who examined them made the usual report; but the next day, an individual belonging to the family

mily of one of them died, as also a third porter
employed on board the ships; and then the
surgeons declared that they had reason to suspect contagious disease.   The matter now began
to assume a serious aspect, and dispatches were
sent off by my father to the Council of Marine
at Paris, and to the Governor of the Province.
The magistrates assembled at the *Hôtel de Ville;*
and all the chief physicians of the city being admitted, stated, that they had discovered evident
symptoms of contagion in a house to which they
had been called.   A guard was immediately
stationed at the door of this house, and all communication with its inmates strictly forbidden.
The next day, however, the person upon whom
the physicians had discovered the unfavourable
symptoms died; and his wife, who was also ill,
soon followed him.   The bodies were removed
during the night, to avoid spreading the alarm,
and buried under the superintendence of a Syn-
dic;—the house was blocked up.   Thus matters

continued for some time, occasional cases of disease and death occurring; but the contagion not appearing to make any progress, and as it had been impossible to conceal all these circumstances from the city, every body began again to breathe more freely, and to hope that the alarm had been groundless. The populace even went so far as to insult the physicians and magistrates, who had recommended the continuation of the strict precautions which had been adopted.

The theatres were again filled with the abandoned and dissipated; who, struck with terror at the idea of such a termination to their vicious lives, had shrunk, appalled, from their usual haunts, and had begun to frequent the churches. The quays began again to look gay and busy; for the preceding events had caused such a panic that every one avoided the neighbourhood of the harbour, as the contagion was supposed to lurk there. My father's house was upon the quay which fronts the mouth of the port, and

from thence we could, with the aid of a glass,
discover the banished ships that were lying still
and lonely at the farthest island. We were now
in the month of July, and the heat of the sun
was intense: the *Mistral*, our preserver from
sickness and disease, had not passed through the
dusty and burning streets for many weeks; and
the sea presented an unbroken line of glittering
brightness far as the eye could reach. Aimée
and I went to our dear Huveaune, and there we
passed a week of peace and freshness, amidst
the green fig-trees and the rich flowers that
flourish there—an Eden in the midst of a dry
and arid wilderness; but at the end of that
week, I received a letter from my father, informing me that fifteen persons had fallen ill in
the *Rue de l'Escale*, one of the streets of the old
town, which you may have observed behind the
right side of the harbour; in whose dark and
narrow recesses one might almost expect to find
the true descendants of our Greek founders.

My father, however, added, that the physician:
who had examined these persons, by no mean
stated positively that they were attacked by th
plague. I determined upon immediately return
ing to the city; and Aimée, to whom I hac
now been obliged to communicate the content
of my father's letter, insisted upon accompanyin¿
me. "Never shall it be said of me, that I re
mained among the cool groves of our *bastide*,'
said she, "and left you to go alone, to risk your
self in that burning and threatening city. No
if God is pleased to visit these devoted wall
with some dreadful scourge, at least I wil
share the perils and labours that it may impos«
upon those whose situation requires exertion.'
We returned : but in our way we met many o
the inhabitants flying to the country, with a
much of their property as they could carr¡
with them. Aimée turned pale as she re
marked them, but said nothing ; and we arrivec
towards evening at my father's. He was no

at his house ; and my mother, whom we found
in great agitation, told us that he was gone to
the *Hôtel de Ville*. Leaving Aimée with her, I
hurried thither ; and inquiring for my father,
was admitted into the room where the Council
was assembled. The physicians were making
their report respecting the fifteen persons who
had fallen ill, and added, that eight of them had
died.   Still they would not give any positive
opinion as to the nature of their disease ; but
the Syndics resolved upon taking the strictest
precautions, and had all the bodies removed at
midnight. The houses where the disease had
terminated so fatally, were all fumigated and
blocked up ; and strong guards posted at the
entrance of the narrow street, to prevent all
communication with it. Fresh alarm was now
again excited ; the quays were all deserted,
and every body hurried through the streets in
suspicious haste. The churches were again
filled with kneeling and terrified crowds, who

made innumerable vows; and the confessional
were thronged with trembling penitents. To
add to the general dismay, a decree of the Par
liament of Aix was sent forth, forbidding al
communication between the country and the
city; and, from the higher parts of the public
walk, parties of troops might be seen stationing
themselves all round the walls, and taking the
appearance of a besieging army, while the vine
yards and fields were filled with tents, and fur
niture, and terrified crowds. I would have sent
Aimée to our *bastide*; but if she would have
gone, that was now impossible; for its quie
groves were probably occupied by the soldiery
who were stationed in that quarter. It was
bitter to me to think that those walks where
we had so lately wandered, and those flowers
that we had watched and watered ourselves
would now be trampled upon by the rude
and careless steps of these men. The ex
istence of the plague within the city was now

positively ascertained ; no further hesitation or doubt remained upon the minds of the physicians, and they had proposed, as a sure preventive to its spreading, that fires should be lighted at sunset through every street of the city. Accordingly, as soon as the evening-gun had announced to all vessels at sea that the harbour was closed for the night, at one and the same moment, the piles of wood which had been heaped up in every quarter were kindled, and spread their red light over the white city. I shall never forget the scene. The flames arose in thick and smoking volumes, and showed, indistinctly, the numerous crowds that were standing around watching their progress ; some of whom appeared almost to imagine that they were to work an immediate and beneficial effect. The waters of the harbour seemed like a sheet of fire ; and the ships that crossed the bay that night must have thought that the city was a prey to some dreadful conflagration. The Syndics

passed through all the streets, accompanied by
a body of troops; and at length the morning
arose bright and cheering upon the still awake
and wandering crowd. I had accompanied my
father part of the night in his duties, but :
quitted him when we reached the *Place Sain*
Ferreol, and hastened to my mother and Aimée
who were together. They were sitting at th
open window of our house that looked, as I hav
said, upon the harbour and quay, and gazing
upon the awful scene before them. My mothe
inquired anxiously where I had left my father
and seemed in the greatest alarm about him
Aimée, my dear affectionate wife, endeavoure
to tranquillize her, though I could perceive tha
she was far from feeling the confidence she wa
endeavouring to inspire. " Dear mother," sai
she, " all will yet be well; Henri here thinks so
—don't you think so, Henri?" Alas! I did no
think so; but I spoke encouragingly to the dea
beings that seemed to look to me for comfort

" I trust and hope it will be so," said I ; " the
wood has burnt bravely, and the whole city is
filled with its smoke and smell, which will check
and kill the plague if it be still clinging among
our garments and houses.   Besides, look at those
clouds yonder, surely they portend the *Mistral*,
whose fresh breath will sweep up the *Canebière*,
and dispense coolness and cheerfulness around.
Cheer up, dearest mother ! let us welcome my
father, after his arduous duty, with smiles.   See,
he is coming now, with that good and gallant
man the Chevalier Rose."   My father, accompanied by the Chevalier, came in, and we anxiously
questioned him upon the state in which the city
now was.   Their account was rather encouraging ; no fresh case of disease had occurred,
and much benefit was expected from the influence of the fires.   " It is singular," said the
Chevalier, " that the government has afforded
us no assistance: our provision must shortly
fail, the city is full of beggars ;—as we are cut

off from all communication with the country,
fear we shall be shortly in great want of sup
plies." At this moment a message arrived fron
the *Hôtel de Ville*, begging the attendance of th
Chevalier and my father immediately; and w
heard a loud uproar upon the quay. The pec
ple were clamorous for bread, as the flour
which the city had contained, was almost all ex
hausted. My mother and Aimée retired fron
the window, which I closed, saying, "This i
nothing, don't be alarmed, a few soft words anc
promises will soon quiet them. Dear Aimée
why do you tremble so?" and she fainted in m
arms. My mother and myself sprinkled he
forehead with water, and when she recovered
she burst into tears. "It is I that am the cow
ard now!" said she; "but, indeed, the sight o
those wild-looking men has filled me with ter
ror; what would become of us if the desperate
populace were to rise?" "Oh! fear not that, m
love," said I; "the Chevalier knows their hu

nour well, and ere now will have soothed them
nto patience." And I was not deceiving them,
or presently we heard loud shouting, and cries
f " *Vive le Chevalier Rose notre bienfaiteur !* "
choed along the harbour. I persuaded my
lear mother and Aimée to take some rest;
.nd, leaving the house, hastened to the *Hôtel de
Ville*, which I found surrounded by a crowd of
ersons of all descriptions. They seemed to be
n the utmost agitation, and repeatedly shouted
Saint Roch! Saint Roch! I recollected that the
ollowing day was the festival of that Saint, who
vas worshipped as our protector and guardian
rom pestilence. The Syndics had determined
ipon preventing the customary procession, as
hey dreaded the great increase of the contagion
vhich might thus be caused; but the ignorant
nd infatuated throng obstinately insisted upon
ts taking place; and such was their fury, that
he Syndics were obliged to give way; and even
he Chevalier Rose, who had tranquillized their

first clamour for bread, was unable to preva
upon them to give up the procession. Ac
cordingly, the next morning by daybreak th
whole city was flocking into the streets; and eve
those who had remained panic-stricken withi
their houses for some weeks, now made their ap
pearance, as if the influence of the Saint woul
dispel all the noxious and poisonous air aroun
them. The procession, accompanied by th
Syndics and a body of troops, set out from th
church, which you may have remarked on on
side of the *Cours*, and passing down the *Rue d
Canebière*, came out upon the quay; there i
halted, and the scene was singularly awful an
impressive. The vessels were all covered witl
flags, and manned with their crews in their bes
attire; while the houses all along the quay
were hung with green boughs and crimson sill
and tapestries. A party of troops, with drum
and trumpets, preceded the procession. A long
line of monks and friars was ranged around

the quay, bearing wax tapers and baskets of
flowers, chanting the hymn that is appropriated
to the service of the Saint.   Behind them,
and extending a little way up the street, stood
the priests of the different churches, with the
bishop at their head, mitred and arrayed in his
richest robes, surrounded by the magistrates,
while banners and olive-branches were waving
in the air above them.   Immediately before
the bishop, was carried a large silver image of
the Saint, the arms of which were extended, as
if in the act of bestowing blessings on all around.
At a signal which was given by the firing of a
gun, the immense crowd, which stood in the
street and along each side of the harbour, sunk
upon their knees ; the sailors knelt upon the
decks of their ships ; and the bishop, in an
audible and solemn tone, pronounced, amidst
the listening multitude, the prayer which is appointed to Saint Roch, and which you may see
hanging up in one of the apartments of the

Consigne. He ceased, and instantly the air resounded with loud shouts of *Saint Roch! Saint Roch! ora pro nobis!* and the bells of all the churches tolled quick and deep. I was looking upon the scene, with my mother and Aimée, from our window; and throwing my arms around the waist of each, we knelt at the signal, and remained some time in true and fervent prayer. I have often thought of that moment since, and wished that I could then have died. My heart was full of affection and devotion, and clasping the beings I most loved on earth, and with such a splendid sight before me, I could have sunk back into their arms, and never should have known the misery I afterwards felt. As we rose up, the hymn again burst forth from the departing train of priests, and was taken up by the crowd on the quays and the sailors, and echoed even over the sea, which lay listening in brightness and calm. "Surely," said Aimée, " our God will hearken to the intercession of the holy Saint, and accept the prayers and praises of such a multitude ; and if the supplication of a humble and affectionate heart be worthy of being accepted, mine has been heard, Henri, dear Henri!" and she threw her arms round me. " Can it be possible, as I have heard and read, that such a vast people as now stands before us could be all in one short week swept off by the withering hand of plague ?   It cannot surely be ; else, long ere now, the disease had spread, and not lingered in one single secluded street." " Alas !" said I, " that all the voices which are now calling on our patron Saint might be, ere long, hushed, or raised in agony, is but too true ; but let us hope the best." The procession now began to return from the quay ; and as the hymn gradually became softer and more distant, as the rich train passed up the *Canebière*, the crowd by degrees fell away, and the influence of the Saint appeared already to have visited them, for they were smiling, and more cheerful than they had been for weeks. But our trials and sufferings were but begun. This very festival, which the people had fondly trusted was to charm away the plague, was the means of its complete triumph; for it was like the fire that may lie smouldering and smothered in the black embers, but, if the match and dry rushes be cast upon it, kindles, and breaks out into a burning flame. The meeting of such a host of persons together, had collected into one centre all the lurking seeds of disease, and before two days had elapsed, the plague was raging in every part of the city in hungry wildness. The Syndics, however, still continued their exertions; and my father was not among the least active. But the labour of prevention and precaution was at an end; nothing now remained to be done but to alleviate suffering, and remove the ravages of death. The city began to wear an appearance of the most frightful desolation and dismay; and from the open windows of the long lines of houses, cries of agony and lamentation were heard. The harbour presented a scene of confusion and dread; the vessels were all drawn away from the quay, along which a strong palisade was erected; and bodies of troops were stationed at different intervals about the city, to protect and assist the Syndics in the discharge of their arduous duties, and to preserve some kind of order. You may imagine the constant and dreadful agitation in which my poor Aimée and my mother were kept, both on my account, and my father's; for I accompanied him every where, and assisted the Chevalier Rose in burying the dead. For to such a height had the disease now arrived, that almost all those persons who had been hitherto employed in doing this, had perished. The beggars and galley-slaves were employed, but they likewise sunk beneath the contagion, in great numbers; and the dead began to accumulate in vast frightful heaps in all parts of the city! What a

dreadful sight it was, as we made our rounds
There were the putrid and decaying corpse
lying all along the streets, and beneath the tree
of the public walks, which are now crowded
with gay revellers. Among them, and surround
ed by these horrid spectacles, lay whole familie
on small mattresses, moaning with pain and hun
ger, and parched with burning thirst. We me
persons wandering about in all the different spe
cies of madness, brought on by intense agony
Some were shrieking and yelling, and wildl
imploring assistance ; and others were langui
and worn out, and roamed along weeping an
wringing their hands. A single night was suff
cient to add more than a thousand carcases t
the already appalling heap; and horrible indee
were those nights. The weather was as calr
and clear as it is now, and continued so fc
weeks together. In vain did we pray for th
Mistral. The sun, as it went down every even
ing, left us no breeze to cool our parched bodies

and the night used to creep on amidst the groans
of the dying, and the howling of the city dogs,
which were likewise infected. Sometimes, at
intervals, we could hear, from the upper end of
the *Cours*, the trumpets of the troops that were
watching our devoted walls, and they echoed
solemnly and sadly over the vineyards. Still,
among these sights of danger and devastation,
my excellent father remained firm ; and through
the exertions of the Syndics and the Chevalier
Rose, and the pious labours of the bishop and
the priests of the different parishes, some scanty
comfort and relief were afforded to the afflicted
and suffering people. But the most heart-rending sight of all, that hourly and momentarily
met our eyes, was that of numbers of infants
moaning in their cradles by the side of their dead
mothers !

But I must pause now, my son ; it is long
since I have talked of these matters, and the
relating of them brings them as fresh before me

as ever. Let us retire into my cell, and refresl
ourselves with some of these ripe grapes anc
oranges ; my mouth is parched, and the sun be
gins to beat through the leaves of these fig-trees
We will remain till the evening breeze rises anc
breathes through the wood."—We entered th
cell ; and the old man, going up to the crucifix
knelt before it, and repeated a low prayer, witl
his head bent down to the earth ; then rising
and pointing to the oranges, " Taste them, my
son," said he, " they are from Nice, that mountain Paradise, and the gardens where they grov
may be seen glittering from the wide sea. You
are not aware, perhaps, that this fruit will no
prosper except in the neighbourhood of the sea
and that, like our restless flies, it delights in the
warmest and most genial spots." I observed to
the old man that I had never been at Nice.
" 'Tis a lovely place," said he ; " and I wonder
not that so many of your sick countrymen should
select it for their graves. Our seas and skies are

blue here; but, then, we have the impetuous *Mistral,* which roots up our woods and vineyards, and choaks us with the white dust of our roads. But there it is far otherwise ;——nestled in the arms of a deep bay, and sheltered by lofty rocks. Nice feels not the rude breath of the *Mistral,* and enjoys, during the winter months, such weather as would charm the unhappy into forgetfulness of the past. All around are rich woods of olives, bathed by the quiet waters, and clothing the rugged and perpendicular sides of the Genoese Alps. I remember when I was there in my youth, with my mother and my lost Aimée, I used to wander, in dreaming and delicious visions, along the myrtle-clad shores. And, I was once particularly delighted with the grand appearance of Corsica, which, in a clear morning horizon, resembled the pinnacles of some magic castle ; for as the sun rose, and his rays flung a misty light over the island, it seemed gradually to fade and sink beneath the waters.

And I recollect that my father laughed at me
when I told him that I had seen it. Why it is
fifty leagues off, said he : but still I had seen
the island, for the fishermen all told me so ; and
I remember too a little chapel built in the rock
and dedicated to Saint Charles, where I used to
go and sit, and look over the rich valley that lay
beneath. Convents and churches, with their
marble staircases and pillars, glittered amid the
olives that covered the high banks of the torrent
river Paglion, that runs through the valley
while in the distance, near the city, were the rich
fruits you see there mingling themselves with
the fig and almond trees that were just put
ting out their pink blossoms ; and then, when I
clambered higher, and reached the old castle of
Montalbano, which was at that time an impor
tant fortress,—then, what a glorious prospect
used I to discover ! The wide bay before me
with its rich green shores, and Antibes sparkling
in the distance ; beneath me the harbour of

Villa Franca, inclosed in a semicircle of wooded hills, and its tall light-house, at the end of the narrow quay ; and behind me the dark rough rocks which overhang Nice, backed by the snowy Alps, like the advanced-guard of a mighty army, whose white plumes might be seen stretching and towering away in unequal and interminable lines.——But come," said the old man, " the sun is sinking behind yon projecting point of the bay, the leaves begin to tremble ; we will resume our seat on the rocks, and I will endeavour to conclude my melancholy story." We went out, and the Hermit sat down amongst the wild herbs, while I remained leaning against the trunk of a large pine, which was growing out of the rock.

CHAPTER XI.

I TOLD you, resumed the Hermit, tha
our eyes were affected and wounded with th
pitiable sight of the poor helpless infants, that la
weeping and sobbing beside the lifeless bodies o
those mothers that could no longer soothe an
hush their cries. Among those women I re
marked, as I was passing through the *Cours*
the wife of one of the porters that had for
merly been employed by my father; and takin
up her poor little infant, which was clingin
to her cold breast, I carried it off in my arm
to our house. My mother and Aimée receive
the child with tenderness and soft compassion
and procured some milk from the goats, whicl
wandered neglected about the city; and the
had the satisfaction to restore the little crea

ture to strength.   We were now in the month of September.   The disease was unabated and unrelenting in its course, and dire and dark had been its ravages.   The magistrates assembled at the *Hôtel de Ville* towards the beginning of the month, and examined into the condition of the city, and the number of deaths which had taken place.   The result of the examination was appalling! For the circumstance of their own number being reduced to one-third of what it had been a month before, was sufficient to impress their minds with an idea of the general extent of the ruin.   Upwards of five hundred persons immediately connected with the *Hôtel de Ville* had perished.   The city guard, which had been engaged in superintending the distribution of wine to the people, and in preserving order, were almost all swept away; and the officers of the police were every one dead.   The magistrates who remained alive, sat looking at one another in silence for some time; till the

Chevalier Rose, addressing them in an encou
raging and noble speech, inspired them wit
fresh hope and confidence. " Fellow citizens,
said he, " let us not shrink from our imperativ
duties. If we are at last to perish by the disea:
which now rages unresisted in the city, let u
at least, while we are lying in pain and solitud(
have the consoling reflection that we have dor
what we ought. Let us imitate the bright e>
ample of our virtuous Bishop, whom I can se
now, through the windows of this chambe
moving among the sick and dying; attended b
his priests and friars, and administering bodil
and spiritual nourishment to those who ai
neglected by all but God and his minister:
Let us remember that the eyes of our countr
are upon us; that our conduct in these peri
ous times will be handed down to the admir;
tion or contempt of posterity." And as h
concluded, the other magistrates rose simult;
neously, and going to him, clasped his hand:

and promised to stand by him firmly to the last. My father had not attended the meeting; he had been engaged in the *Place Saint Fer-reol*, in superintending the carrying away a vast pile of bodies that were heaped up in the centre. I left the *Hôtel de Ville*; I joined him in the *Place*; and there stood the few remaining galley-slaves, clothed in large loose dresses, with wide hanging sleeves, dragging the bodies with long iron hooks, and tossing them into carts. I recognised among these appalling heaps, which were training amid the dust, and distorted with the last pangs of distraction and delirious pain, some that I had been accustomed to pass many happy hours with upon that very place. The galley-slaves began, however, to be refractory, and refused any longer to work; and my father and myself were in great perplexity and difficulty, when the Chevalier Rose arrived. "How now!" he called out to the desperate and rebellious slaves, who had cast themselves upon the

earth, and hid their faces in the long sleeves
of their garments;—" how now, ye wild and
wicked wretches!—is it thus that ye expect to
obtain pardon for your crimes? Is it thus
that ye expiate the dark and deadly deeds
whose mark ye bear? Do ye not hear the
groans and shrieks of the dying around you,
and who are wandering in misery through the
city? Such will be your eternal fate, unhappy
men! such is the hell that awaits your guilty
souls, if ye will not do our bidding! And of
what do ye complain? Are ye exposed to
greater danger than your magistrates? Do ye
see us shrink from duty?"—and seizing from
the hands of one of them an iron hook, he continued, " Rise! rise! the Chevalier Rose never
asked man to encounter peril which he himself
would shun! Rise, and follow me!" And
having thus spoken, he began himself to drag
the corrupted carcases, and fling them into the
cart. The galley-slaves, used to his well-known
voice and influence, rose; and giving him a

oud cheer, continued their labour. The heavily laden tumbril then passed slowly down the street, and along the quay, rolling on towards the *Place de la Tourette* ; where, doubtless, my son, you, who love the glorious sights of Nature, have stood. Beneath that place had been discovered some dark subterranean caverns which communicated with the sea, whose waters echoed among them. The promiscuous and livid bodies were hurled down into the gloomy depths ; and the dashing of the breakers, and the screams of the sea-birds, were their only requiem. You have, perhaps, seen the painting which represents this awful scene ; it is, I believe, in one of the chambers of the chateau *Borelli.* I replied, that I had seen it; as also another, at the *Consigne,* displaying the terrible effects of the plague, and the heart-rending scenes of sorrow and separation which it had caused.——The old man clasped his hands together, and casting his eyes up to Heaven, said : Of separation and

sorrow, indeed ! God knows it has been so to me !
A father, mother, and a young new-made bride,
all, all, swept off ! while I was spared to linger
out a long and lonely life. When I saw so
many dying around me ; when I felt their hot
breath upon me, and listened to their cries, I
thanked God for my life, and hurried back daily,
after attending my father, to my affectionate
Aimée. But when I had none left to return to,
when none sat watching for me at the window
which looked towards the *Hôtel de Ville*, then I
could and did pray for death. But I have
somewhere read, as I read much now, that there
are persons so constituted, that the danger in
which they may be placed, only serves to keep
their blood in that wholesome agitation and
warmth which prevents them from sinking
into the dangerous lassitude of fear ; and that
le peril monte à la tête comme le vin, I think
the expression was. For though I was daily
and nightly engaged in assisting my father in

the performance of his duties, yet the hand of disease passed harmless over me. Not so did it spare my father! For towards the end of September, one morning as he was passing through a narrow street of the old town, his foot slipped, and he rolled among a heap of the festering carcases. The shock, the disgust of this circumstance, affected him so much, and had so tainted his blood, that upon his return home, which he immediately did, he complained of sickness, and before the next morning was in the last agonies of the disease. We all, you may conceive, were stricken to the heart. The whole night we had watched by his restless pillow; and Aimée had supported his burning forehead in her arms. She would not quit him; and I stood looking on, in dreadful anticipation of what might yet follow. The poor little babe lay sleeping softly in its cradle, unheeding the fearful scene which was passing around it. My mother knelt before the crucifix which was

at the head of the bed, and occasionally sprin
kled my father's forehead with perfumed water
He, alas! knew us not, his senses wandered, h
fancied himself still endeavouring to extricat
himself from among the fatal heap of bodies
and he struggled and strove to free himsel
from our arms;—but all was soon over! anc
Marseilles lost another of her best and mos
useful citizens. We could not bear the idea o
burying him instantly, as our safety seemed t
require; but a few hours after his death, m
mother, who had sat silent and inattentive t
every thing by the side of the bed, lookin;
upon the fast-changing features, complained o
violent pains in her head. Aimée and mysel
both shuddered at her words, and we had reason
for ere the sun had cast his last beams upon ou
windows, my father and mother lay by eacl
other, in rest from all their pain! Aimée anc
I knelt before the crucifix, and offered up ou
prayers for their departed spirits. But the bit

ter thought that they must be buried directly, that our lives, my precious Aimée's life, might be endangered if their bodies were allowed to remain, soon presented itself to me.   But could I see them thrown into the yawning pits of the *Tourette ?* (since, in those times, there were no distinctions of rich and poor funerals,)—impossible ! and I determined upon bearing them myself to the garden, which was behind the house that belonged to my wife's father, who was then in America.   I sprinkled them with vinegar; and wrapping myself in a wide cloak, I conveyed them separately away, and laid them with my own hands in one grave, beneath the almond-trees.

Thus had I, at last, begun to feel in my own family the desolation and blank which the destructive ravages of the disease had caused ; and all I had now left in the world to live for, was my Aimée.   But she was spared to me ; and I made a vow to the Holy Virgin, that I would dedicate my first daughter to her service, if both our days were lengthened, and our lives spared to see our children flourishing around us. The first period which passed after our loss, was dreary and disconsolate; I had been my poor father's companion in his difficult and dangerous duties; and now I went forth alone, and bitterly did I lament the painful privation. But I soon gave up my former exertions; a secret and undefinable dread began to hang over me, and I was unwilling to quit Aimée for any length of time. She, innocent and tender as she was, began to recover her spirits; and as the autumn advanced, when the heat decreases, and the chill *Mistral* sweeps up from the north, with its dark train of clouds, we both hoped that some diminution of the disease would take place. For increase, it scarcely could. The harbour before our windows presented a frightful appearance;— its waters were covered with the floating carcases of men and animals, and the ships lay silent and gloomy upon the corrupted waters.

All along the quay were scattered the precious, and now useless cargoes, which had been intended for a healthy and happy city; but some of which had, perhaps, caused the ruin that lay around them, and mocked the rich productions of America and Italy. And when I ventured into the streets to examine into the state in which the city was, what a sight presented itself! It had seemed, weeks before, as if nothing could have added to the dismay and darkness of the scene; but though the contagion was then at its height, it had not accomplished all its wild work. The long wide street of *La Canebière* was filled with beds, and furniture of all descriptions, thrown from the windows of the houses, which looked white and desolate, like a long range of tombs. At some of the windows were a few pale and emaciated wretches, who were leaning upon their withered arms, and

looking down towards the sea, as if the sight of
it could have refreshed and cooled the poison of
their blood. Higher up in the *Cours*, and close
to the gates of Aix and Prome, lay a vast heap of
goats and horses, which had died of hunger and
disease, while black swarms of mosquitoes were
humming and hovering about them. Here and
there among the piles of human bodies, which
were spread in every direction, lay the Friars
and Monks of the different Orders which the
city contained; their hands crossed upon their
breasts, and clasping their beads. For terribly
had the good brothers suffered in the exercise
of their Christian and compassionate ministry.
Capuchins, Jesuits, Observantines, Recollets,
barefooted Carmelites, Trinitarians, Dominicans,
and many others, to the amount of three hundred,
besides the greatest part of the *Curés* of the different parishes, were scattered all through the
city, in death and decay. The hospitals had become incapable of containing the sick; for the

moment any symptoms of contagion appeared
upon any one, he was frequently, and instantly,
deserted by all his kindred and friends, and left
to die in his lonely chamber of hunger and pain,
or obliged to crawl to the hospital.   But those
establishments soon could contain no more, and
thus thousands were compelled to drag their
weak and wasted limbs to some shady corner or
doorway, where they might lie unmolested and
die.   Thus passed away the month of September
and part of October.   The Chevalier Rose, and
our pious Bishop, ceased not to pass among the
afflicted people, like protecting prophets, of whom
it might have been said in the words of the holy
King David, "A thousand shall fall beside
thee, and ten thousand at thy right hand, but
the pestilence shall not come nigh thee."   The
month of October at last concluded, and the
first of November our holy festival of All Saints
arrived.   Who would have thought upon that
anniversary a year before, that its revolving

successor would have presented such a spectacle as that day rose upon? Then, all was still and solemn, the religious crowd were quietly and slowly pacing to the churches, to pray for their departed relations, and the city was at rest from its labours, but not as it was at that moment. Those who had knelt and asked the interces sion of the blessed saints, for the suffering souls of the dead, were now, perhaps, themselves all mingled among them, and expiating their own sins.

It had been determined by the few remaining Magistrates and the good Bishop, that upon this day, an encouraging and unusually solemn ser vice and procession should take place; and that a new festival should be instituted, in memory of the destruction which the plague had caused, and as a means, possibly, of appeasing the wrath and awakening the pity of God. There were no longer the same reasons to prevent the celebra tion of this ceremony, as had existed some months

before with respect to that of St. Roch. Then
we were endeavouring to baffle the insidious
pest, and to detect and quell its silent course.
Now all was different : its fury and fire had
gone the way they would, and worked their
pleasure, and we had but to pray for relief and
future alleviation. On that morning Aimée and
I had gone to the garden where our parents
were buried ; and kneeling upon their graves,
and clasping each other's hands, we had poured
out our supplications to the interceding Saviour,
and his blessed Mother. When we returned,
Aimée took the laughing infant from the servant's arms, and, going to the window, stood
playing with it and fondling it there. The
heat was so intense still, that we were compelled
to throw open our windows, to admit some of
the fresh sea-air, though the sight that lay before us was so dismal. But long habit had somewhat accustomed us to it, and my wife could
now for a short time enjoy the cool breeze when

it visited us.   I placed myself at her side, and
putting my arm round her waist, I told her o
the ceremony which was just about to take place
" God bless our Bishop, and the noble Chevalier
said she.; they have supported and soothed the
sinking courage and spirits of us all, and long
will   their   names   be   loved   and   remembered
Hereafter, dear Henri, as we stand upon th
Tourette on some cool autumnal evening, and
look down upon the city and healthy waters, and
once   more   busy   quays,   we   shall   talk   of   thes
days   with   shuddering   recollection,   and   com
pare the cheerful scene with that which now lie
before us.   We shall talk of the good Bisho
aud our friend the Chevalier, who will then b
saints in heaven ; and as we sit upon the scan
tered blocks of marble, while our children   an
around us, we shall feel the gale playing upo
our faces, we shall hear the Catalan's evenin
song, as he sails into the peaceful harbour
and we shall feel our hearts sad but grateful

the remembrance of these burning days." " May it be so! may your anticipations be accomplished, my best of treasures! said I; thank God! I too, have done my duty, and in times like these may say so. Not for worlds would I have to reflect upon my having selfishly consulted my own safety, and shrunk from sharing the dangers which my fellow-citizens have encountered. But for thy sake am I spared; thy innocence and love have interceded for me, like yon misty vapour, that is just gathering about the sun, and will prevent his burning rays from falling upon the holy procession. And thy soft and compassionate care of that sleeping babe will plead for us both, and rising up to heaven with the prayers and incense that our priests will soon offer, may at last appease the angry Saints. See! the Magistrates and the Chevalier are passing along the quay, and proceeding to join the procession; they wave their hands to us. I leave thee, Aimée, I go to pray for us all before the holy

sacrament, but will not tarry long." As I said
these words, the bell of the cathedral from
whence the train was to set out, slowly tolled
and swung its solemn sound down upon the
quay. At its deep knell, the sick, the dying, the
desperate men, women, and children, that were
scattered and spread along the brink of the
waters, as if they had hoped to find some relief
upon the cold stone-work which hung above
them, raised their feeble limbs, and staggered
and tottered toward the *Cours,* where the solemn
service was to take place. I hastened thither, and
an affecting and striking appearance did it pre
sent. At one extremity was erected a tempo
rary altar surrounded with green branches and
boughs, and covered with fair white muslin
Above it hung a rich crimson canopy, bordered
with golden fringes and tassels, and surmounted
by white plumes of feathers. Upon the altar
were placed tapers and flowers, and bright
golden vessels ; while all around were strewed

fresh leaves and roses. The steps which led up to the table were covered with precious tapestries; and upon the canopy was worked a large bleeding heart, surrounded by the words *Sacré Cœur de Jesus*. From among the trees which lined each side of the *Cours*, waved painted banners and pictures of Saints, mixed with mirrors and crosses, and blessed beads. But the living scene was sadly and mournfully contrasted with the pride and pomp, and sumptuous show of the holy preparations. There lay the dying upon their mattresses, which they had contrived to have placed as near the altar as possible ; and as they tossed and turned upon their feverish beds, they ceased not to fix their eyes upon the sacred heart. Then came crowding round, those whom the disease had yet spared, but who looked as pale and palsied as if they had risen from their graves. Their staring eyes, and skeleton bodies, mingled themselves horribly with the banners and branches which

hung above them; and their anxious features
were reflected all down the *Cours* in the mirrors,
which, as they swung about in the wind, seemed
to multiply them in endless and ghastly lines.
Presently we heard the voices of the priests and
friars approaching, accompanied by the hoarse
and lengthened tones of the trumpet, which
seemed, indeed, to be spreading its miraculous
sound among the graves of the world, and sum-
moning mankind before the Eternal Throne!
I thought then upon my poor parents, and I
bowed my head upon my hands in prayer.
Daily and nightly do I kneel before yon crucifix; but never, never have I offered up my
heart to God with such fervour and intensity
as upon that well-remembered day! The procession came slowly on; the thronging people
listened in silence, and the restless and dying
sufferers lay still upon their beds. But, alas!
how different did it appear from what it had
been some months before! Then, there was a

long train of priests and friars, and magistrates, and military pomp; while the bishop, arrayed in his mitre and splendid stole, looked with encouraging and noble countenance upon the faithful people. All this was changed. Attended only by the Chevalier Rose and two or three magistrates, which were all that remained; a few of the canons of the *Acoules*; and the *Curé*, and some priests of the parish of *St. Ferreol;* he walked in humility and mortification; clothed in coarse garments, the rope of penitence round his neck, the cross traced upon his breast, and barefooted, the pious prelate ascended the steps of the altar, and threw himself in deep and ardent devotion at its feet. Then rising and turning round towards his kneeling flock, and spreading his hands above them, he bestowed upon them the consoling and comforting benediction, the *Dominus sit vobiscum!* which recalls the wandering mind to its duty. Then consecrating the holy wafer, and murmuring over it the mysterious and unheard prayer, he held it up to the expecting multitude, who bent their bodies to the earth. And having partaken himself of the blessed sacrament, and distributed it to the ministering priests, he solemnly dedicated the city to the *Sacré Cœur de Jesus,** and instituted and appointed the day to be kept as a festival once in every century. He then descended the steps of the altar, and passing among the thickly spread mattresses, he anointed the now hushed and grateful sufferers with the consecrated oil; and many, as his fingers completed the Christian sign upon their foreheads, looked upon his face and died.

I remained praying and kneeling in admiration and awe; but the thought of Aimée, who

* Upon the banners which are carried at this procession, the Saviour is represented with a heart upon his breast, surmounted by a cross, and encircled by a glittering glory, to which he points, as if bidding mankind confide and appeal to his love.

must be expecting me, made me start to my feet, and bowing my head to the bishop, who was standing close to me, I hurried away. My house was close by, and, as I hastened up the stair, I heard my wife laughing, and the little baby crowing and chuckling with joy. When I entered the room, Aimée was playing with a ball of cotton, which she was throwing and making roll about the room to amuse the child. "Bless you, my love!" said I to her, "it is indeed refreshing, after such a sight as I come from, to find you thus; come, let me, too, join in your sport;" and I strove to snatch the ball from her, which she playfully hid in her bosom. "Oh!" said she, "you cannot have this, it came here from a young and gay knight that was lingering beneath my window; and, I suppose, contains soft and sugared words." "What do you mean, Aimée?" said I; "you are become too poetical and mysterious in your language for my understanding!" and I believe I looked angry.

" Fie, Henri !" said the gentle creature ; " what
are you envious of my new acquirements ? I
thought you loved me better than to be vexed a
my prating folly : let us not quarrel about thi
toy," and she threw it on the ground. I looked
at her, and saw the tears starting to her eyes
my heart smote me, and I flung my arms round
her neck, while the babe played with my hair
" Oh ! there stands my knight," said Aimée
pointing to a little boy who was upon the qua
just below our window ; " see how wistful he look
up to us." " What do you mean, my love ?"
said I. " Well, if you must know this might
secret," said my wife, " that careless rogue i
playing with his ball, (poor fellow ! it is well fo
him that he has health and spirits to do so,
flung it up through the window, and then ra
away, frightened at his fault ; see, one of th
squares is broken." I took up the ball, an
threw it down to the boy, who ran off immedi
ately ; but seeing the Chevalier passing toward

the *Hôtel de Ville*, I kissed Aimée, and hastened
after him.

The Chevalier had just received a report from
the remaining physicians of the city, stating that
the disease was sensibly diminishing. "Thank
God!" said he, "our gates will soon be opened,
and the assistance of money and provisions, promised us by the Parliament of Aix, will soon
arrive.   Henri, my friend, I have supported
myself through these trying scenes by God's
assistance! but I know not what I should do,
did they last much longer.   To see so many of
our best and dearest friends and citizens lying
dead and deserted ; and to think of the dreary
void that must be here when health returns to
us! Great God! look at this silent hall!" continued he, as we entered the council chamber ;
" look at that circle of chairs ! almost all those
who filled them some months ago, and were con-
gratulating themselves upon the success of their
precautions, are now—where shall I say ? for I

know not—flung, perhaps, amidst the slaves and
the beggars into the caverns of the *Tourelte*. I
shuddered at the recollection of the scene which
I had witnessed there, and said, " At least, my
dear Rose, my own father and mother are
buried in an unpolluted, though it be not a consecrated grave. The almond-trees with their
green leaves and pink blossoms shade the earth
which covers them ; and the breeze which
sweeps along the vineyards, breathes freshness
among the flowers that my Aimée planted
there." We looked out upon the harbour,
whose vessels were beginning to assume a
healthier appearance ; the sailors being employed
in washing their decks, and hanging out into the
air the beds of those whose bodies were floating around. The men had hitherto remained
indifferent and inactive ; and with the reckless
desperation of their disposition, had passed the
little time they expected to live, in intemperance
and blasphemy. But the holy ceremony seemed

to have changed the hearts and elevated the hopes of all, and some were even singing their long-neglected songs. The Castle of St. Nicholas, on the opposite quay, was deserted and dreary, very different from the appearance it had presented when I had anchored beneath it five months before. But it was no longer bathed by the same untainted waters; heaps of human carcases floated along by its walls, and the green and gangrened limbs of various animals were piled up on the rocks at its feet. " Look," said the Chevalier, " look at yon vessel which lies close to the *Consigne*; she is but small, and yet the pestilence which has swept off so many thousands from this vast city, came lurking among her precious silks. Those fair forms for whose pride and pomp they were woven and wafted hither, are now a prey to the worm and the water-rat. And how is thy wife?" continued he, " does she still hold up in cheerfulness and confidence? Thou art indeed happy in having such

a comfort under these afflictions. I think I can
see her at the window of thy house;" and in fact
Aimée was leaning out of the window upon her
hand; the child was not with her, and I supposed
that it slept. I waved my hand to her, but she
saw me not, else I knew she would have kissed
those white fingers to me. A friar just then
came up to the *Hôtel*, and inquired for the Chevalier. We descended from the balcony where
we had been standing, and found the religious
below. He was the bearer of a message from the
Bishop, requesting the Chevalier's assistance in
distributing the bread and wine which the virtuous and venerable patriarch had daily bestowed upon the hungry people. Hitherto they
had received it in tranquillity, and trembling
anticipation that they might never need more;
but now, since the mass, they had recovered
their hope and strength, and numbers who had
wandered about before, careless of nourishment,
now rushed towards the episcopal palace, and

ressed upon one another in close and crush-
ng confusion.

Such was the report of the friar, and the
Chevalier's powerful interference could alone
erhaps prevent this additional evil. He has-
ened off with the messenger, and I returned
o Aimée. She was still leaning upon the win-
low; and as I passed under it, I looked up,
ind smiling, said to her, " Here I am, my love;
you need not lean and linger there now, to
vatch for me; here I am, come to complete
our peace." She smiled upon me, but spoke
iot; and an unpleasant and uneasy sensation
assed across me, as I looked at her languid
yes. I hastened up the stairs, and into the
oom; the infant was not there; and Aimée, hear-
ng me come in, turned round and held out her
iand to me. There was something in the way
he did this so unusual, so unlike her general
manner, that I stood still for an instant, looking
ipon her in silence. Her countenance was still

cheerful and smiling, but there was an expression of lassitude and debility in the features, and
a slight redness hung about her eyelids ; her
hands were hot, but so were the sun's rays, which
had been beating upon the window as it was
sinking into the sea ; and I said to her, " My
inconsiderate, careless Aimée, is it thus you consult our happiness, by making yourself ill, and
exposing your delicate frame so long to those
dangerous beams ? Here, taste these oranges,
which you know have been preserved here ever
since my return from Cadiz : they will cool
your tongue and parched lips ;" for she complained of thirst, and said that her mouth seemed
burning. She took the oranges, and, dividing one
into two parts, gave me one, saying, " You too
must be weary, my dearest husband. Alas ! we
weak women require so much care and cherishing,
and yet remain inactive and useless ! while you,
proud in your strength and courage, seem re-
gardless of fatigue and danger." The moist syrup

seemed to relieve her ; and being anxious to know if the tumult and trouble around the bishop's palace had been appeased, I tenderly embraced my wife, and telling her where I was going, I left her, as I thought, refreshed and restored from the noxious effects of the sun. I hastened up to the palace, and there I beheld indeed the influence of heroism and piety. The vast crowd was hushed and tranquil ; the excellent Bishop stood upon the steps, surrounded by the priests, one of whom held up a large silver cross ; the Chevalier was just below him. The obedient people came, one by one, in patience and gratitude, and received upon their knees, from the hands of the good Belsunce, the strengthening donation. The venerable man blessed each as he knelt down, and the Chevalier addressed to many of them some encouraging expressions. " That is well," said he to one man whom he had observed before as among the most violent, " that is well, my good man ; your fellow-citizens

can now partake in tranquillity of these alms,
and your next confession will be more acceptable
to your priest than if you had converted the
Bishop's charitable exertions into a scene of disappointment, and perhaps death. "*Oui, mon
Chevalier*," said the man, "if ever God descended upon the earth to befriend the poor, he
is among us now. When I look at you and our
merciful Bishop, I am sure that ye are the angels
appointed to assist us in our distress." "So, my
pretty maiden," said my friend Rose to a young
flower-girl, "could not you find a lover to come
and receive your mother's portion, without being
compelled to struggle and strive with those slender limbs among the crowd?" The girl blushed
as she saw those near her smiling, and said,
"Oh! Sir, to be sure, Adolphe would have
come directly, but, thank God, he is at Paris,"
clasping her hands as the Bishop blessed her.

Well, my son, the blessed and Christian office
lasted till the moon rose, and even after; for the

aged and infirm, who could not advance before,
now made their feeble way up to the Bishop's
feet; and a beautiful sight it was to see them, as
the moonlight fell upon their furrowed faces,
holding up their shaking hands, and themselves
blessing the holy priests. I could have lingered
much longer there, but Aimée was alone; and I
walked slowly back towards my house, among
the retiring people. As we passed along the end
of the *Cours*, we saw sitting, upon one of those
benches under the trees, where probably, my
son, you have often sought shade, a Turk who
had long dwelt at Marseilles, and was noted for
his skill in medicine. His name was Hassan;
and he had perhaps, by his spices and prescrip-
tions, preserved numbers from falling a prey to
the pestilence. He was sitting calmly and
gravely amidst the bodies which still lay around,
and held in one hand a pipe, which he was
smoking, while the other was concealed in the
folds of his robe. As we passed by him, the peo-

ple saluted him, and seemed to do so with a sort of awe. Hassan replied to their address with a slow and tranquil bow, seeming to be perfectly indifferent to the living and the dead around him. It was a striking and strong instance of that system of fate and fixed destiny which you have probably heard of, my son, and the believers in which feel neither hope nor fear, but await the inevitable event in complete composure.

I reached my house, the windows were closed which surprised me, as I knew my Aimée loved to stand and gaze upon the waters of the harbour as the moon shone upon them, and which had been during the afternoon freed in a great degree from the putrid bodies, by the sailors who, moving about in boats, had pushed them with long poles towards the mouth of the harbour, from whence they floated away round up to the rocks along the coast. But my wife, I thought, might probably be performing her evening devotions ; and as I drew near the door, I heard her voice in low and confused murmurs. But, Mother of God ! how did I find her ! I had left her sitting at her embroidery, at a table near the window, and I looked towards that part of the room. She was not there. The rest of the apartment was in darkness, and the moon just threw a few beams upon the table, which was covered with painted roses and velvets, and shining silks. I was alarmed ; I heard however her voice, and stepping on, my foot (and the old man shuddered) struck against something which lay upon the floor. It was my wife. She knew me, called to me; " Henri, raise me up ; I am ill, my feet are weak and wavering, and, in crossing the room to fetch my guitar, I have fallen here." I raised her up, and supporting her in my arms, I bore her to the couch. Her hands were like fire, and her lips, as I kissed them, almost clung to mine. " Aimée, my precious creature," I asked in agony and horror, " what dost thou feel ? what means this strange weakness ? Are you in pain ?" " My tongue is blistered, my forehead throbs," said she, " and I could drink the worst and dullest water." I put one of the oranges to her lips, but she seemed to heed it not, in spite of her wish for moisture. The truth now at once flashed upon my distracted mind : the pestilence had breathed upon her ; but how, and in what manner, and from whence had it come ? Aimée had never once quitted the house, and the servant was too terrified to do so, and, I knew, had not. Suddenly the circumstance of the ball darted across me. It was even so,—the infected cotton had communicated its poison to my wife's heart's blood. She continued to lie in my arms, but still and tranquil, as if my embrace had power to refresh and soothe her ; but soon she complained of shooting pains in all her limbs, and seemed growing worse. I called wildly for the servant ; and telling her to watch by her mistress, and whis-

pering my suffering Aimée that I would soon
bring her relief, hurried away to the *Cours*.
The Turk, Hassan, was still there, and I rushed
up to him. "Come with me, come fly, Hassan!"
I almost shrieked out; "bring hither thy simples
and spells, for they are all needed." The Maho-
metan looked at me calmly as he slowly rose;
and said, "*Allah! il Allah!* there is no God
but *Allah!* and Mahomet is his Prophet. What
is to be must be. The camel may not strive
against his master, nor the slave against the whip;
nevertheless, I will go with thee, young man."
He gathered up his long garments, and walked
on, but so deliberately, that I was tempted to
upbraid him with his cruelty. When we got
back to my house, the pest had not lingered in
its course : my poor wife was delirious, and her
cries wrung and racked my heart-strings. I
sunk upon my knees by the side of the couch,
and took her clenched hand into my own. She
knew me not ! Her words were wild and wan-

dering, and she raved of harps, and saints, and sleeping angels. "Give me the babe!" she shrieked out; "give me the babe! see, they ask me for it! they frown upon me, and wave me away, and point to it. Give me the babe! Ah now," and she clasped my hand; "now I have him, the blessed Virgin opens her arms to me, the angels tune their harps!" And fatigued and exhausted by the paroxysm, she then lay still. Hassan stood at the foot of the couch, looking down upon her in silence; and when she ceased to rave, he slowly shook his head. "The Black Spirit hath been here," said he; "I see the point of his sable arrow, even now, festering in those boils which are upon thy wife's neck : not all the herbs and frankincense of our spicy groves could now sweeten or heal her blood. Thy fair Palm-tree must die, young man; the hot blast of the Simoom hath scorched her."—If you, my son, have ever lost something which seemed to form a part of your existence, and your words would lead me to suppose that you have, then can you feel for me, and conceive what I suffered as the Physician Hassan spoke thus.

" No! no! say not so! good Turk," I cried, " say not so! I will give thee gold and merchandise sufficient to make thee Vizier over thy native city, if thou wilt heal this sweet saint." " It cannot be," said Hassan, "alas! pity it is that so fair a creature should die an infidel, and be for ever cut off from the blessed gardens of our Paradise, and the songs and pleasures of the favoured Houris. But it cannot be! the Angel of Death is even now covering her with his wings;" and the death-pang began indeed to rattle in her throat. But I cannot, I cannot tell thee how she died; I scarcely know. I remember something of her clinging to my neck, and kissing my forehead, and the screams of the servant, and the odour of essences and spices; but nothing distinct remains upon my recollection. I became delirious, as they told me afterwards, and knew no one, not even my friend Rose, who never left me. When I recovered my senses, after a month's darkness and distraction, all was blank. My loss alone stood before me, like yon rugged island, which is surrounded by a cold unfathomable waste. My wife had been buried in the same grave with my parents, by the care of my affectionate Rose!

During my derangement the month of November had passed quite away. December arrived, and brought with it the *Mistral,* and the malady, as they told me, was dying away; and need, indeed, it had to do so, for it had little left to ravage. The parliament of Aix, towards the end of the month, withdrew the line of troops from before our walls, and the new year opened encouragingly upon the reviving city. But it brought no change of prospects to me; I was like the vineyards which lay around us, and which had pined away during the plague, untended and forgotten.——Your sorrows, my son, have, no doubt, made you pious, and a reader of the Scriptures, as it did myself.   I used to sit at my window and look upon the rejoicing crowds which again thronged the quay, and compare myself, as I saw them smiling and greeting each other, to the field so beautifully described by the Prophet son of Amos.

" I will water thee with my tears, O Heshbon and Elialeh ! for the shouting for thy summer fruits, and for thy harvest is fallen ; and gladness is taken away, and joy out of the plentiful field ; and in the vineyards there shall be no shouting ; the treader shall tread out no wine in their presses ; I have made their vintage-shouting to cease."   And soon, my son, I became indifferent to the world : I had none to labour or live for; and I determined upon quitting those scenes which only increased the bitterest of my recolections.   I gave up my property to my Aimée's father, who had returned from America to mourn with me over her loss, and retired hither.

The sacred dust of the three beings who had made my past life happy, I removed; and it now lies mingled and awaiting mine in the marble tomb below. Many a long year has gone by since that time, and I little thought that I should have lingered so long after them upon the earth."

CHAPTER XII.

As the hermit concluded his story, the ves-
per-bell tolled from the village below; and I
found that my attention had been so occupied
by listening to him, that the day had passed
away unperceived. The moon had risen, and
threw her full unclouded light upon the rude
and winding paths which led down from the cell:
I rose, and asking the old man's blessing, who
seemed exhausted and depressed, I returned
through the perfumed wood to my house.
When I arrived there, I found that my friend
the vigneron had left me a new-year's gift. It
was a pretty basket, made of rushes, and filled
with rich grapes; and my servant called it a
Cophin. The singularity of this appellation
struck me, and I immediately recognised another

of those traces which remain in these countries of their ancient Greek colonists; *cophin* being evidently a corruption of the Greek κοφινος, a little basket.

The history of these colonists is one of those circumstances which furnish to the studious mind a wide field for thought and pleasing reflection. Some of the Greeks who had taken up their residence in that part of Asia Minor which is bathed by the Ægean Sea, and which lies between Troy and Smyrna, had been expelled from their country by Harpagus, one of the generals of Cyrus: they were called Phocæans; and, after wandering about for some time like pirates, reached, at length, the coast of Provence. Upon their arrival, delighted at the appearance of the country, which, with its bright sun and vines and green fig-trees, reminded them of their own, they determined upon concluding their unsettled mode of life, and fixing themselves in this inviting region. But, in or-

ler to effect this peaceably, it was necessary to
lespatch an embassy to the rude Prince of the
Provençals; who then resided at, it is supposed,
he modern Arles. Upon the arrival of the Pho-
æan messengers at that place, they found that
he inhabitants were engaged in celebrating a
estival, which the King of Arles had proclaimed
or the purpose of choosing a husband for his
laughter. The ambassadors were introduced
nto the hall, or, perhaps, wood, where were
ssembled the Provençal chief, with his daughter,
nd a long train of suitors, and courteously
ntertained. But to the astonishment and dis-
nay of the native wooers, the Princess, who was
llowed the singular privilege of choosing for
lerself, immediately bestowed her hand upon
he leader of the stranger guests. Of course,
y this marriage the Phocæans became friends
nd allies to the father of their Queen, and
vere allowed the permission which they had requested, to build for themselves a city, of which,

the foundations were immediately laid, and which were to form the city that now lies below me. They called it Massilia, for which name various learned reasons have been given, which I neither understand nor can enter into. The city Massilia, from whatever circumstance so called, silently and gradually increased in opulence and importance ; while her harbour was thronged with ships, and her internal government was wise and pure. Six hundred of the most esteemed citizens formed the principal council or senate ; of whom, fifteen were selected to transact all the more immediate and urgent affairs. No one, unless he had children, could form a part of this council ; the natural affections of the heart being considered, in the simplicity of those times, the best security which could be obtained for the freedom and welfare of the state. Their manners were correct and simple ; all licentious amusements were forbidden ; and the attention of the people was entirely bestowed upon the increase of their commercial fame. But there prevailed among them one singular custom, which the philosopher will consider with curiosity; the Christian with pious horror; and the unhappy with deep interest. When any person, after having suffered unusual misfortunes and misery, lost all hope and courage, and considering himself deserted or detested by the Gods, determined upon dying, the Senate required that his purpose should be intimated to them. That body then assembled in the Hall of Audience in solemn state, and the unfortunate and desperate person was brought before them. He was then questioned as to his resolution; and if he still persisted in it, was ordered to unfold to the assembly his reasons; which he did:—giving an account of his afflictions, and confessing his despair. The senators then deliberated upon the case; and if they considered the man before them a fit object for relief, delivered to him a portion of the hemlock, which was preserved for this express purpose in the gardens of the Senatorial Palace, and sanctioned, by a recorded decree, the dreadful act which then followed. This melancholy abandonment of what mankind in general so fondly cling to, is one of those problems in the mystery of our nature, which set all reason and philosophy at defiance. For the wise and the weak alike fall by their own hand ; the warrior, the statesman, the eloquent orator, and the poor drivelling and desperate mechanic, have all sunk beneath the intense gloom and agony of mental depression. Yet, in this smiling climate, it would seem impossible for a man to become so totally and hopelessly darkened, as to require the juice of the fatal hemlock. For since I have dwelt here, I have found my heart grow calmer, and my spirits lighter. I have thought upon the past with less bitterness, and have even been, at times, almost happy. But then, the words of others would awake again the scotched snake,

nd the sun would seem dull and misty.   And so
nust it ever be ! It is not the sumptuous palace,
ior the quiet cottage ; it is not the golden gar-
len, with its statues and founts and marble ter-
aces; nor the simple hedge-rows of wild roses
nd honeysuckle, winding among the green
anes, that can give rest or peace to the mind :—
t is its own place, and in itself

    " Can make a heaven of hell, a hell of heaven."

We may change our clime, we may dwell
mid the olive and the vine, beneath the cataract
nd the snowy mountain ; but though, thus sur-
ounded by beautiful nature, the chain which
iinds our hearts may for a time be slackened,
et, anon, the inquisitor Care tightens and
wists its links, and the iron again enters into
ur souls.

Montesquieu, in his Spirit of Laws, says,
' That while the practice of suicide continued to

be general among the nations of antiquity, their Republican virtues were sterner and stronger, than when a Roman senate had learned tamely to obey the nod of an imperial despot." It certainly did not diminish the activity and independent spirit of Marseilles. She planted colonies, she assisted Rome against her great rival, and was numbered among her most faithful friends and allies. But amidst that mighty struggle for the world, between Cæsar and Pompey, the Greek city sunk beneath the brighter star of the Dictator, and became his tributary. Time passed on ;—Emperor after Emperor delighted or disturbed the world, till at length Constantine, at the commencement of the fourth century, became the first Christian Prince and Pontiff of Rome, and Marseilles ceased from her Pagan superstitions. Upon the death of Constantine, and the partition of the empire among his sons, Marseilles was allotted, among the other cities of Transalpine Gaul, to Constantine the

younger; and became, during his reign, the
scene of a remarkable tragedy.   The young
prince had married Fausta, the daughter of
Maximian Herculius; who, compelled by the
failure of his projects and plots against his own
son Maxentius, in favour of whom he had hastily abdicated the crown of Italy, was living a
fugitive at the Gallic court.   Maximian, however, though foiled in his previous attempts to
regain sovereign power, was not contented to
live in security and tranquillity.   He formed a
dark conspiracy against his son-in-law and bene-
factor; but his machinations were discovered,
and he was obliged to fly.   He hurried to Marseilles, with the hope, perhaps, of saving himself by sea; but Constantine, having rapidly
pursued the traitor, with a party of troops, was
admitted secretly by a postern gate into the
city, and Maximian fell into his hands.   He,
however, piously refused to punish, as he
might justly have done, the father of his wife;

and life was spared, and liberty restored to the
fugitive. But the abdicated sovereign could no
continue an obedient subject ; and he again con
trived an ungrateful plan of rebellion and mur
der ; darker and more deceitful than the last
since he had endeavoured to corrupt the faithfu
tenderness of his daughter, and induce her to
unite with him in his bloody design against her
husband. Fausta feigned compliance, and pro
mised to dismiss the guards which were always
placed at night in the royal chamber,—thus leav
ing the prince an easy prey to the assassin ; but
the unhappy daughter and affectionate wife had
disclosed all to Constantine; and one of the
Eunuchs of the palace was commanded to lie
down in the devoted bed. In the dead of the
night, Maximian, feigning to awake suddenly.
rises, and, amidst an affected and artificial agita
tion, hurries to the chamber of his son-in-law, to
communicate some ominous dream. There he
exultingly despatches the unsuspecting Eunuch ;

nd coming forth, proclaims to the palace the leath of the Emperor. On a sudden the trumpets sound, the Imperial eagles are seen advancing amid the torches of the Prætorian guard, nd the Emperor himself, surrounded by his fficers, stands before the terrified and confounded Maximian. All further generosity to the ncorrigible and unnatural parent would have een useless and impolitic. The melancholy hoice, however, of the mode in which he would ie was allowed him; and the baffled tyrant laced about his own neck the rope which terminated his dangerous life.

END OF VOL. I.

LONDON :
PRINTED BY S. AND R. BENTLEY, DORSET-STREET.

THE

JOURNAL

OF

AN EXILE.

IN TWO VOLUMES.

VOL. II.

LONDON:
PRINTED FOR SAUNDERS AND OTLEY,
BRITISH AND FOREIGN PUBLIC LIBRARY,
CONDUIT-STREET, HANOVER-SQUARE.
1825.

JOURNAL.

CHAPTER XIII.

Jan. 4. 1822.— I STROLLED this morning to the village, where I had first been with the hermit. As I entered the narrow street, I saw several persons collected before the door of the house which I thought was Auguste's, the preserved mariner; and I hastened on, expecting to find, perhaps, the joyful preparations for his wedding in full course. But when I had reached the cottage, a very different sight presented itself. Seven or eight peasants were assembled in silence, looking upon the melancholy decora tions of a village funeral.   Across the door of the house hung a black cloth, which just left sufficient space beneath its folds to allow the persons without, a view into the interior of the apartment.   That was dark and dismal, the windows were all closed, and the only light which the cottage received was from the darkened door and a few wax tapers, which were placed in rude wooden stands, and surrounded an open bier.   Within this, I could just see the pale features of the dead person, which were, however, partly concealed by a white pillow, which lay upon his breast, on which was placed the cross.   Near the bier stood a small vessel with holy water, and a little brush for sprinkling it.   I must acknowledge that my heart smote me when I saw the old mother sitting by the body: I had hoped that these preparations had been made for age and infirmity.   It was not so! Auguste, the young, the hopeful, was dead! and I looked round

for Claire. I saw her near the poor mother, clasping her shaking hands in her own.
I ventured not to enter the cottage at such
a moment; the presence of a stranger and
foreigner might have been disagreeable. I
passed on, therefore, to the church, which was
at a little distance. Its doors were open, and,
just as I reached them, the *curé* came forth,
preceded by a man bearing a tall cross, and
carrying his black cap in his hand. I uncovered
my head as he passed, and entered the church.
It was simple and unpretending in its appearance, except in its altar. That was, as usual,
loaded with flowers and tinsel ornaments, and
a glittering painting of the patron Saint, re-
clined against the little pavilion in which the
precious wafer was contained. A few votive
paintings, and some fresh vine-leaves, hung
round upon the walls, and completed the decora-
tion of this rustic temple. My mind recalled to
itself the village churches in my own country;

and I felt my heart and reason give the preference to the latter. Here, the gaudy trash and trappings of the altar conveyed no lesson to the simple peasants, but could only please and flatter their eyes. The priest, as he knelt before it, and moved backwards and forwards the vessels and Saints in solemn mummery, muttering some obscure and unintelligible prayer, could work no lasting effect upon the minds or hearts of his flock, who only obey, because they do not understand. How different is the scene in the sweet and humble English village! At the sound of the church-going bell, on a bright Sabbath morning, what a happy and holy sight is there! Wordsworth has beautifully described it in his " White Doe of Rylstone."

" From Boehm's old monastic tower
  The bells ring loud with gladsome power ;
  The sun is bright, the fields are gay,
  With people in their best array

Of stole and doublet, hood and scarf,
Along the banks of the crystal Wharf,
Through the vale retired and lowly
Trooping to that summons holy.

And up among the moorlands see
What sprinklings of blithe company,
Of lasses and of shepherd grooms,
'That down the steep hills force their way,—
Path, or no path, what care they?
And thus, in joyous crowd they hie
To Boehm's mouldering priory."

And then, when they reach it, the low Gothic
porch, with its stone benches, upon which the
aged and weary rest themselves till the bell rings
quickly in; the rustics in their doublets and
stoles ranged in long rows up the aisle; the low
murmuring from the vestry of the parish-school
as the minister's daughter listens to the Cate
chism which some of the lisping lips can scarcely
utter; and the sullen sound of the opening and
shutting of the pews. Then, the minister in a

plain white surplice, holding out the cheerful promise of absolution to the truly repentant; very different from the mysterious secrecy of the confessional, and its paltry penance of abstinence from flesh. Heywood, one of our old poets, has sarcastically described the arrogant system of Romish absolution and indulgence.

" With small cost, without any pain,
　　These pardons bring them to Heaven plain.
　　Give me but a penny or two-pence,
　　And as soon as the soul is departed hence,
　　In half an hour, or three-quarters at most,
　　The soul is in Heaven with the Holy-Ghost."

Then, too, the simple psalm sung in full ambitious chorus by the musical spirits of the village, who are all assembled, with the clerk at their head, and the bassoon in front in the large gallery, and, as its loud and ringing tones cease, the minister's voice is again heard slowly recalling the attention to the decalogue, as he stands at

the rude wooden table; on one side of which
hangs our Saviour's prayer, and, on the other
those commandments which he is endeavouring
to enforce. Finally, the clear Christian dis
course, adapted to the understanding and heart
of all, alike removed from the gloomy threaten
ings of the Puritan and the licentious lesson of th
Neapolitan Friar. But here, the peasants may
troop to the mass with their gay jackets and
nosegays, and shining crosses; their hearts may
be humble and good; yet the communion o
prayer, the spirit of that encouraging part of ou
service which prays all that may be there as
sembled, to accompany their pastor with a pur
heart and humble voice in the supplications, i
wanting.

The ignorant peasant prays, but knows not t
whom, whether to the Saints, the Saviour, or hi
holy Mother. He listens to the Latin invoca
tion with stupid astonishment, and thinks that i
must be a fine thing to be so near the altar an

the host as *M. Le Curé.* I was interrupted in
my reflections by the approaching sound of
voices, which announced the advance of the
funeral, and I heard the attendants singing one
of those hymns which are particularly adapted
to this part of France. As the strain came
stealing on, I could compare its effect with that
produced by the gradual approach of the same
mournful train in England ; and, again, the
latter claimed the preference. The stillness
which reigns around, broken only by the
closing of the hearse-door, the neighing of the
plumed and pawing horses, and the thrilling
words of the clergyman as he precedes the
coffin, "I am the resurrection and the life,"
are far more awakening to the dearest feelings
of our nature than the artificial hymn that
now echoed through the church as the procession entered it. Slowly advancing, the
bearers placed the open bier in the middle,
and stood round it. The priest, after having

knelt and bowed and knelt again before th
altar, performed the funeral service, and th
hymn for the dead was chanted. The ol
mother, who had attended the corpse, supporte
by Claire and her daughter, suddenly fell to th
earth, as the deep voice of the assistant pro
nounced the *de profundis clamavi*, and was car
ried out. The ceremony then concluded, the pries
having sprinkled the pale face with holy water
and they all left the church to proceed to th
cemetery. I was anxious to inquire about th
poor old woman, and hastened to the cottage
She had recovered, but was in great misery
" The will of the holy Saints be done!" said she
" but indeed it was a hard thing to lose my bo
thus : better had it been that he had never com
back, for then I should not have known how h
suffered. But now I shall always think 1 hear him
(and I thank God that I could not see him) speaking more and more weakly every day, and ye
so gently and sweetly, and clasping my old hands

with his thin wasted fingers." Poor Claire and the sister said nothing : they were standing at the window looking towards the cemetery, where the dreary business was seen drawing to an end. The scene distressed me : I could be of no use or comfort, so I left the mourners unmolested, and returned to my house.

I found my friend the pedestrian waiting for me. My little pupil was there too, and was attacking him with some of those terms of abuse which are bestowed upon Englishmen in this country, and which children catch up without knowing what they mean. We were both much amused at his arch impertinence, and my friend said to me, " The mutual ridicule with which the natives of different countries are disposed to treat one another, is in no case so strongly exemplified as in that of France and England. The Spaniard, the Italian, the Swiss, the German, the Russian, and even the Turk, do not regard each the other with that consum-

mate and captious contempt which influences th
untravelled Frenchman and Englishman. Th
latter, when he first arrives in this country, i
prepared to consider the people, the manners
the customs, and the country, as inferior to hi
own, as perhaps the Chinese thinks the institu
tions of the Europeans are, compared with thos
of his Solon, Confucius. All the pride and pre
judices of an islander are awake, and he passe
among the officious and smiling Gauls with tru
British scorn. France! what is it full of, bu
dancers and tumblers, weak soups, frogs, fid
dlers, and fripperies? and adopting the unsparin
creed of that intolerant literary pontiff Johnson
he exclaims, as he shivers before a smoky wooc
fire, and gazes with despair upon the cold tilec
pavement of his room, "*Extra Britannian
nulla salus.*"

"The Frenchman, on the other hand, crosse
the narrow strait, to which he has given the sin
gular appellation of the Sleeve; and concerning

which, I once saw a French caricature. It represented Bonaparte endeavouring to creep into the sleeve of a coat ; while a great staring figure in red, intended for *Le Roi George*, stood over him with a drawn sword, saying, " *si tu oses, tu y resteras.*"

" To return to our traveller. He lands in good humour aud good will : he has been very sick, *Mais un peu de bouillon arrangera tout cela.* The commissioners of the hotels crowd round him, and he proceeds to the *Tete du Roi tenue par Podevin.* But soon all his latent prejudices are put into action, *Point de bouilli, une soupe comme de l'eau, du vin comme de l'encre, et rien qu'une sauce blanche. Quel pays d'Herctiques ! cent Religions, mais qu'une sauce !* Then on his journey up to London. The rapidity of the diligences affrights him ; the exorbitant charges at the Inns make him wish himself again at *Beauvais* ; and the dark foggy atmosphere of London, as he descends the precipitous steep

into Greenwich, recalls to his terrified mind
the pistols and the poisons, and the suicidal taste
of the country, where the sun never shines. Nor
is his distress alleviated, when he arrives at the
White Bear. All is Babel and confusion around
him; nothing but cries of *Coach, Coach,* and
frequent attempts of the porters to carry off his
sac de nuit to a *fiacre.* His fare is demanded
by a man who keeps his hat on his head;
and who, instead of a profound bow, for the
munificent *pour boire* of twelve *sous,* throws them
into the kennel, and calls him a French fool.
When he has at last succeeded in discovering his
friend in Poland-street, he finds him half English,
eating beef and potatoes, and drinking porter.
He sets forth in search of a *Restaurateur,* and
dans un carreau, as he calls it, or square, actually discovers a real undoubted one. He enters delighted, orders his *julienne,* his *frican-
deau,* his *omelette aux fines herbes,* and his
demi bouteille de Bourgogne. He has omitted

to examine the *carte;* "*mais c'est égal,*" he knows well enough the price of these articles. *A la bonheur!* he exclaims as he finishes his portion of Parmesan, and calls for the note. *Mais, Grand Dieu!* ten shillings! Why he could have a superb dinner *chez Very, la demi tasse* and *petit verre* included, for less. He has scarcely recovered from the dismay which this occurrence has excited within him, when he strolls into a coffee-house. He takes his hat off as he enters, and makes a bow to a lady, who happens to be sitting at a table, waiting till her husband comes down stairs, and whom he has mistaken for the *dame du Comptoir.* He addresses his conversation to a gentleman near him, who scarcely answers him, and looks at him suspiciously. Baffled in his attempt to procure a game at dominoes, he calls for coffee, which is brought to him in a large silver vessel, surrounded by a labyrinth of basins and cups. The coffee seems like the scourings of the boiler at the

Café de Foi ; and his grimaces and annoyanc
are prodigious. He rises to leave the *café,* an
gracefully pours the contents of the sugar-basi
into his pocket, amidst the laughter of the pei
sons who are near, and the indignant expostula
tions of the waiter. And to crown all, the foui
pence which he had laid down upon the tabl
and the one which he presents to the waitei
are both scornfully rejected, and two shillings ai
angrily demanded. Such are the miseries whic
await many an unfortunate native of this countrj
who crosses over to England, with all the vai
and pert prejudices of his nation, which, thoug
differently shewn, render him just as ridiculou:
and really uncomfortable, as the sullen Englisl
man."

CHAPTER XIV.

My friend the Pedestrian proposed, that we should walk together to the Lazarette, as I had been long anxious to see this singular building. It is built upon a rising ground, to the right of the harbour, and open to the influence of the *Mistral.* This wind, which, I have had frequent occasion to mention, is one of those peculiar phænomena which affect particular districts : it blows from the north-west, and, when gentle, diffuses an agreeable and refreshing coolness upon the parched vineyards and thirsty fields. But it frequently sweeps over Provence with the utmost fury, howling along the troubled waters of the Rhone, shaking, and sometimes shattering the bridge of boats, which connects the ancient town of Tarascon with its opposite neighbour, Beaucaire, so well known

as the Leipsic of France. And then spreading
itself away through the country, it snatches up
the thick heaps of white dust, that have lain accu-
mulating for months upon the roads, and whirls
them in a blinding cloud upon the passenger and
the pasture. And I myself have seen the air as
thick for miles round with this dust as if it were
snowing. It has been known to continue for
weeks and months together, and to disappear
for as long a period ; as for instance, during the
miserable days that Marseilles passed, when
oppressed by the plague. For it is considered
in the Provençal harbours a great dispeller of
the unwholesome air, which may, and probably
does, arise from the beating of a southern sun
upon a tideless sea. The waters of the ports
upon the Mediterranean are not renewed and refreshed by the influx of pure waves ; all the mud
and filth of the city run into them, and a dangerous steam must arise from the corruption
and constant contamination which thus take
place.

The Lazarette is a very large establishment : but, as I have before set down an account of its regulations, it will not be necessary for me to record much concerning it now. We were admitted within an outer gate, upon which might well be inscribed those lines which Dante has placed over his Inferno :

    " Per me si va nella città dolente,
      Per me si va nell' eterno dolore,
      Per me si va fra la perduta gente !"

Beyond the gate we found a long passage separated from the rest of the building by a treble screen of iron, behind which the persons who are performing quarantine stand when they wish to communicate with their friends. Several were then engaged in this agreeable employment, but looked extremely ridiculous thus caged up. They had more the appearance of the royal lions and tigers which I remember to have been so delighted with when a child, as they roamed backwards and forwards in their

iron dens, lashing their bodies with their spir;
tails, and glaring out through the bars upoi
the impudent intruders.   But yet, appalling re
flection! those men, were they but admitted t(
the embrace and society of their friends, migh
work as much, aye and more, horrible mischie
than the wildest and worst of savage beasts
Look at the sad history of the Plague, and ever
now the frightful condition of Barcelona.   Th(
last accounts from that place were indeed distress-
ing ; it had become a second Marseilles under the
fearfullest influence of pestilence ; but, alas
unlike her, in the devotedness and heroism of
its citizens.   For they are divided against themselves ; the pest of anarchy has united itself in
most unholy league with the fever's yellow
banners ; and they march on unchecked, nay,
even aided by the mad and parricidal civil war-
fare of the Catalonians.   I am informed that the
deaths exceed 1500 a-day, and that some
wretches have been detected in mixing poison

among the fish in the public market : that, o
the physicians who went down thither from
Paris, in noble emulation of the two Charitabl
Sisters, one has died, and another is in grea
danger : that the disease has spread all along
the coast of Spain, and that Cadiz herself begin
to tremble : that the suburbs of the city ar
covered with the dead bodies of persons who at
tempted to make from the city, and who wer
instantly shot by the Sanitary Cordon. It ha
been asserted, that the establishment of thi
latter precaution, which has also taken place i
France, is more likely to introduce the infectio
than avert it ; as it will be impossible to preven
the troops from having communication witl
some diseased persons: And this has given ris
to an anxious discussion respecting the nature o
the yellow fever, whether it be contagious o
infectious. I am not sufficiently versed in thes
matters to decide the question ; but from the in
quiries I have made here, I should rather be in

clined to consider it as infectious simply, and not contagious. I say, simply, because it appears to me that it is much more easy to take precautions against such diseases, than against those which are contagious. This has been proved in the present instance, with respect to Marseilles; for it is now well known, that a man who had been employed on board one of the suspected vessels, in discharging her cargo, and had been allowed, finally, to come on shore, died a day or two after of the yellow fever. He lodged in one of the streets of the old city, where the plague first broke out, and must have communicated with the other inmates of the house. The authorities got intelligence of the circumstance, and the house was instantly blocked up, the man buried in quick-lime, and his wife, and all the persons whom they could possibly suspect of having had intercourse with the deceased, sent to the Lazarette. This happened some time back, and was not, I believe, generally known for some days

But when it did become known, it excited great alarm here. Many families quitted their houses, and fled away to Avignon, and some even to Lyons. The news of our position reached Paris ; every body there considered us as a lost people, and I certainly saw a letter, stating that in that city it was very positively affirmed, that we were dying by twenties and thirties a day.

" Extemplo Libyæ magnas it Fama per urbes.
  *   *   *   .
Parva metu primo mox sese attollit in auras,
Ingrediturque solo, et caput inter nubila condit.

And I have no doubt that very shortly, though *parva metu primo*, she would have hidden (not her *diminished* head) among the clouds, and that thirty would have been made, according to Falstaff's arithmetic, three hundred. Nay, so far was this report carried, that an Englishman who left this place six weeks ago for Naples, has just returned as he went ; for the vessel was refused admittance into the harbour, as coming from a diseased port ; and so said he to me, " I am come back *re infectâ*. But, thank God, this second visitation was averted from these walls, for nothing further has occurred ; and it would appear, from this circumstance, that the disease is clearly only infectious ; for had it been contagious, we should be now, perhaps, spread about the streets in agony, with no Chevalier Rose or good Belsunce to console and comfort our bodily and mental pains. The symptoms of this complaint may be easily mistaken for a common headache, till the fatal black vomit appears ; then, indeed, there can be no uncertainty. It has been said, that if between the paroxysms of this fever strong doses of bark and port wine be given to the diseased persons, a cure may be confidently expected.

We saw, through the grating, the captain of the American vessel that was wrecked the other day, watched closely by a guard. His reflec-

tions could not be the most agreeable during his
captivity ; nor would, I imagine, those of any
person be, thus imprisoned, in the midst of
death and danger.　No communication is permitted between persons who are in any way suspected as to their health ; and thus a man stalks
about like some blighted and deserted sinner,
and is reduced to the amusement of scrawling
upon the walls of his prison, impatient and que-
rulous sentences ; such, for instance, as " *La vie
est une quarantaine pour le paradis.*"　Looking
down upon the sea when we quitted the Lazarette, we could perceive some of the exiled ships
riding at their anchors, and boats engaged in
bringing off either their sick, or their cargoes.
These latter, as I have I believe before remarked,
are conveyed to the Lazarette, according to their
nature, where they are subjected to the opera-
tion of being purified.　The merchandize which
is considered capable of communicating the infection, consists of silks, linen stuffs of all kinds,

cotton, sponges ; nay, books, chaplets, and rosaries. The boats were slowly labouring along
with their dangerous burthens, and I thought I
could almost see some sickening yellow wretch
drinking in the light *Mistral*, which he hoped
might cool his burning entrails. " Let us descend towards the harbour," said my companion;
and on our way thither we passed an old gate, the
only remnant then left in these streets of their
old Roman masters. It was neither remarkable
for beauty of architectural ornaments or form,
but it might perhaps have been the entrance by
which Constantine had been secretly admitted
into the city, and through which the body of
the strangled Maximin, which was discovered in
the eleventh century, in a marble tomb, might
have been conveyed, when Raynambauld, the
Archbishop of Arles, ordered that the pagan
bones should be cast into the sea. We passed
on, and reached the quay. It was crowded with
the idle and the industrious, the merchant, the

sailor, and the politician. Greece, England, Spain, Paris, supplied ample food for all ; and the crowd and conversation seemed to be as varied as the rich piles of fruit and goods that lay along the wharfs mixed with ropes and huge iron rings, and casks of oil. The fishermen, in their red caps and coarse rough brown jackets, were dropping about in their Spanish-looking boats ; and a watchful gendarme was lounging along here and there, and occasionally snatching the forbidden cigar from the detected sailor. For the use of this luxury is strictly forbidden upon the quay, lest some unlucky spark might communicate with the vast quantity of hemp and flax which Marseilles imports from the north. As we walked down toward the mouth of the harbour, a large brig came sweeping in with a considerable part of her stern torn away ; and as she passed between the two forts of St. John and St. Nicholas, and beneath that of Nôtre Dame, which, perched upon a barren beetling rock above the latter fort, seems to be looking down upon the city and waters at its feet as its peculiar charge, the crew uncovered their heads, and reverently crossed themselves. They had probably been hard pressed at sea, as the appearance of their ship denoted, and they were thanking the blessed Virgin for her intercession. " The superstition and strangely contrasted behaviour of sailors in danger," said I to my companion, " is a singular feature in their nature. At one time, brave and bold as the waves they are climbing over, they dare and defy the storm, the cannon, and the concealed battery. But, should they happen to sail from a port on an unlucky day,—should their beads be wrongly numbered, or their paternoster be pronounced imperfectly, depression and dread hang upon them ; and they feel all the old influence of the omen and the augur. Those men who are now moving by, and offering up their thanksgiving for their preservation, were probably encouraged in the working of their ship during her dangerous troubles, by some favourable sign, some unusual brightness of the lamp that was burning near the picture of their patron St. Nicholas. Else they had perhaps yielded to the terrors of th e tempest, and the splitting ship would have echoed with their drunken and desperate cries. " We ascended the *Place de la Tourette*, in whose pits lies the dust of a city. Magistrates, Priests, nobles, slaves, and fair female forms, were all cast into the moaning caverns ; and those impressive lines of Virgil, in which he describes the husbandman ploughing a field of battle, might be here applied to the fisherman :

" Grandiaque effossis mirabitur ossa sepulchris."

We proceeded up to the church, which stands at the end of the terrace, and which is said to have been built upon the site of an ancient temple of Diana. It is mean and neglected, as are all the

churches of this city, and very unlike the sumptuous cathedrals of the Netherlands, where,
however, I am inclined to think no deeper devotion prevails than in these southern climes.
For, if the piety and sanctity of a Christian
temple are to be estimated according to the number of holy relics which it contains, *l'Eglise
Majeure*, which is the name given to this church,
may fairly boast of its illustrious origin and treasury. It is asserted to have been founded by
St. Lazarus himself, the brother of Mary Magdalen, who were both, together with St. Martha
and Joseph of Arimathea, exposed by the Jews,
in a vessel without sails, to the winds and waves,
which, less cruel than their persecutors, wafted
the saintly band to the shores of Provence.
They dispersed themselves with holy zeal over
the sinful country ; but Lazarus remained at
Marseilles, and founded this church upon the
ruins of the Phocæan Temple. Mary Magdalen, the humble penitent, ever mindful of her

former guilt, and of its necessary penance, retired to the barren mountain of St. Victor, which
looks down upon Aix, and shews itself to the
mariner far out at sea. There she inhabited a
grotto hollowed out of the rock, and there,
amidst self-denial and mortification, she died.
But her influence and memory still lingered
about the rugged walls which her tears and
trials had hallowed ; and many a pilgrimage, and many a vow, were accomplished within their still recesses. Louis XIV. and
his mother Anne of Austria, both knelt at
the feet of the Colossal statue of the Saint,
which then existed, but which the Revolutionary
crusade against the images of God and man
struck down into dust. The legend is firmly
believed by the simple peasants ; and even the
more enlightened and enlarged mind may pause
before it rejects entirely the fond imagination.
The enthusiastic feelings which arise at the
fancied presence of the dust of heroes or poets,

may be alike excited towards holier things; and
he who is warmed to patriotism by the idea tha
he stands near the ashes of Nelson or Washing
ton, in which are still living their "wonted fires,'
may feel his heart becoming more humble and
devoted to God by the contemplation of those
spots which tradition has invested with the odou:
of sanctity. When the fierce Crusaders, red
with blood and slaughter, and trampling upor
the malicious and turbaned Infidel, had planted
the Christian banner upon the holy hill of Zion
the sight of the stony sepulchre in which they be
lieved the wounded body of their Saviour to hav
been laid, softened and subdued their impetuou
vengeance; they knelt in awe and admiration be
fore it; and casting away their shields and drip
ping swords, and clasping their mailed hands ii
unanimous prayer, they felt, for a time, the pre
sence of the God of peace and love. In wha
were the morals of the French people benefited
by their contemptuous annihilation of those le

gends and holy places, which form so considerable a part of the Roman Catholic Religion? Did it make them kinder or better? No. On the contrary, they became more wicked, and more frantic. The very populace of Marseilles, who would have formerly trusted in the intercession of their Saints, and have endured misery in patience, became, upon their abolition, the most licentious and lawless of the Republican banditti.   *   *   *

An Abbé, who is collecting alms for the poor Christians in Palestine, is to preach to-morrow in the principal church, and I propose going thither.

Jan. 9. I went this morning to hear the Abbé Demahures deliver his discourse. The church was crowded to excess. There was no mass; it was simply an exhortation and address to the charitable feelings of his fellow Christians.

The Abbé was a man apparently about forty, dressed in a large black robe, and from his chin hung a long black beard. His text was taken from Isaiah : " The wilderness, the solitary place shall be glad ; . . . and the desert shall rejoice, and blossom as the rose." He began by explaining the text in the sense in which he wished the words to be particularly understood by his congregation, and endeavoured to impress upon their minds the importance of his mission. He then went on to describe what that mission was, and concluded his sermon with a pathetic entreaty, that his hearers would believe implicitly the tale of distress he had told them ; that his humble voice might not be raised, as that of one crying in the wilderness, to pillars of sand and suffocating winds ; and that, by their powerful aid and assistance, they would cause the poor destitute churches of Palestine to be glad and blossom again, as the refreshed rose. The scene was striking. The church was filled with all descriptions of persons, and all apparently listening in deep attention. The voice of the

preacher, as it echoed down the aisle, and talked
of the suffering pilgrim, the persecuted hermit,
and the pious protection of those who listened
to him, sounded like that of the venerable
Peter, as he animated and excited the surrounding multitude to the first Crusade ; and I almost
expected to hear, as he concluded, the unanimous shout, "It is the will of God ! it is the
will of God !"

CHAPTER XV.

JAN. 20. MY friend the pedestrian came up yesterday, and asked me to accompany him to Nice; but I declined, at least for the present. I have become attached to this place, and my health is in that state that I cannot bear the fatigue of travelling. He remained with me the whole day, and afforded me very great amusement, by relating to me some of the various scenes he has passed through since he had resided in this country. He has lived in different parts of the Continent, and remained a considerable time at Lyons, which he described to me as a noble city, rich in trade, and in the beauty of its position.

He is an enthusiastic admirer of Nature, and told me that he used to pass much of his time in wandering along the high woody banks of the Saône, which unites itself with the Rhône below the city. He particularly described to me, with considerable ingenuity, a small island called *l'Isle Barbe*, which lies in the centre of the Saône, close to the village of that name, about two miles from Lyons; and which, on the Patron Saint's day, with its gay tents and flags, and waving trees, and high-capped peasants, presented the appearance of some gay triumphal galley, slowly making her way down the river ; and he also mentioned to me, the splendid effect produced by the procession of the holy Sacrament upon the *Fête Dieu*, as it spread itself down the long *Quai du Rhône*:—the cloudless sun shining full upon the silver censers, the waving plumes of the canopy, the military escort, the altars, like blooming bowers, placed at intervals all along as far as the eye could reach, the white streamers hanging in long lines from the windows of the houses, and the bare heads of the thousands that lined the stone parapets and bridges, and the broad river beneath, slowly pacing on, and almost lingering about the rushy banks, as the priest held up the glory-encircled Host.

" After having wandered over different parts of France for nearly a year," my friend continued, " I began to feel anxious to know something about my friends in England. I determined upon leaving Lyons, where I then was, and returning towards the coast of France, by way of Switzerland and the Rhine. I quitted Lyons one evening just before sunset, after the heat of the day, in the month of June. As I ascended the eminence which stands at the end of the *Quai du Rhône*, and which commences the road to Geneva, I paused, to look back upon the city I was leaving. The Rhône ran below me, and making a majestic turn, held on its mighty course by the long white quays, with their trees and steeples, and lofty houses; while

the *Pont Morand* threw its slender arches across
the waters, which rushed through them in rippling eddies.　Beyond, on the other side, were
fields, and vineyards, and long low marshes, and
promenades ; while the mountains of Dauphiné
were spreading themselves in the distance.　But
more to the left, rose up in the clear evening sky,
a dome, solitary and gigantic.　It was the crest
of Mont Blanc.　Its distance was probably, in a
straight line, eighty or ninety miles, and yet I
saw it distinctly, and apparently near.　I am inclined, as you may have observed, to think deeply
upon all I see ; and I have always found that
the effect produced upon me by beholding these
stupendous works of Nature at a distance, is
greater than when I am beneath them.　They
leave an impression of mysterious awe upon my
mind ; and I can compare the feelings with which
I looked at Mont Blanc to nothing else than
those with which I contemplate eternity.　There
it was still and stately, nor could any one

assert, that its foundations were not laid in the
wilderness of glaciers and torrents. But betweer
me and it, all was unknown and untrodden; a
wide space of meadow, garden, vineyard, and
rocky glen must be passed, ere it could be
reached; and yet it was as certain, that the
mountain was beyond, as that the bell which I
heard tolling from the cathedral, and which
swung its sullen sound even to my feet, was
hanging, though out of my reach and ken, in its
gothic tower. I turned to proceed: the sur
suddenly sunk behind the dome, leaving it of a
deadly white and livid colour, as the dark rock
showed itself here and there through the snow
I paced on through the old provinces of Bresse
and Bugey, towards Geneva. These two provinces formerly belonged to the Duke of Savoy,
and were obtained from him in exchange for Susa
which commands the mountain-pass into Piedmont, by *le bon Roi Henri*. I need not mention
his numerical position; as unfortunately the ap-

pellation which describes his character, at the same time points out to all who have read history, this among the few bright exceptions to the usual catalogue of kingly names.   He was accused of having by this exchange made peace, *comme un marchand*, in giving up the town which commanded an easy access into the Promised Land of Europe ; but Henry was content with the simple merit of having strengthened his frontier, without desiring the more brilliant possession that might have caused another Pavia.   My road lay along the banks of the Rhône, which came rushing down from its native glacier.   It was swollen with recent rains, and its dark rippling waters swept by the winding banks like a flying host. The country through which I passed, after my three days' march, was wild and mountainous, and seemed to be gradually swelling from the wide plains of France, into the rocky spires and snowy crags of Savoy."

" I passed the gulph where the angry Rhône

sinks into its rebellious channel, and is almost lost, till at some distance it rises again, at first gentle and repentant, but soon resumes its stern and stormy course as it hurries away to the Mediterranean. I remember I was asked for my passport there. The Commissary, who was a short pursy man, with a red Burgundy face, sat at a small desk in all the dignity of a village authority, and stared at me through his spectacles, as he read in good French my title of *gentilhomme Anglois*. My general appearance certainly was not much like that of a *nobleman*, having an old cloth knapsack on my back, a hat which might very well have passed for General Monk's in Westminster Abbey, and a coat which was very like a poet's. My shoes were still in worse plight, for the stony road of the mountains had so maltreated them, that I was literally in the situation of Peter Pindar's pilgrim on his way to Loretto. However, as *gentilhomme Anglois* I certainly was described;

and the man, looking at me suspiciously, asked
me where I was going, and said with a sneer,
" *Ma foi! Monsieur, si j'étois gentilhomme, je
ne voyagerois pas à pied. Je suis bon pieton
pourtant.*" His appearance, however, I pre-
sumed within myself to think, was very unlike
that of a man capable of toiling up a mountain,
for his legs were so thick and fat, and his neck
so short, that I should as soon have suspected
a barrel of being a pedestrian. However, the
Commissary of *Blanchy* had a right at *Blanchy*
to be what he pleased, but none to sneer at me ;
so I very shortly told him that if he wanted to
know where I was going he must look at my
passport, and, as for his preferring any other
conveyance than that of his own feet, it was no
affair of mine. A few boys that were lounging
at the door of the office, and the deputy's deputy,
seemed thunderstruck at my disrespectful reply,
but nothing further passed ; and the man having
examined and signed my passport, I marched

on. I passed the night at an inn just above
Geneva, in a small village; and my fondness for
odd incidents had very nearly involved me in a
serious inconvenience."

" The innkeeper, seeing that I was rather a
singular-looking traveller, treated me with little
ceremony, as my title was in my pocket, but my
worn-out shoes stared him in the face. I reach
ed the inn about sunset, and the man was sitting
before his door. I asked if I could have a bed
for the night. The innkeeper examined me from
top to toe, and then said, " *Mais je pense que
oui.* There is a room, is there not, Jeannette ?"
calling to his daughter, who was engaged in pre
paring supper within. The girl came immedi
ately to the door with a piece of veal in her hand
into which she was inserting little pins of lard
and which made the meat look something like a
red cribbage-board. She was a pretty *bruette*
enough; and if I had been in better funds
than I was then, and more like a *Seigneur*, I

had not fared ill in the hands of *la Demoiselle de l'Auberge.* But my present appearance was enough to banish all that kind of thing; and she said rather too haughtily, I thought, since she was addressing me, " *Oui, vous pouvez avoir un lit.*" This reply, however, was ambiguous, as it frequently happens in these small inns that there is only one room, which contains three or four beds. However, I made the best of it; and unbuckling my knapsack, I sat myself down on a bench at the door."

" The evening was uncommonly beautiful, and from my seat I could see part of the range of the Jura mountains, which were "up-heaving their broad bare backs to the sky." " *Il paroit,*" said the innkeeper, with that sort of look that a man assumes when he is endeavouring to say something impertinent in an easy jocose manner —" *il paroit,*" nodding at them with his head, " *que ces souliers-là s'ennuyent de vos pieds et de leur longue route. Ils seront bien contents de se reposer chez le savetier.*" All this was quite true; and as I have always found it the best way on these occasions to take such things in good humour, I replied, that I thought so too. My patience under this attack made us friends directly, and calling to his daughter, he told her to bring us the *goute*.* "Come, Sir," said he, "*choquons*† to our better acquaintance." I did not omit making my bow to the *demoiselle* as I drank " to our better acquaintance;" and my bow certainly neutralized the effect of my shoes, for she said, the gentleman is tired; perhaps he would like to have his supper, and retire early. I seconded this proposition, and ordered some warm milk and bread. The innkeeper seemed disposed to recommence hostilities at this death-blow to his usual supper charge of 3*f*. 10*s*.

---

* This is a small glass of brandy, which answers to our stirrup-cup in some instances, and in others, as it was used here.

† Let us hob-and-nob.

but I added directly, " and let me have a
bottle of wine now." The storm passed off
instantaneously ; and we were soon seated
at the table with our *Vin de Beaujolois.*—
" Here 's to the health of your comrades,"
said the innkeeper, swallowing a large glass
of wine that I had poured out for him : " I
have seen many of them, and capital walkers
they are ; a little wild though, and not much
like scholars." What the deuce does he
mean ? thought I, and I was going to ask him,
when he continued, " *Ma foi!* you German
students had better mind your Greek and Latin,
than go wandering away to fight against the
Turks. It is a poor business, and the Greeks
won't thank you much, after all, for they want
money more than men." Here was a curious
mistake ! However, I determined upon humour-
ing it, as there appeared to be no gensdarme stationed in the inn. " Why, as to money," said
I, " to be sure we have not much of that," and

the innkeeper eyed me again; "but we have stout hearts and arms, and we know pretty well how to fight." "*Diable!*" said the man, "that is a curious life for a scholar; I thought you fought only with your pens and your books. But pray, what part of Germany are you of?" I had it all before me where to choose, so I resolutely replied, of Stutgard. "*Ah! la jolie ville*," said mine host, "*je la connois bien.*" You have the advantage of me then, thought I. "It is upwards of three and twenty years ago, before you were born, young man, that I was there with our army, and well do I remember the time; — we were commanded by Moreau, *le traitre!* but we all loved him then; ay, and if he had wished, he might have been our general now. *Pardi!* we had hard work of it there; the Archduke never let us rest, and soon beat away back to the Rhine the other army that was commanded by Jourdan, which was to communicate with us. And, after all, *nous voilà*

in full retreat, too, across the Devil's Forest;
for it was black and gloomy as himself; and
many a man found Hell or Paradise among its
desperate defiles!*   But a noble retreat it was,
harassed as we were by the Austrian Duke, and
that emigrant Bourbon." "Which?" said I. "Oh !
l'Enghien ! d'Enghien ! he that got his deserts
afterwards; and yet that was a black affair, too.
As to Moreau, what a pity it was that a man
who could bring off his army so well, should go
and have his legs shot off in an Austrian camp !
Mais à la santé des jolies filles de votre Ville," and
he winked at me as he savoured the wine, which
he seldom tasted at his own expense; " I used to
drink to their healths when I was there, in bright
bumpers of Rhein wine.   I was quartered in

* In the Black Forest there was an inn, which took
for its sign " The Kingdom of Heaven," and the pea-
ants used to say, that, in that wood, either Heaven or
Hell were found.

the house of a woman that sold fruit; and in
one of the skirmishes about the city was
wounded; she took care of me, and so did her
daughter, my dear wife, God rest her! I married her, Sir, after the peace of Leoben, and
brought her here, and we lived as happily as we
could with our little girls. My wound here,"
pointing to his leg, which, I had not observed
before, was lame, "kept me safe with my wife.
But she died, Sir,—as we all must! Our *Curé*
said that 'she made a good end;' and I know
it, if he did not say so, for she had been kind
and charitable. Perhaps you may know the
house she used to live in; it was close to the
Museum, a small low building, not far from
the banks of the little river there."

I began now to repent a little of my new character, and proceeded to *battre la campagne*, as
the French say. The innkeeper asked me various questions respecting people he had known
at Stutgard; and concluded, by commencing

a conversation in German with me. "*Komen mein Herr*," said he, "*lieben sie diese Wein ? er ist recht gut ?*" I have acquired a little acquaintance with that language since, and should have been glad to have had the same then, for the man might as well have talked to me in Arabic. I knew, however, that Ya was German for Yes, so I hazarded the monosyllable. "*Das ist wohl*," said the innkeeper; "*diese Wein ist nicht travaillé*, as we say in French." "*Ya*," responded I again, and instantly perceived my blunder; for the man, luckily however in French, attacked me. "*Comment, Monsieur l'Etudiant*, what do you say there? that my wine is doctored?" "Oh! *non, non*," I stammered out; "but I left my country so young that I have almost forgotten my own language." "*Tant pis*," said the man, rather surlily, and I thought suspiciously; but just then came the smiling Jeannette to the door of the house, and informed me that my milk and bread were ready. " *Bon*," said I, " *j'ai faim*, and I went into the house, where my suppe was set out. The innkeeper came in, and sa himself down before the kitchen fire, which could just see through the door of the room was in ; and at a round wooden table sat tw *rouliers*, or waggoners, taking their suppe of harico beans. I was of course anxious t avoid all fresh conversation with the innkeeper which might have further betrayed my *incognito* so, after I had finished my milk, I called Jean nette, and she showed me my room ; which wa at the top of a narrow staircase, and had a smal window looking upon the road. I told Jean nette that I intended to start very early in the morning, and paid her my reckoning, and gave her a franc for herself. " *Oh, Monsieur !*" said she, " you can easily open the door ; *et je couche moi tout près de vous*, so that I shall hear you."

Now there are some wandering adventurers that this *couche tout près de vous* would have instigated to some harumscarum trick ; but, as you perceive, I am too much of a philosopher to become a Don Juan. Jeannette wished me good night, and drawing to the door, which had, as usual, no lock, left me to myself.

My apartment was singularly furnished : some large wooden chests stood there ; one of which I ventured to open, and there beheld Jeannette's Sunday finery, and a magnificent cocked hat and coat of the old regime, that had belonged probably to some *seigneur du village*, and had fallen to the share of the innkeeper's father, who was of this part of the country, at the destruction of the noble pigeon-house and chateau. For you must know, that it was considered formerly a distinguishing mark of nobility to be entitled to a pigeon-house. To return to the furniture of my chamber: in one corner was a strange-looking closet, something like Bluebeard's ; and the same curiosity was excited within me to inspect it, as impelled the unfortunate

Fatima. Besides, some bravo might be concealed within it ; and before opening the door, I cautiously felt about the room for the chinks of a trapdoor, through which my mangled body was to be cast. I opened the closet, which turned out to be a very *safe* one, for it contained sundry pieces of cold *bouilli*, and butter and bread. It was, however, a mark of confidence in Jeannette, to leave me alone with them ; and I prepared to undress myself in great security, when I heard a noise in the road below, and saw two gensdarmes ride up to the inn, escorting a couple of runaway galley-slaves, as I guessed them to be from their peculiarly haggard appearance. I just saw them dismounting by the light of the moon, and calling for the innkeeper to take their horses. The prisoners were chained together, and clanked into the house after the gensdarmes, who made the kitchen resound with their calls for supper, and the stamping of their heavy boots. *Votre passeport, Monsieur*—the *il Bondo-*

cani talisman of the Police, darted across my
mind; and I felt myself in a cold sweat as I
recollected my inconsiderate assumption of the
suspicious character of a German Student and
Crusader. The innkeeper, I thought, would most
assuredly mention his having one of those public
personages in his house, and my imagination represented me chained, as an impostor and dangerous spy, to the slaves, and led away to Lyons.
I remained perfectly quiet, however, listening in
much anxiety to the conversation below, and expecting every instant to hear ' *Ma foi, il faut bien
faire attention à ces pietons-là*, go, my girl, and ask
for his papers.' But to my great relief, nothing
of this sort passed, and the noise below gradually
died away. I could not however sleep, as I was
considering how I should get off in the morning,
which, as it broke into my room, found me feverish and perplexed.

I got up and dressed myself. I took the precaution of removing all my baggage from my

knapsack, and put it into my pocket, with the
knapsack, which was small, and could just contain my necessary changes of linen ; then, taking
my shoes in my hand, I cautiously descended
the stairs. When I got down, the door which
separated it from the kitchen was shut, and I
peeped through the glass above it : one of the
gensdarmes was fast asleep near the fireplace
and the other was standing at the door of the
inn, and seemed to be examining the appearance
of the weather. I hesitated a moment before
emerging from my reconnoitring post ; but it
was better to have to do with one than two, so
out I came. The noise I made in opening the
door made the gensdarme turn round, and the
runaways who were chained to a strong wooden
bench, which was fastened to the wall, and were
lying on one side of the room, turned their
heads and looked at me. The gensdarme quitted
the door, and entering the kitchen, said, " You
are early this morning, friend." " *Oui*," said I

in my best French, "*J'ai loin à aller ce matin ;*" and putting on my shoes, I was quietly passing the man, when he said, "*Allons ! Allons !* you are in a great hurry, *prenez la gouté auparavant,*" and he poured out two small glasses of brandy, one of which he presented to me. The devil take his *gouté*, thought I ; but in for a penny, in for a pound, as they say, so I swallowed my brandy, and made a second attempt to retreat. Whether my evident uneasiness struck the gensdarme, I know not, but something seemed to do so, for he suddenly said, " *Apropos, mon homme*, have you a passport ?" My blood ran cold, when just at that moment down came Jeannette. " *Ah, ma joliette*," said my persecutor to her, " *te voilà aussi, ma foi !* every body seems in motion this morning." I made, during this interval, a third effort to extricate myself from my critical position ; and the good-natured girl, seeing that I was in some difficulty or other, said to the gensdarme, "*Laissez le aller ; nous le connoissons—il n'y a pas de danger ;*" and making an awkward bow, away I went.

CHAPTER XVI.

I took care, said the pedestrian, to walk slowly while in sight of the house, lest I should excite some suspicion; but the gensdarme, who came again to the door, seemed quite satisfied by Jeannette's mediation, and calling to me, said, " You will find the path down by the river dry now, and the bark is mended ; if I were you, I would go to Geneva that way."

Now, he might as well have talked to me of a path in the moon, as I had never seen the country before ; but I presently overtook just at the turning down of a lane, three men I hailed them, and asked them my way to Geneva. " Oh !" said one, " we are going that way ourselves ; come with us, and we will guide you." Accordingly, we all four pro ceeded on, and soon descended into a rich valley of meadow and corn field, all green and fresh with the recent rains. From the conversation of the men, I found that they were Savoyards returning home from some of their wide and wandering journeys. They were men, but had probably passed their youth amid the streets of Paris or London. Sent off in their earliest years from their native mountains, with a marmot or an organ, and a few *sous*, the hardy Savoyard journeys

" With humble ware and pipe of merry sound ;"

and daunted by no distance or difficulties, paces away with his wild music along the roads of a foreign clime friendless and forlorn. When he reaches any considerable city, there he takes his stand, and collects a curious crowd around him by the exhibition of the little animal, his constant companion, or the miraculous machinery of his organ. Thus, perhaps, he may contrive to scrape together a scanty subsistence ; but it is, indeed, scanty, and often the gateway of some house, or the bench before some door, is his bed ; or if he attempt, by industry, to gain a better livelihood, the vilest employments are assigned him ;——he clambers up the dark chimney, or polishes the shoes of the hurrying *calico*, at Paris; or he becomes an itinerant vender of images, or the exhibitor of monkeys and dancing dogs in the British capital. And when he has succeeded at last in hoarding a little treasure, his green valleys and wooden cabin present themselves before him, and he hastens back to pass the rest of his days amidst the winding recesses of *La Maurienne* or *La Tarentaise*, two of the beautiful defiles of Savoy.

Such characters I found were the men I had joined ; and we continued our way together, and, gradually descending, reached the banks of the Rhône, which ran racingly by. We hallooed for the bark, which was upon the other

side, and which presently came swinging across
by means of the pulley which is fastened to a
rope stretched from a post on one side of the
river to another on the opposite side. We all
got into the bark, and floated slowly back, as the
stream was so rapid that it impeded the transver-
sal motion of our vessel : all our dependence was
upon the strength of the rope which retained the
boat ; had that broken, we must have been hurried off, or perhaps swept down into the gulph
which swallows up the unwilling river. We,
however, arrived safely on the opposite bank,
and I began to feel that I was on Swiss ground.
But we were yet a considerable distance from
Geneva ; and after walking on for an hour or
two, I invited my companions to enter a small
inn, and called for some wine. They drank, of
course, to my health ; but the wine was detesta-
ble, cold and sharp, something like that which
is produced round Paris. My Savoyards, however, appeared to relish it well enough, and said

to one another, " *Bon, bon ; ceci vaut mieux que la mauvaise bière de Londres.*" " What, then, you have been in London ?" said I. " Yes, we have been there," replied one of them—" I and my comrade here ; but he," pointing to the third, " has always lived at Paris." " And how did you like London, my friends ?" said I to the two who had been there. " *Ah ! Monsieur, pas trop ;* we poor wanderers never wish much to live in such large cities ; every body despises us and our broken words, and many a cold comfortless night have we passed upon the steps of some fine Palace. *Mais vive St. Maurice et notre chère vallée !* we shall soon forget all when we get back to Chamouny."

I could have wished to have made them my guides to that place, and to have visited the mighty *Archiprete dei monti ;* but my finances were in that state which requires a strict adherence to some settled route ; and this I had resolved should be along the shores of the Lake of Geneva on the Swiss side, and so across the country by Fribourg to Berne and Basle. The country through which we passed after we had quitted the inn, did not strike me as differing particularly from any other, the wide plain on which Geneva stands being hidden from my view.

We continued, however, gradually to advance; and as we passed among the long green lanes which lead from the river to the city, the Savoyards struck up part of that beautiful air which was so popular at Paris, and which these men had probably learnt there.

Aux montagnes de la Savoie
Je naquis de pauvres parens,
Voilà qu'à Paris l'on m'envoie,
Car nous étions beaucoup d'enfans,
Je n'ai apporté, helas ! en France,
Que mes chansons, quinze ans, ma vielle et l'innocence.

When we had arrived, as they informed me, within half a mile of Geneva, my companions told me that their path lay in another direction, that they had far to go before night-fall, and taking off their hats, and wishing me a *bon voyage*, they all three dropped down into a narrow winding road which turned away to the right ; and I continued my journey alone.

I soon got a glimpse of Geneva, spreading before me with its two towers, looking like those of the Tower of London ; but I was still a considerable time before I reached the gates. I entered them from the Savoy side, where the two roads branch off ; one towards Chamouny, and the other leading away to France. I confess that its appearance disappointed me ; I had heard so much of Geneva ; of its being such a Paradise ; of the beauty of its site, and the charming richness of its environs. I saw nothing but a wide extent of country, varied, to be sure, but not so picturesque or agreeable as that about one of our English watering-places,—I mean Tunbridge Wells. The Jura mountains rising like giants, and sullenly bending away towards Basle, were the only interesting objects in sight ; or when I looked towards the Alpine recesses of Savoy, all was cloud and obscurity. But as I advanced, I saw the blue lake glancing in upon me occasionally through some break in the houses ; and I hastened on in all the anxious anticipation of having one of my first wishes gratified. Again I was disappointed ; instead of a magnificent sheet of water spreading itself out in majestic extent, I perceived that the lake at Geneva only shewed part of its charms, like an artful coquette ; and that all its love and beauty lay retired behind the green banks of the *Pays le Vaud*. Still it was a fresh and cheering sight, as the waves came whitening round the point of land which forms its bend, and made two or three boats that were rowing up from Lausanne, heave and roll as if at sea.

I roamed about the town, beneath its dark sheds, and ascended the terrace, whence I again saw the lake. But I always become tired in a short time of a town ; its museums and galleries, and libraries, never interest me ; my imagination speeds over the country which surrounds them. Besides, my finances were so narrow, that they only admitted of my enjoying the unstinted beauties of Nature ; and the constantly repeated franc at the door of these shows, would soon have made my little, less! I visited, however, the old church, from whose pulpit the gloomy Calvin may have dictated his Pontifical decrees, and, perhaps, fulminated the deadly sentence upon Michael Servet.

It is a singular reflection that two of the Lake cities of Switzerland should have been the scenes of parallel instances of bigoted zeal in two rival religions. Constance beheld the intrepid Huss sacrificed, either to the weakness or treachery of the Emperor Sigismund ;

and the Pope of Geneva imitating those, against whom he preached, condemned his Arian opponent Servet to be burned alive.

As my funds were in this state, you may conclude that I did not dine at the *table d'hôte* of the expensive inns of Geneva. I just planted myself in the corner of one of the small rooms at the *Traiteur's*, a house looking upon the lake ; and enjoyed my simple fare with that companion before me, more than if I had swallowed soups and sauces in a crowded chattering room.

After dinner, I strolled about, and looked up at the windows of the house in which Rousseau was born, with that enthusiastic pleasure that one feels in beholding the former residence of a favourite author. It is almost like grasping the hand of an old friend ; all the passages of our former pleasures and amusements flow in upon our hearts.

I saw many of my countrymen lounging about ; none, however, that I knew ; and probably if I had, neither I, nor they, would have been desirous of claiming acquaintance, as our mutual pride would have held us back : I, because I was poor, and they, because they were rich. I had, however, somewhat improved my costume ; I had sent my shoes, according to the innkeeper's hint, *de se reposer chez le Savetier*, and I was shod in a splendid new pair, which were, however, rather like the seven devils, more wicked than the others, for they pinched my feet cruelly.

I had left my baggage safely at the inn, a small place somewhere in the street leading along the lake ; and as I rambled on, saw several carriages hastening away, filled with glittering company, towards the country. I walked in the same direction that they took ; but presently I saw them all returning, slowly and silently, with the same inmates, but some of them in tears : the circumstance surprised me ; I spoke to some person who was returning on foot, and he told me that the ball to which the carriages had hastened, was stopped by a fatal accident. A little boy, one of the sons of the lady who gave it, had been playing in a cart, the cart had upset and fallen upon him, and the child lay in agony, and probably expiring. It was further said, that the poor mother, when told of the occurrence, thought not that it was so serious; but when the physician, who had been to visit her little boy, came into the room to make his report to her, she asked him if the ball could go on ? " Ball ! Madam," replied he, " in twenty-four hours your child will be dead." The mother fell senseless, and never recovered completely the shock.

Upon returning to my inn, I mentioned that I intended to set out early the next morning. The people of the house asked me if my passport had been signed ? " No," replied I ; " I thought that in Switzerland there was no necessity for that." They laughed at me, and I found that this Republic had imitated the suspicious care of its neighbours, and that the traveller was obliged to add another link here to that chain of superintendence which lengthens as he goes. I set forth, therefore, to the Senate-house, where, after waiting some time as obsequiously as in the *Bureau des Affaires Etrangères* at Paris, I was favoured with the signature of the Swiss ædile.

I then went and stood upon the bridges that unite the two parts of the city, and beneath which the Rhône seems to speed away, as if it feared a second annihilation in the rival lake. I was not a native of Geneva, and yet I almost felt that faintness of heart which Rousseau describes himself to have experienced as often as he crossed them—*Un defaillement de cœur*, as he calls it. I returned to my *hôtel*—a name goes a great way; and went to bed. Next morning, before sunrise, I was up, and in motion. I left the inn, and emerged shortly upon the road which leads towards Lausanne.

There is no one but the pedestrian that can tell or feel the delight of this commencement of his day's march in a bright breezy morning.

> " Cheerful, at morn, he wakes from short repose,
>   Breathes the keen air, and carols as he goes."

Every thing pleases him ; he may be said to feel his existence, and the singing of the birds, the waving of the trees, the distant lowing of the cows, make him stride on like a giant re-freshed.

On I went, and as I met the peasants carry-ing in their milk and fruit to market, I re-galed myself with the delicious and still warm liquid, which, with some fruit and bread, made me a capital breakfast, and equalled the rich *ieben Frauen milch*, which I afterwards tasted in Germany. You are too independent and inquisitive yourself, my friend, to see any thing in this, but an ardent devotion to simple and natural tastes; and you can, I am sure, understand the pleasure I feel in this mode of breakfasting. There are many, I know, who would smile upon me with scorn, and perhaps might call me mad ; but I can reply to them in the words of the Roman : "*Malim cum 'meipso' insanire, quàm cum aliis sapere.*" I had rather enjoy a fresh morning on the shores of Geneva's lake, though I fasted on bread and water for days, than dine upon turtle or venison, washed down by the brightest champagne.

" You are right," replied I. " He who loves Nature and all her works and wonders, can, indeed, say that he is independent. The smiles of mankind pass away, their hearts grow cold towards us, and if we are unfortunate, they either quite neglect us, or look upon us with that sort of pity which the rich man bestows upon the beggar. But Nature, glorious, gracious Nature,

s ever unchanged ; and if storms for a time de-
ace her fields and ruffle the glassy surface of her
akes, she soon, like a hasty but affectionate
nother, breathes comfort to us again, and show-
rs upon us her sweets and flowers.   When I
ame hither, my heart was almost broken, life
eemed a blank to me, and I looked around upon
hose glittering walls and houses, as upon the
vhite tomb that was to relieve and rest me.
But the precious breezes of that sparkling sea
lave brought some coolness to my burning soul ;
he endless peace of these skies has lulled my
lnquiet thoughts to some repose ; and I have
ound that to sit and muse on the past amongst
he wild herbs which grow in the wood beneath,
s less painful than if I were in crowded streets
or chambers.   The slumbering passions of my
lature are not roused by the sight of forbidden
ruits ; and though I am for ever banished from
he world's Eden of domestic bliss, yet the fiery
lashing of the restless sword falls less fiercely

upon my eyes. But pray continue your account."
" Well," proceeded my friend, " I paced on in
the full enjoyment of my greatest pleasure. I
had been recommended to go to Ferney to see
Voltaire's house, where, if I chose, I might sit
in his chair; but Voltaire never was a favourite
with me, and the mere sight of an author's
dwelling, unless he has been my companion and
friend, does not tempt my curiosity. So I
passed on amid the shady avenues of trees which
border the commencement of the road, and
shelter the numerous villas that are scattered
along the banks of the lake. This I could not
see, for it was hidden by walls and gardens,
except when it sparkled in upon me through the
trees of some orchard, whose wall was not so
high as the rest. At last, however, my view
was unimpeded, and I could walk close to the
dimpling waters. I reached Nyon, but passed
beneath it, and loitered on, dreaming and delighted. The frowning black cliffs of Savoy

reared themselves on the opposite side, just leaving space enough between themselves and the lake for a road, a village, or town; the lake lay like a precious amethyst, with the dark mountains reflected within its surface, and whispered and wound about the shore at my feet. And what a contrast did that shore present to the other side. It was like hope to despair!—the one, green, flourishing, and fruitful; the other, brown, barren, and blighted. Nyon, Rolle, vineyards, smiling villas, white churches, and liberty, were around me!—beyond, were squalid cabins and despotism.

I dined at a small inn, somewhere on the road between Rolle and Lausanne; and towards the afternoon, when the sun's heat was a little past, continued my route. But soon the magnificent full view of the lake opened upon me, as I reached an eminence at some distance from the inn; and my eyes impatiently darted their view away down to its extremity, where some white shining specks told of Vevay and Chillon, and on the other side, La Meillerie.

Evening was coming on, and I sat down upon the bank; a dark cloud was hanging over part of the waters, and I thought portended one of those magnificent lake storms which sweep out from the Alpine treasures of tempest and trouble; but the cloud passed slowly away, leaving the unspotted lake pure and harmless, as it looked up to the smiling sky. I would not yield the remembrance of the sensations I experienced while resting myself, for that of the most brilliant success of ambition. I took out a small tin cup, which I carried with me constantly, and drank some of the cool waters; and I can well conceive the feelings which made Rousseau, as he roamed along those shores, mingle his passionate tears with the blue waves. There is no explaining in detail, the intensity of the delight of a true adorer of Nature, when surrounded by her choice works, —he cannot explain it himself. He feels that his heart is identified with the beautiful objects which are spread around him, and he remains in apt and rapturous contemplations. When I indulge this holy enthusiasm, those rich lines of Beattie have always come into my mind, and I have *felt* them :

O how canst thou renounce the boundless store
   Of charms which Nature to her votary yields ?
The warbling woodland, the resounding shore,
   The pomp of groves, and garniture of fields,—
All that the genial ray of morning gilds,
   And all that echoes to the song of even,
All that the mountain's sheltering bosom yields,
   And all the dread magnificence of Heaven,—
   O how canst thou renounce and hope to be forgiven ?

The bell of Lausanne, as it ' swung its sullen roar o'er the wide water'd shore,' warned me that it was time for me to return to reality ; and towards dusk, I found myself ascending the steep eminence upon which that city stands. It was Saturday evening, toil was at an end, and the inhabitants were slowly sauntering along upon the terrace, which is the first object that attracts the attention. I paused as I passed across it, and looked down again upon the lake. Its character was changed. The moon had risen, and a pale golden path seemed to connect the rival banks; that of Savoy looked still darker and drearier, while a few solitary lights glimmered along its frowning line. I turned to proceed, and made my way to an inn, (not the Faucon, I should just as soon think of going to the Clarendon in London, but a smaller and more modest one.) I was furnished with my usual repast of bread and milk, and went to bed.

But it grows late, said my pedestrian acquaintance, and I have some distance to go; some other time, I will relate to you the rest of the circumstances which I have met with in my travels."

CHAPTER XVII.

January 20.—I WENT strolling about the country to-day, away beyond the Château Borelli, and
reached another *bastide* or villa, which lies near
the mountains.   In my way thither, I passed a
solitary-looking Château, where, they told me, the
present King of Spain had lived for some time,
when he had been kidnapped into France by the
king of the fortune-tellers, who built up castles
and coronets for others, but, like the blind wandering gypsy, could not control his own fate.
Many of the Peers and Princes that he made are
now high and haughty in their golden galleries
at Paris ; while the Aladdin himself has lost
the magic lamp, and sleeps on the enchanted
and solitary rock of the Atlantic.   The house

itself presents nothing remarkable,— a few fig-
trees and vines are scattered about it; and Fer-
dinand must have bitterly regretted the shady
groves of Aranjuez, while wearing his degraded
days away upon this parched soil. The villa,
which I visited afterwards, was of a very different description;—it belonged to some rich
merchant of Marseilles, and its gardens were
laid out like a little Versailles. Statues and
fountains and pavilions, in mimic microscopic
mockery, brought the stately avenues of that
splendid palace to my recollection. But here the
resemblance failed, for as I sat beneath the shade
of the fig and almond trees, and as the bee
and the blithe bird hummed and hovered about
me, I thought of the damp and dingy atmosphere that was then hanging over the leafless
elms and oaks of the northern chateau.

As I was returning home, I overtook a peasant
driving a mule, laden with the roots of olive-trees
and their branches, which he was carrying home

for fuel. Those branches make a delicious fire, especially when mixed with the almond wood;—they diffuse a rich perfume around the room, and fill it, as it were, with incense. I am very fond of a wood fire;—there is something venerable, hospitable, and, I may almost say, poetical, in the sight of a wide chimney filled with bright bickering logs, that crackle and sparkle and seem to rejoice themselves in the cheerfulness they create. The "*ligna super foco large reponens,*" is, in my opinion, much more calculated to dissolve the cold than coal, for there is nothing to impede the circulation of the hot air from the chimney; and the feet, the most important part of the circulating system, are kept infinitely warmer than when the fire is contained in an elevated grate. And then the faggots blazing upon the ample hearth carry us back to olden times, to the days of the ancient hall hung round with banners, of the dais, and the volcano of a chimney, that mingled its roaring with the wild wassail that echoed along the gothic benches; some remnant of which antique state may be found in the halls of our colleges at the Universities;—there are the raised and privileged *high table*, the frowning pictures of some of the knightly founders, mingled with the grave bishop and the sagacious lawyer; and the pomp and ceremony of dining, such as it must have been when the Baron perhaps gave the same signal for dinner as the presiding *Fellow* does at present. The long train of attendants, bearing in the dishes after the conclusion of the short grace, to which attention is called by the single blow of a small hammer upon the tables, has always recalled to my mind these lines of Suckling.

> " Just in the nick, the cook knock'd thrice,
>   And all the waiters, in a trice,
>   His summons did obey;—
>   Each serving-man, with dish in hand,
>   March'd boldly up with dish in hand,
>   Presented, and away."

Alas! these recollections of the former passages of my life, when I was in the full bloom
of youth and hope, fall mournfully now upon
my heart.   And yet there is a pleasure derived
from thinking upon the past, though the present
be miserable and comfortless; such as the mariner feels as he sees, in his mind's-eye, his
wife and smiling children, and cheerful hearth,
while surrounded by darkness and roaring
breakers.

I recognized the peasant I had overtaken as
the same I had before seen at my friend the
hermit's; and the recognition was mutual.

" *Bon jour, bon jour, Monsieur!*" said he,
" *voilà ce diable de Mistral.*"   The north-west
wind had suddenly got up, and was flying away
over the plain, pouncing upon the dusty roads
and lanes, and scattering the white powder in
our faces.

" Yes, my friend," said I ; " but it will do
us good ; it will keep off the yellow fever."

" Ah ! I don't think of that," said he ; " *ma foi, non !* the fine folks in the city may talk about that if they will ; but we *campagnards* have enough to do to mind our fields. But what do they say about the war ?"

War ! what could he mean ? I had not then become so utterly indifferent to what was passing around me, as to be ignorant of a war.

" *On dit*," added the peasant, " *que le général a été pris.*" I recollected to have heard something about a General Berton that had been hatching some annual plot in Saumur, and concluded that the man alluded to him.

" Oh !" said I, " all that will soon be over."

" *Tant mieux*," said the peasant ; " for though fevers don't much concern us, war does ; we are obliged to pay our taxes, and more *droit* upon our wine, and every *sous*, you know, Sir, counts to a poor man."

" Make yourself easy, my friend," said I, " your tranquillity will not be disturbed."

" *Ah! vive la tranquillité!*" exclaimed the peasant.

We were approaching the village where my companion lived, which lay near the sea. The little tinkling bell of his mule brought out two or three children from the house up to the little court of which he drove the animal, and who began to stroke its ears, which he took very lovingly. The wife came to the door with a small dish of lentils in her hand, into which she was pouring some oil,—probably for their dinner. It was a sort of inn; I was tired, and the sun was at its greatest heat; so, upon the invitation of the peasant, I went in with him.

" *Allons, ma femme*," said the man, " let us have some of our best *saucisses,* and our best oil, for the gentleman. We have no butter, Sir, you must go away beyond the Isère for that, but our oil is fresh and sweet."

I had never tasted any thing dressed in that

way before, so I made no objection. Our meal was soon prepared, and we sat down. The children had napkins carefully tied about their necks. The peasant said a short grace, and the wife prepared to do the honours of the simple board. My walk had given me some appetite, and I really found that their oil was not so disagreeable as I had expected. The peasants were quite pleased at my apparent satisfaction; and the man said to me,

"Ah! my good gentleman, one sees well that you are not like the proud dainty seigneurs that sometimes come this way, and tell us that our country is good for nothing. The other day there came two fine ladies and a handsome cavalier to see the chateau, where you have been this morning, and they stopped here to refresh themselves;—but, *diable!* they wanted fresh butter and white bread, and bright knives; and said, that in their country every *auberge* had such things; and the gentleman wanted Champagne and all those dainty wines, and said that ours was no better than English beer."

" Why," I replied, " I am not so rich as they are, perhaps, and must put up with humble fare. I certainly like butter better than oil ; but we cannot have all we would wish in a foreign land."

" You may say that with truth," said the peasant ; " and no man knows it better than myself. When I was eating black rusk at Algiers, I used often to think that I would be content to live upon walnut oil all my days, if I could get back to the place where they made it."

" Do they make an oil from walnuts ?"

" Oh yes, Sir, down by Valence on the Rhône ; and we get some of it here sometimes, mixed up with the innocent olive oil."

" And what do you mean by Algiers and black rusk ?" said I.

" What do I mean, Sir ?—why, that for a year

I was groaning among those cursed pirates, and looking wistfully enough at the rice and the mutton that my old devilish master used to devour; and I should be there now, perhaps, had it not been for the good old Hermit of Saint Joseph." ..

" How did he contribute to your liberation?" I asked.

" How?—why by paying the ransom for me; which I might as well have waited to pay myself as to dine with our *prefet*, although my good Annette here toiled in the heat of the sun, with her oar, in the hope of scraping up something for me."

I expressed my curiosity to hear the circumstance to which my host alluded; and he immediately said, " Certainly, Sir, if you will come and sit with me under the large mulberry-tree where the little ones are playing, I will tell you all about it;—and try and make us a little coffee, Annette," added the man to his wife.

" *Oh ! oui, pour le Monsieur ;* my good Louis, coffee is too dear for us," said Annette.

" *Ah bah !*" replied the husband, laughing, " you are as bad as my master Hamet, an old cruel devil, that used to tell me that I was a very expensive slave to him, because I drank so much water, that he should soon be obliged to sink a fresh well."

Annette seemed to be alarmed by this terrible comparison, and set about preparing the coffee ; while my host and myself sat quietly down under the tree.

" *Ma foi !*" said the peasant, " I have told the story often enough to all my neighbours, and yet my blood runs cold every time I think of it. You have seen the small vessels that come from the ports along the coast, Sir, with fruit and flowers ?"

" Oh, yes, I have often seen them discharging their pretty cargoes."

" Well, Sir, I used to belong to one of those

little things, and made one or two voyages as far as Genoa. We were coming back from that place, and just put into Nice, to take some oranges on board;—we were soon all ready again, and the wind came fair; so one bright May morning we worked out of the bay, with a famous freight of fresh fruits and flowers, and our deck looked just like the garden of one of our *bastides* here. The wind, as it blew among our sails, seemed quite sweet; and I plucked one of the almond-blossoms, and threw it upon the water. ' *Va*,' said I, ' *va trouver Annette*, and tell her that I am coming.' I was a young man then, Sir, and you know, perhaps, that we do many foolish things at that time."

I said nothing—I could not; but bowed my head in assent.

" Well, Sir, on we went; and our captain said, that the weather was so fine there was no use in creeping along the coast; he should bear out to sea, and so get away to Marseilles;

and you may be sure I did not object. So away we went, all sail hoisted, and Antibes soon looked like that white speck of a hut on the mountain yonder. It was a glorious sight, as the little ship floated along so easily upon the waves; and many a wistful look I cast towards the quarter that I thought Marseilles lay in; but I could see nothing except a light mist, that the captain told me was hovering about the coast. But, said he, we shall see the sun shining on the Catalan boats by to-morrow evening, and we shall, I hope, sail in with them. The night came on; we were all steady, as the captain said, and the stars were all out. We went down to bed; the man at the helm began to sing over my head one of the songs that are such favourites among the coasters, and I lay listening to him till I fell asleep."

" Do you happen to recollect it?" said I.

" I will try," replied Louis, and considering a little, he began the song, the original of which

I have lost, though I preserved the following
translation of it :—

My comrades all have said good night,
But the helmsman's heart with hope is light,
For he must see, while alone he wakes,
Our Lady's Fort as the daylight breaks.

My comrades all have said good night;
But the stars are shining still and bright,
And the flowers that stand around my feet,
As gentlest hours of sleep, are sweet.

My comrades all have said good night;
But our vessel holds her course aright,
And long ere next the sun be set
They 'll see her from the high Tourette.

" I don't know how long I had slept, but I was
awakened by a terrible bustle over head. The
morning was just breaking, and I got up, and
went upon deck ;—*par la Sainte Baume!* I trem-

ble even now at the thought, there was a large ship coming right down upon our vessel, with all her sail set, and bristling and foaming upon the waves like a great fish.   There was a mist hovering about us, so that I could not distinguish her deck ; but I heard some strange shouts, and our captain ran about like a madman : the man at the helm stood firm, and tried to take the wind of her, as the captain kept crying out ; but it was too late ; and in seven or eight minutes she was close up to us.   Three or four men, in turbans, instantly jumped upon our deck, bellowing out, " *No paura, no paura,*" and began to grin and nod at us, as if we were old acquaintances.   *Ma foi !* such acquaintances as those are none of the best.   The rascals turned away our man from the helm, took out the fruit, and then hoisted us all up into their cursed black ship ; at one end of which the captain was sitting, an old man with a long white beard, and a large shawl tied round his neck ; a brace of pistols was sticking in his breast. Our poor little boat they sent adrift. Our captain seemed to understand their jargon a little; and the old pirate laughed, and talked with him, and he told me afterwards, that he had been thanking us for our fruit and flowers, as he had one of his favourite ladies on board. Well, Sir, we prisoners were sent down into the hold, and there they kept us, feeding us with some black stuff, that I would not give to my mule; and there we stayed for six days, among the cables and blocks, and tormented by thirst: they only allowed us to come upon deck for half an hour. We did not much care about that, for those wretches got round us, and jabbered their gibberish, and seemed like evil spirits. *Mais allons, Annette, le café, le café;* and Annette came forth with it. The children, seeing the white sugar that had been produced for me, came stealing up, and peeped round from behind the trunk of the tree under which we were sitting. " *Ah! les polissons,*" said the father, " *viens ci, mon petit Louis, viens à ton grand père,"* and he took the youngest on his knee ; who looked boldly up in his face, and at the same time possessed himself of a very respectable piece of sugar. " Oh! Louis, you spoil that child," said Annette. " Well, well, my wife, he is like his poor father, and I can't help fondling and indulging him. Our boy, Sir, was killed at Waterloo, and this is his son ; there stands his sister ;—here, Josephine, come and speak to the gentleman, and he will give you some sugar too." The girl came slowly up to me, and held out her hand, into which I put my sweet donation, and off she ran to display it, I suppose, to some less fortunate companion. Our coffee was excellent ; and as we sipped it, Louis continued his story.

CHAPTER XVIII.

" WELL, Sir, there we lay—the captain, the other man, and myself, melancholy enough, and wishing for some lucky Levanter, that might set the pirates at their wit's ends, and perhaps give us a chance of working the ship, as the captain said ;—but the infidels had the upper hand of us that time ; and though we all prayed and told our beads, the Virgin had a mind to make us taste of slavery ; and if, as they tell me, our good King Saint Louis was in the same plight, why, I don't know that we had any right to complain. On the sixth morning we heard a desperate howling and yelling over head ; and one of the black dogs called to us into the hold, and told us to come on deck and see Algiers, ' *Veni can d'infidel, veni, ecco la Algiere.*' I have remembered the words ever since, for the Captain crossed himself and said, ' The Holy Saints have mercy upon us now !' Up we went upon deck, and there, sure enough, was that devilish purgatory straight before us.——Did you ever see Villa Franca beyond Nice from the sea, Sir ?"

" Never," said I.

" When I first looked towards the land, my heart beat, and I thought that it was all a dream, and that I was just off that place ; there were the green banks to the right, and the high rocks behind, and a fort up to the left, that might have been the castle of Montalbano, and the lighthouse and the mole just as they are at Franca ; but, then, there were two or three odd-looking towers, just like those large oil-flasks you see yonder ; and the sun glittered upon something else there, that looked like the moon when she has a mind to be leaving us. And sure enough it was no dream ; for when we got into the harbour, instead of the pretty-look-

ing peasants that used to come, with their black
silk nets twining among their hair, and buy our
gay flowers, there was nothing but a parcel of
savage black men in turbans, and some sad
pale fellows in chains, that looked like galley
slaves, except that they were almost naked.
And I whispered the Captain, that the Turks
seemed to be like us in that respect, and did not
cut off a poor man's life because he was unfortunate and guilty. The Captain turned his face
upon me,—*pardi!* I see him now,—and said, with
a deep groan, ' We shall be like them to-morrow, and perhaps worse,—they were once as we
are.' My heart sunk as low as one of our wells,
and I did not speak another word. And, indeed, I had no opportunity, for when we got
close up to the mole, the boat was ordered out,
and the old Jew of a Captain made us get into
it, and away we went to the shore. When we
landed, we were marched off directly along the
dirty dismal streets, just like those in the old

town ; and we presently stopped at a house they said was the Dey's palace, and a dismal-looking place it was, with its small grated windows. But what do you think we saw directly before us at the entrance?—*Mon Dieu! ça me fait mal au cœur même à présent. Voyons Annette, donne la goute. Allons, Monsieur,* to your better health. *Bois, mon petit chat,*" said he to the child that was sitting upon his knee ; and the infant suspiciously sipped some of the hot liquid.— " We saw, Sir, three bleeding heads lying on the ground, and my foot slipped in some of the blood and brains that were spread about. Holy Saint Victor ! thy name be thanked for bringing me safe out of that tiger's den. The old Dey was sitting up in his room upon a cushion, smoking ; a parcel of pigeons were flying about him ; and, as we saw him through the window, he looked just like one of my goats there, with his beard and his fur tippet and the half moon that was stuck in front of his turban. They

made us kneel down in the mud, and make the
salem, as they called it!—*Diable!* to kneel to an
Infidel Satan like that!—I don't know what they
said, but when we got up, we prisoners were all
separated, and my poor captain led away by
the man who had commanded the ship that
took us. I and the other followed a man
they called an Aga, and, as we went along,
the malicious Moors did nothing but shriek in
our ears, *schiavi! schiavi!* They should have
known better, for they were all coming from
their churches, as my companion told me, who
had been there once before. Well, Sir, when
we got to the Aga's house, he stripped off
all our clothes, and put on some of the rags
and remnants that had served for some other
poor devils; and told us, in his *lingua franca,*
that we might be thankful we had fallen to so
good a master, for that, when his slaves offended him, he never gave them more than forty
lashes! while every one else gave theirs fifty!

My shoulders began to tingle, and my companion looked very grave; but, as it was getting dark, we were sent away into a black hole of a place like a dog-stable, to sleep. Next morning, by daybreak, we heard a fellow shouting, *A trabajo, a trabajo can del Christian;* and the task-master came in with a long whip, and bade us get up. *Ma foi!* there was no alternative, so up we sprang; and all that day did we broil and blister in a hot Afric sun, with nothing but some black crust and water for our food. And when we faltered or flagged, crack, crack came the long whip about us, till our legs smarted again. My companion soon fell away, and looked as meagre as one of our cows here in Provence, that have no taste for shrubs and burnt grass. I was young and strong, and I thought of my dear Annette, and endeavoured to keep up my spirits; but when my work was done, and I had a little time to myself in the evening,

it was then I used ·to feel lonely and lost. I
could see from my master's garden the sea
and the little ships flitting along in the distance; and when the weather was clear, I
could see the opposite land. And I used to
think, if I could once get over there, I would
easily beg my way to Marseilles and Annette.
But the cunning heretics watched us too close,
and I might have sung, as they say one of
our Troubadours used to do, when he was shut
up somewhere in Germany I believe." The song
to which the man alluded, I recollected to have
before seen; and having referred to it in the evening, I amused myself in translating it, as follows,
as far as the sense and obscurity of the old language would admit. The metre is extraordinary;
as appears by the first stanza of the original.

> Jà nul home près non dira sa razon
> Adreitamen, se come hom doulen non
> Mas per conort pot el faire canson
> Prou ha d'amicz, ma paûre don li don
> Honta y auran se por ma rehezon
> Sony fach dos hivers prez.

Since he, who lies in binding bonds, his story cannot
       tell,
To comfort him in this distress, and all his longing
       quell,
I counsel, that he make a song, and try its soothing spell.
Now great will be your shame, my friends, your false-
       hood dark as hell,
If thus, because, to ransom me, your lands ye will
       not sell,
           'Two winters see my chains.

And let them think, my subjects all, my lords and ba-
       rons bold—
Those English, Norman, Gascon knights, who of me
       fiefs do hold—
There's not a serf that I possess, but, if to bondage sold,
Could make his prison gates fly back, and pass forth free,
       for gold.
I will not call my liegers false, yet, if the truth be told,
           Two winters see my chains.

Alas! the weary captive's heart hath neither friend nor
       kin ;
They think not of his pining, as they sit their halls
       within ;
The thought of that torments me more than all the
       pangs of sin.
And should I die, thus far away from battle's glorious din,

What knight, on those who leave me thus, his faith again
    could pin?——
        Two winters here in chains.

Nor is it strange that thus I yield to dark depression's
    sleep;
The King of France, with spear and brand, doth o'er my
    fiefdoms sweep,
And break the peace that he hath sworn by Holy Rood
    to keep:
And well I know, that many a Prince and King do hold
    me cheap,
Since I have passed my weary days within this dungeon
    deep,
        Two winters thus in chains.

But, mark ye! fierce and haughty foes, whose hearts are
    now so high,
Because that thus, in traitor bonds, King Richard now
    doth lie,
When these long tedious hours of pain are past, that
    make me sigh,
Ye'll see once more, and quail beneath the lion's fiery
    eye.
Cheer up! my brother troubadours, though thus are
    lingering by
        Two winters o'er my chains.

ister, Countess, listen well, it is not thee I blame,
ind yet, because I kept thee safe from worldly suit and
     claim,
          My days are such as these.

Jo longer can I masses sing to Chartreuse Holy Dame.
          La Mene Loeys.

To return to the peasant, " But I trust that
rou did not remain as long as poor Richard
mong those cruel gaolers of yours?" said I.

" You shall hear, Sir. I told you that my
ompanion wasted and pined away, and he soon
ied, leaving me sad enough! Fight or nine
nonths passed, or crawled on I might say, after
is death, and I began to give up all hope and
rish to follow him; when, one day, as I was
itting down near a well I had been sinking,
nd eating my black cake, who should I see
oming towards me but one of the Fathers
f our Holy Trinity, that are all now dead or
:attered, God knows where! You that are in
  foreign country will understand, Sir, what

I felt when I saw him,—I fell at his feet and wept. The good father raised me, and told me to be comforted; ' Thou art free, my son, said he, ' thy ransom is paid, and thou wilt ere many days be past, see thy friends.' You may imagine, Sir, that I was happy, and to happy to speak, for I looked at the good man, unable to utter a word for joy: and when, at length I did speak, I said nothing intelligible. The kind friar bade me be tranquil and compose myself Well, Sir, I followed him to the quay, and there were a number of other happy creatures like myself, singing and shouting, *La patrie! La patrie* and we all embarked; and many a curse did we bestow upon the wicked place as we left it. But we kept our chains, and said that we would not pull them off, till we had shown to the city the dreadful state to which its Christian natives are often reduced. And merry and gay we were, and we made the ship ring again with our vintage songs. I thought that the good Fathers of the Trinity had paid my ransom, as they were used to do every year, till they were all turned adrift—poor Saints! But the others told me that they had heard the Consul talking to the friar about me, and that he had said, ' that though the money was in his hands, yet the friar had better seem to pay it among that for the rest. It was an odd story, and I could scarcely believe it; since, if that troubadour king could not find friends to ransom him, how was I, that had nobody but my betrothed Annette? And impatient enough I was to have it all cleared up. We had a glorious passage; and when we saw the old mountain of *La Victoire*, I thought that the tunny-fish would be all frightened away by the shout that we set up. They made us perform quarantine for a few days; but we were all right, and we sailed straight up to the quay, close to the *Hôtel de Ville*. They had been expecting us, and the windows were all

hung with flowers and silks; and the rest of
the Holy Brothers were all there, with their
Abbot; and as we cast anchor, the little boy,
that carried the bright silver cross before the
monks, raised it aloft, and all the people that
were standing about threw up their caps, and the
bells tolled, and the Abbot blessed us. When
we landed, they made us march two and two,
with our chains, and as we went up the *Cane-
biere*, we pointed to the marks which the long
whips of those African imps had made; and the
ladies waved their white hands, and threw roses
upon us, and came and took off our chains. But
all that did not satisfy me; I was looking about
for Annette, and, sure enough, I saw her standing
under the trees of the *Cours*, just as we reached
it, and weeping. I could not bear the sight, and
stay where I was, so I darted out of the procession
and rushed up to her. She knew me directly,
and giving a loud shriek, fainted in my arms.
I had my chains still about my hands, and as I

put them round her, I thought that if she had been always with me, I should not have so much cared to have worn them longer. But a kind lady came and took them off, and sprinkled my Annette's face with sweet water, and she opened her eyes, and flung her arms round my neck, and sobbed for joy. And all the people seemed as delighted as ourselves; for the men had tears in their eyes, and blessed us as they passed. But when I looked again at my Annette, my heart smote me, she was so pale and thin, and her clothes were worn and old, and her hands blistered; and I said to her, My Annette, my dear Annette, what! have you been a slave too? you look as wan and weak as myself."

" Oh ! Louis," said she.

" Ay, ay, *ma femme*," said the man to his wife, who had stolen up from the door, and was listening behind the tree, " we are talking about you, and listeners hear no good of themselves."

" *Eh bien! mon homme*, say what you will about me, for you ought to know me well after thirty years' acquaintance, and I am not afraid of you."

" Ah, no," said Louis to me, " she has no reason, indeed, for she knows that I love her as well as my preserver from the Turks. Why, Sir, she used to labour day after day, in one of the little boats that you may have seen plying about the harbour, in hope of scraping together something for me; but she would have worked long enough ere she could have got sufficient to content those greedy, griping sharks. But the Virgin protected her, Sir, as I always tell her, and made her labour profitable. Come here, *ma femme*, and tell your own story. Here, bring your wheel and your stocking, and let us have a few of our sweetest grapes that are

hanging up near the chimney." The wheel and
the grapes were brought, and Annette sat down,
while the little boy, who had been for some
time impatient of his thraldom upon the knee of
his grandfather, (who seemed like others to have
acquired a taste for confining others, by having
been confined himself,) now crept down, and
began to make sad confusion among the ball of
flax which was upon the ground. "*Reste tranquille donc, mon piccion,*" said his grandmother.
' *Je vais conter une histoire* ;" and the child,
cheated into a belief that the *histoire* was to
be one of fairies and fine castles, sat himself
down quietly among the leaves of the tree that
had been blown down by the recent attack of
the *Mistral*.

"My husband, there," said the French female
peasant, " has made me tell my story so often,
that I begin to be ashamed of it; and a gentleman,
like you, I fear, won't find much to please you in
it. When the news came of one of our coasters

aving been robbed by the Pirates, and the men taken away for slaves, I was sitting with my mother in our little stall that we used to have near the Museum. ' *Voilà une triste affaire,*' said some of the other flower-women that were standing there, ' some of the finest and first flowers and fruits all gone, not to mention the men. It is a shame that the king does not hang all those robbers.' I was expecting my Louis home every day, and when I heard them talking so, I asked what they meant. ' Why, one of our best coasters, the Emilie, has been sent adrift by the Algerines, who took good care to have all out of her that was worth any thing,—the poor fruits and flowers, and the men too.' That was the name of my Louis's ship; and I jumped up, and without saying any thing to my mother, who called after me in vain, away I ran down to the port, and there, sure enough, I saw the poor little vessel just brought in by one of the Catalans. Oh, Sir! what I felt then! and how I wished that I were rich and great that I might give all I had to buy back my poor lover ; but it was of no use to wish, so what do you think I determined to do? Why, I will tell you, Sir. Said I to my mother, There now, I shall never be married, for the only man that I will have is taken by the Algerine pirates for a slave. ' Nonsense,' says my mother, ' you 'll find plenty besides him ; there's Charles the porter, that you know always offers to carry our flowers from the port for nothing, and a kind-hearted fellow he is. *Dieu merci!* never be married !' But my mother might say what she pleased, I was determined to have my own way. No! says I, no! no! *ma Mère*, I will never forsake dear Louis, that you know used to smuggle us in many a pretty thing from Genoa, made by the nuns there ; so you may stay here to mind the flowers, and I shall go and try to earn some money by working in one of the little boats. Mayhap some kind Christians will pay me more than the rest, when they know why I do it. So, Sir, I did so. And many a burning day I laboured; but every body laughed at me, and said I was a fool to make myself a galley-slave, because my lover was one. Yet, Sir, for all that, I went on, and I thought that I was doing the same thing as my Louis. Well, one day, there came a gentleman down to the quay, and told me to carry him over to the castle of St. John, that's close to the *belle Tourette;* and while we were crossing, he told me that I was too weak to work in that way; and asked me if I had no friends to get me a place in the city.— Oh, Sir, said I, the only friend I have, except my mother (and she can't do any thing for me), is a slave, and can't marry me now."

" Poor woman!" said the gentleman, " and how long has he been so?"

" Oh! about nine months, Sir; and may be nine years, unless God is pleased to do something for us, since I shall never be able to earn enough for his ransom. 'Poor woman!' again said the gentleman, and so sweetly and mournfully; and as we had got to the other side, he gave me a crown, and went away. I put it with the rest I had saved, and kept on labouring, and every evening when I went home I hid my money; and my mother scolded me; and the porter Charles kept coming about the house;—but still I trusted in the Virgin, Sir, that always protects faithful hearts. But mine was heavy enough, as I saw the tenth month come, and no hope yet of buying Louis; and when I heard that the friars were gone to Barbary, to deliver as many of the slaves as they could, I used to pray every day up at our Lady's Chapel in the fort on the rock, and promise her a bouquet of roses and jasmin, if she would send my lover back. But they told me all the names of the men that the good religious had ransomed, and his was not there. So when they came back, I could not bear the sight; and I was standing as miserable as any

one could be, when whom should I see, but th
very man I was crying about! Oh, Sir!
thought I should have died; and when I reco
vered, (for I fainted,) Louis and I went home t
my mother's, and she seemed glad to see him
and we were married two days after. But w
could not think who had paid the money for us
till I happened to think of the kind-spoken gen
tleman I had carried over the port a month be
fore; and said I one day to my husband, I hav
it,—as sure as there's a true tear of our Saviou
in the old church treasury, I know the goo
man that has done this for us. So I kept a goo
look-out for him, and one day I saw him comin
along the Rue St. Ferreol, just as I was returnin
from the fruit-market, with some figs I had beer
buying. So I ran up to him, and fell down a
his feet, and took his hands, and put them to m
lips, and told him that God and the Saints woul
for ever bless him, here and hereafter, for hi
charity. But he seemed angry, and told m

that I had mistaken him for some one else, and broke away from me. But I was determined that I would find out the truth, and I spoke to Louis about it. ' Oh !' says he, ' I have a friend that lives with the banker that does all the business for Algiers ; I 'll ask him about it.' And so he did ; and the clerk told him that a gentleman, describing the very same that I thought, had come to their house, and paid in the money for the ransom of a slave named Louis Faushet, then at Algiers. And a few days after I saw him again ; but this time I would not be put away, and I wept bitterly, because he seemed so unwilling to speak to me. And the good Samaritan at last confessed what he had done, but told me to keep it a secret ; and so I did ; but it's almost the only one I ever kept."

" That 's true enough," said Louis.

" He used to give us money after, but he seemed very unhappy ; and at last told us, one day, that he was going to live up at Saint Joseph,

in the hermitage there. And he soon went ; but
made us happy and easy for life, with some of
the money that he said was of no use to him.
since he had lost every body he loved in the
plague. My husband's uncle died soon after,
and left us this house ; and here we have lived
ever since. But we have had our troubles too ;
for our boy was killed at Waterloo, and his wife
soon followed him, leaving us these two little or-
phans. We try to make up their loss to them as
well as we can ; but we are old, and must soon
be taken from them like their own father and
mother."

" Thank ye, my friends," said I, " for your
story. Some other day I will come and pay you
another visit ; but I must be hastening home.'

I quitted the inn, and reached my house in
about two hours. I then read for a considerable
part of the night.

*   *   *

CHAPTER XIX.

February 10.—I have been for some days past a prey to all my former depression and despair, having no pleasure in any thing, not even in the affectionate fondling of my pupil. The snake within me is only scotched, not killed ; and the whole bitterness and blankness of my fate at times come back upon me. At a period of life when man begins to look round upon the world with the eye of experience and understanding, when the boiling impetuosity of his very first youth subsides into the clear majestic current of confirmed manhood and rational direction, I am deprived, for ever deprived, of all the benefits which others derive from the remembrance of their faults, like the lawgiver of the Jews, who was shown from the top of Mount Pisgah those lands flowing with milk and honey, which he was never to enter, though he had passed, like the rest, many a burning sand and stony desert. I remember when I came here, two years ago, after my extrication from the difficulties and distresses which then embarrassed me, I thought that I might still hope for future and better prospects, though the path of my life had commenced but roughly. The novelty of the country, the beauty of its climate, and the anticipation of again returning to my country, from whence my misfortunes had banished me, elevated and encouraged my spirits. I was younger, too, and the veil of delusion and dreamy delight had not been entirely cast aside from the sober realities of life. Fancy, with her fairy wand, still stood by me, and " Hope smiled and waved her golden hair," as the magic Palace of Enchantment glittered before my eyes. But all that is passed! Hope and Fancy are gone—Indifference and Despair remain! I now see all face to

face, not as through a glass, darkly.   I may say
with Spenser—

> " All is but feigned, and with ochre dyed,
>   That every shower will wash and wipe away ;
> All things do change, that under heaven abide,
>   And after death, all friendship doth decay.
>   Therefore, whatever man bear'st worldly sway,
> Living, on God, and on thyself rely :
> For when thou diest, all shall with thee die.

*   *   *

February 14.—My pedestrian friend, who
had, as he told me, become anxious about me,
came up here yesterday.   His conversation generally amuses me, and his manners and tastes
correspond so much with my own, that I do
not feel his presence as any intrusion upon my
privacy.   He again repeated his wish that I
would accompany him to Nice, where he is
shortly going ; but I have given him no posi-
ive answer ; I care so little for change of place,
have so little pleasure to expect from it, that

I would fain remain quiet. My friend perceiving that I was much depressed, said, " I am
very sorry that you seem to be relaxing into
your former uneasiness of mind ; if you will
allow me, I will continue the account of my
pedestrian pilgrimage to Boulogne, which was
my destined point ; perhaps it may dissipate your
melancholy for the present." His motive was
good-natured, and therefore I acquiesced in his
proposal ; and after we had taken an early dinner
of fruits and bread, which we both prefer, in this
climate, to meat, thus imitating the natives, my
friend continued his narrative in nearly the following words :

" You may remember that I had arrived at Lausanne, when I broke off in my account. I went
to bed, as I told you, and the next morning was
awakened by the *garçon d'écurie*, who brought
me my shoes unusually shining and splendid
The man told me, that there was another English gentleman below, who had come in after

me. I got up and went down, and found him. We entered into conversation, and he informed me that he had been pedestrianising too, having come as far as Dijon, from Paris, in that manner. But he had since sprained his foot, had come to Lausanne with a *voiturier*, and was now calling hastily for a surgeon, as he fancied his foot had grown worse. The surgeon came, examined it, and recommended that he should bathe it in hot water, *dans de l'eau chaude*, and went away. But the Englishman was no Frenchman, and he made sad work of the *eau chaude* " *Je faut mettere mes pieds dans chaude eau dans une tube*," said ie to the servant, who appeared at his summons, and who stared at him in hopeless astonishment. I explained, however, to her what the gentleman vanted ; and the water was, I suppose, carried to iis room, for away he limped.

I took my breakfast, and afterwards walked out. t was Sunday morning, and the Protestant popu-ation of Lausanne were all in motion, and hastening away to the cathedral. I followed them, plunging down the steep streets of the town, and then ascending again to an open square, where the church stands. I saw nothing to distinguish it particularly from others; it contained, however one singular tomb, that of Felix Amadeus the Eighth, of Savoy, who was first a king, then a pope, and lastly, a simple individual.

In fourteen hundred and thirty-four, he abdicated his crown, and retired to the Priory of Ripaille, where he founded the chief Order of Savoy Saint Maurice, which with that of the Annonciade of Piedmont, are the two principal orders of the Sardinian dominions. The origin of that of the Annonciade is singular, and might be compared to that of the Garter.

Amadeus, Sixth, surnamed the Count de Verd, was a gay and gallant prince, and probably often enlivened his warlike pursuits by dancing, as our Edward the Third, with the fair ladies of his

court.; One of these, touched and delighted
by the attentions of the graceful monarch,
worked a bracelet for him with her own hair,
and marked upon it as its device, the initials
of four French words, denoting that both in
ove and arms the happy Amadeus would ever
be successful. The gratified prince made the
circumstance an occasion for establishing an order of knighthood; but, unlike our English king,
he at once acknowledged in its title the favour
which had been shown him, and called it *Les
Lacs d'Amour.* But the pacific and pious Ama-
leus the Eighth was unwilling to retain a name
which seemed to perpetuate the memory of some
icentious intrigue of his ancestor, and by him
the order of *Les Lacs d'Amour* was converted into
that of the Annonciade.

Still, however, its origin was not entirely effaced, for the knightly badge consisted of a rich chain
of gold, whose links were mingled with white and

red roses of enamel; but to counteract the impure ideas which the chain and the roses might have excited, the future Pope caused a golden image of the Annunciation to be suspended from the enamelled flowers.

Amadeus the Eighth died at Geneva, and was buried at Lausanne; perhaps, because he might consider its church holier than that of Geneva, since it is said to have possessed among its reliques one of the ribs of Mary Magdalen and a rat that had eaten the Sacramental bread

I had been so long absent from my country and used to nothing but the mummery and show imposition of the mass, that the simple and plain Calvinistic service was quite refreshing to me It was like the unpretending conversation of a truly well-informed man after the pompous puff and preaching of some would-be Solomon.

When I quitted the cathedral, I strolled to the terrace, from whence I had a view over the

lake, and a magnificent scene it was.   The
day was gloomy, but the sun still asserted his
authority among the clouds that lay in immense
masses above the lake.   Clouds have often
been compared to mountains, but the resemblance never struck me so forcibly as then;
there they lay in wild terrific confusion, precipice and crag and yawning cavern, while,
to complete the noble illusion, a long dark
arch extended itself directly across the lake,
taking the appearance of some gigantic Alpine
bridge.

They were worthy rivals of their neighbours,
the true mountains, which seemed to sink into
nothing beside them; — and yet these were no
mean ones.   There were the rugged rocks, directly opposite, of *La Meillerie* hanging over
the town, brown and threatening;—there was,
to my left, the *dent de Jaman*, protruding its
red tooth above the rest of the mountains

about it; and there was the commencement of the *Bernèse Alps*, or *diablerets*, as they are called in the country, rearing themselves up as if to look, like their inferior familiars, at the beautiful lake.

But there were other points of interest which lay around me, besides the magnificent one in front. There was the willow-tree in Gibbon's garden, where he had composed his glowing History, and glowing, indeed, it must have been with such a scene before him ;—for the man of imagination and ardent mind will always write better and freer, and with more fervour, amidst the glories and beauties of Nature. Then there was *Beaulieu*, where Madame de Staël and her father had lived. The cathedral, with its singular tower, stood perched upon the highest part of the town, with the old turrets of the college beneath it, and the rich hills spread up above, covered with little *chalets;* a few peasants were passing along, with their straw peaked hats; and I could have stayed where I was till night. But I was anxious to reach Vevay that day; and as my object in travelling was not to lounge about towns where I knew no one, and which presented nothing within themselves very remarkable, I returned to my hotel, and paying my bill, departed.

The road to Vevay lies along the lake, upon an elevated part of the shore. I cannot describe to you, in detail, all the villages I passed, and the number of miles I travelled before I reached that place. I went rambling on, with the green terraces of vines above, and the noble amphitheatre of the lake before me. A few boats were spread upon the waters, and I might have imagined one of them to contain Julie and Saint Preux in their excursion before the storm. I was upon the shores of the lake of Leman, and was satisfied. I sought not to analyse the properties of the soil, or speculate upon the altitude of the mountains, or the breadth of the water; it was all beautiful, and I felt, without wishing to know what I felt.

I arrived at Vevay towards evening. I went straight to the inn, which was somewhere below the church. Here I found that my *incognito* would serve me nothing, for the Swiss being themselves a pedestrian people, they never make any difference between a pedestrian and a man who travels in a carriage, provided he goes to the best inns. I was received with as much attention as I could desire, and a little more; and, after reposing myself for some time, I set forth, and mounted up to the church-yard of Vevay.

Whenever I arrive in a village or town, one of my first lions is that spot, where I have often experienced much more pleasure than if I had been toiling along gilded rooms or stately gardens:—the still silence which prevails, interrupted only by the tinkling of the sheep-bell;

the stones shining in the sun, some with their almost effaced histories, while others are fresh and black with the pride of new mortality; the simple grief of the peasant contrasted with the lengthy lamentation inscribed upon the loftier tomb; all these things afford, to me at least, ample room and range enough for passing many an hour.

But every one who professes to admire the grand scenes of Nature, must visit the church-yard of Vevay. When I reached it, the sun had ust set; the evening was still, and the boats I had seen in the afternoon were slowly making their way towards Villeneuve. The lake was now shut in by high projecting points, and I seemed to have penetrated into all its secrets. Chillon, Clarens, looked white and silent, and some lights began to glimmer in the opposite little town of St. Gingoulph. Could I have had Rousseau for my companion at that mo-ment, I should have been content—others

might have ridiculed my feelings. Then, just
where the mountains, retreating on both sides,
leave a chasm, through which the infant Rhône
flows into the lake, rose up, Alp upon Alp, peak
upon peak, the august glaciers of the *Valais;*
—there they were, wrapped in their snowy man-
tles, standing and seeming to look at me. I
declare to you, that the sight of those solemn
forms, between which and me a great gulf was
fixed, made me tremble. Had I known that
amid their frightful depths some desperate deed
of wickedness was then perpetrating, I could
not have felt more dread than I did then in
looking at them. And presently the calm moon
came forth, and the shaggy mountains brightened, and the lake rolled in light, and the glaciers looked like the ghosts of the world, wan
and misty.

I remained, I know not how long, enjoying
this magnificent view, when I heard a noise
close to me. I turned, and there stood a man,

who observed to me, that I seemed to admire the prospect. I replied, that I did indeed; and we began to talk about the town and its inhabitants, and the surrounding country. " We are very happy," said he, " our government is much liked, and we thrive well with our little trade in watches. We are much better off than we used to be under the *Bernois*, to whom this Canton formerly belonged; but in the Revolution we were made independent." And here, by the way, let me remark to you a circumstance which has always struck me as singular, and as at once demonstrating the vast effects of the French Revolution :—Upon the Continent, whenever I have conversed with persons concerning it, whether they were Italians, or Swiss, or Germans, or Dutch, it is sufficient if we say, in speaking of that terrible period, " *the* Revolution," which is at once understood, just as an inhabitant of Lisbon may be supposed to say " the Earthquake."

Continuing the conversation with the same person, I talked of General Ludlow, who is buried in the church of Vevay. The stern republican would not lay his bones in his own country, since there were kings within it again; but preferred the free soil of Switzerland, the country of William Tell, who had freed his country from tyranny, without becoming after-wards its oppressor. Ludlow came over to Eng-land to offer his services to William against James the Second, a curious instance of animo-sity towards the son of Charles the First; and not unlike the subsequent conduct of Moreau, who, though as determined a republican as the rest, united himself with the Allied Sovereigns against his own country. I presently wished the person good night, and went to my inn.

Next morning, before leaving Vevay, I went once more to the church-yard, to take a farewell view of the lake I might never see again, and which, if I ever did, I might behold with other and colder feelings. I might be old, or harassed by disease, and the enthusiasm of my youthful days would perhaps, and probably, be looked upon in the same contemptuous light with which others may regard it now. My favourite poet Beattie, in his Minstrel, alludes to this melancholy change in our tastes.

> Yet, at the darken'd age, the wither'd face,
> Or hoary hair, I never will repine;
> But spare, O Time! whate'er of mental grace,
> Of candour, love, or sympathy divine,
> Whate'er of fancy's ray, or friendship's flame is mine.

I continued my route towards Friburg, ascending the deep gorge at the entrance of which Vevay is placed. I will not fatigue your attention by recounting to you all that occurred to me, in detail, during the rest of my journey. The remembrance of that ramble is even now fresh and delightful to my mind; but the relation of it might be tedious to others, who may, perhaps, not see things in the same way as myself. The singular town of Friburg, half French, half German, with its rocks, banks, and its romantic river; the Spanish-looking Berne, with its long colonnaded street and its terrace, from whence the magnificent chain of the German Alps is distinctly seen, with the towering *Yung Frau*, like some mighty Amazon Queen; and the graceful cap of the *Bernoise* women, looking like a dark airy butterfly spreading its filmy wings above their heads.

But let me not forget to mention the worthy host at the *Abbaye des Gentilhommes*, where I lodged. He is indefatigable in his attention, and persons who travel like myself, should always go to his house. The sounding title need not affright them, for the charges are very moderate, and there is no other house in *Berne* where a person, who wishes to be respectably, and at the same time moderately lodged, can go.

The next canton to Berne is Soleure, a Catholic one, and the difference was striking; beggars and bigotry staring you in the face in every street. Then came Basle, the capital of which I reached after crossing a part of the Jura, called the Ober Hauenstein, which separates the ancient bishoprick from Switzerland.

There is a curious legend attached to a clock upon the bridge at Basle, which is always half an hour too fast. Some plot had been laid against the city, and a body of armed men were to have been admitted at a certain hour of the night; but the plot was discovered. This clock, which was to give the signal of attack, happened to be half an hour too fast, and the party, that was to have been silently admitted, having shewn itself before the appointed time, was observed, and baffled.

From Basle I passed on to Strasburgh, and Baden, buried in woods and rocks, and teeming with gay company and baths, with its castle perched upon the green cliffs above. Within this castle there was once a terrible dungeon, deep and dark, called the Virgin's Embrace; above it was a trap-door, upon which if any one stepped, he fell instantly down into the deadly gulf. Some years ago a dog had fallen in, and in extricating him, remnants of clothes and bones, and instruments of torture, were found.

From Baden, where neither my health nor my finances required me to stay, since the former was good, but the latter rather ailing, I continued my walk by Rastadt, a small city where there is a great brick palace belonging to the Duke of Baden, in which, I believe, he never resides. From thence I proceeded to Carlsruhe, which is a beautiful little toy of a capital. The streets are all straight as arrows, and in their disposition not unlike those of Nancy, in Lorraine.

There is a very handsome royal château, and some pretty gardens, to which, they told me, the Grand Duke himself paid particular attention. The court was not then there, and I felt no great curiosity to see the palace.

Shortly after quitting Carlsruhe, the following morning, in my way to Heidelberg, I was over-taken by a female peasant, who asked me her way to that place. I had begun to acquire some little acquaintance with the German language, but not enough to pass for a German; so she discovered by my stammering, that I was a foreigner. She made out, however, that I was going to Heidel-berg, and seemed disposed that we should conti-nue our route together. She insisted on carrying a small packet which I had in my hand, and which had replaced the defunct knapsack. So on we trudged, convèrsing in German, God knows how! and I thought that my friends in England would smile a little, if they could see me thus attended. She was an excellent walker, and when we reached Bruchsal, she told me that she was going to a friend's to breakfast, and would wait for me.

I had begun to be rather annoyed by the acquaintance I had formed, as I saw one or two persons smile, rather sarcastically I thought, as they passed us; so I went to an inn, determining, after my breakfast, to cut her, as they say. I procured my bread and milk, and after paying very moderately, I proceeded; but, to my great displeasure, I saw my friend waiting for me at some distance, beyond the town.

I was determined, however, to break off this singular connexion; and when I reached her, told her, rather abruptly, that she had better hasten on, for that I meant to linger along the road, and should probably not reach Heidelberg till late. She seemed very unwilling to go, but at last she did, casting occasionally some kind looks at me, as she gradually disappeared.

I mention this circumstance to you to show that the pedestrian is in the way of meeting with infinitely more novel circumstances, than could ever possibly happen to the rich traveller in carriages. I reached Heidelberg in the afternoon, and proceeded to the inn I think they call the *Cour de Bade*. I dined at the *table d'hôte*, and there I was myself again, for I found persons who spoke French. After dinner I mounted the rock, upon which the ruins of the old Palatine Castle stand in green and beautiful decay.

Passing along the corn-market, and ascending by a path winding gently up the mountain, I arrived at these charming ruins; and from among them enjoyed a magnificent view of the Neckar, that was coming down from among the rich vine-clothed hills of the valley, to pay its tribute to the mighty Rhine.

The beautiful bridge that unites the two banks was covered with peasants, who were hastening away to some village *fête*; and beyond it, far away in the horizon, were the wide shores that border the Rhine before its retreat into the dark mountain of Bingen, bounded by the blue Vosges mountains, which stretch into the old bishoprick of Spire from Alsace.

I entered the ruins by the gate of Elizabeth, which takes its name from the unfortunate daughter of James the First, who, like the rest of her line, was fated to know all the miseries of dethroned royalty.

A beautiful terrace, planted with flowers and trees, first presents itself ; and a large tower, in which were two niches, containing the colossal and ivy-covered statues of two of the old Princes Palatine, of Louis the Pacific, and of the unhappy Frederick, who might have been named the sufferer, wandering, as he did, with his wife in almost beggary.

I rambled over the ruins till evening, and supped there ; for I found that a family had taken up their abode in a part of them, and I procured some delicious milk, that was brought out from the cool vaults of the castle.   As I sat amid the turrets and mouldering halls, I reflected upon the very different scenes that probably presented themselves there, before the scythe of time and of war had swept over the now desolate pavements.   The fair Elizabeth had, perhaps, presided at the costly banquet that had glittered within the hall of knights, whose rich front I could see from my seat, little thinking that she would ever be compelled to ask assistance from her father, and be denied it ; and still less, that the arch and banner, which spread above her, would be as now they are.

Instead of the dance and the song and the tournament, that had oft been held within the Ducal Castle, there were now but the low murmuring of the Neckar, the warbling of the birds that seemed to rejoice amid the ruins, and the monotonous humming of the wheel, as the woman who had given me the milk, sat

spinning.   The reflections which thus arose
within me, I ventured to throw into verse,
and if you will listen to them as a friend,
and not a critic, I will repeat them." I said,
" I am not one of the '*Judex damnatur cum
nocens absolvitur ;*' pray let me hear them ;" and
he went on : —

      Ye that hither come to gaze
      On the pomp of vanish'd days,
      Think that once these halls were gay,
      Where the long grass waves to-day;
      Where the bird hath made her nest
      Many an eye hath sunk to rest ;
      Many a maid from turret height
      Hath look'd for her long-delaying knight ;
And the trumpet hath sounded, and call'd to the list,
And the warrior his gauntlet to beauty hath kiss'd ;
And the harper the chords of enchantment hath swept,
And a queen, at the ballad of sorrow, hath wept ;
And the dance hath resounded, and minstrels have sung,
But mute is their melody, silent their tongue !——

And the queen and her grandeur are low in the grave ;
And where men ever revell'd, the trees ever wave ;
Then remember that ye will be passing away,
And forget not to-morrow the scene of to-day.

As I was returning through the garden, I saw in a small retired spot, almost concealed by the trees and ruins, a tea-table set out with all its appurtenances, as the lawyers would say, and looking just like the preparation for the same feast in our country. The Germans, indeed, resemble the English very much in their habits of living ; being as opposite to the French as ourselves in the chief customs of society. In-stead of all the machinery of French dishes, they have generally plain solid food like our-selves ; the higher families may live, per-haps, in the French style, as is the case in England ; but it is not among the higher classes of a country that the true national tastes and manners are to be sought for. We

must look for them where affectation and excessive refinement have not reached, as we
must dig deep beneath the surface of an artificial garden to discover the true nature of
the soil.

CHAPTER XX.

IT was in the evening, continued my friend, that I was nearly involved in the dispute which I have before mentioned to you, with one of the illustrious students of Heidelberg. This University is, I believe, the most ancient in Germany. It was founded, I understand, by Robert, the first Count Palatine of the Rhine; and its regulations somewhat resemble those of our Universities. The Grand Duke of Baden, to whom the Palatinate now belongs, is the Rector. The direction of the University is intrusted to a Council and a Senate. The first is composed only of five or six persons, and the other, of all the Professors. Then there are Professors who are appointed to superintend the morals of the students, resembling in some degree our Proctors; and a Bailiff, who has the same municipal authority as the Vice-Chancellors of the respective Universities.

Quitting Heidelberg, I continued my route by Darmstadt, with its musical Duke, and Frankfort, with its unmusical merchants, to Mayence where I arrived upon the third day. There I proposed embarking myself, and going down the Rhine as far as Cologne.

Mayence is an old city, and contains an old cathedral; it is famous for hams, and that is all I can tell you about it, except a curious story of one of its Bishops. He was originally the son of a carter, and used to drive his father's team. By the turns of the *wheel* he became Archbishop of Mayence; and in order to perpetuate the memory of his origin, he took for his arms two cart-wheels, which are even now the arms of the city.

We left Mayence early in the morning, and glided slowly along between the flat banks, where the river seems making an orderly retreat into the dark fastnesses. We passed Hockheim, of which I need say nothing, as you of course have heard of the wines which take their name from it; and gradually floated on till the dark rocks of Bingen seemed opening to receive us.

We swept by the rippling whirlpool, and the gloomy tower of Hatton, to which is attached a singular legend. An Abbot of Hatton, who became afterwards Archbishop of Mayence, had, they say, in a great famine, refused assistance to his hungry diocesans; and when they came about his palace, he would laugh, and exclaim, " Hark, how the rats squeak!" But vengeance was to overtake him! For, some time after, like the king whose miseries made Whittington's fortune, his palace became infested with rats to such a degree, that he was obliged to fly from it, and build the tower which lies below Bingen. There, however, he found no refuge; for the rats pursued him, scaled his castle-walls, and devoured him alive! His spirit is said to appear occasionally upon the tower, in a mist.

You have doubtless read descriptions of the noble scenery of the Rhine, both in poetry and prose. Whatever you have read must convey a very inadequate idea of its real beauty, which may be truly called by a name which is so often used unintelligibly—Romantic.

The Genius of Romance seems to brood over the dark defile, surrounded by her ruinous towers and arches, and spirit-haunted hills. Every vine-clad rock has its legend; and the boatman, as we drove down with the fleet current, sung me the following song, which I have written down, and which I will read to you. It is

founded on a legend attached to an old castle
on the borders of the Rhingau, called Lorch.
Its Baron was very avaricious, and one night
refused admittance to an old man, who had
requested it, during a storm.　The old man
was, (so says the legend,) in truth, a spirit,
and in revenge spirited away the Baron's
daughter up to a high cliff called Kedrick,
perfectly inaccessible.　A young Knight, who
dwelt near, undertook to deliver her ; but was
returning in despair from the perpendicular precipice, when he was accosted by an old woman,
who gave him a little bell, and told him to go to
a cavern in the wood, where her brother lived,
and say that she sent him for a ladder as high as
the Kedrick.　The Knight obtained the ladder,
and subsequently the lady.　The boatman gave
to his tale the name of

THE DEVIL'S LADDER.

Now list to my story, now list to my song,
  As our bark it glides merrily down;
And when I have done, for it's passably long,
  We shall anchor at Bacharach town.

The Lords of the Rhingau are wealthy and great,
  And their castles are lofty and bright;
And they live, as they should, in their princely estate
  And their halls are a glorious sight.

For the Heidelberg tun could never contain
  The wine that flows merrily there;
And the dainty wild boar, that the hunters have slai
  Will give each happy vassal his share.

But the Baron of Lorch is a cross-grain'd churl,
  And his heart is as cold as his hall;
For though he 's as rich as the Nassau Earl,
  His cheer is the worst of all.

Now list to my story, now list to my song,
  As our bark it glides merrily down;
And when I have done, for it 's passably long,
  We shall anchor at Bacharach town.

The winds they did howl, and the trees they did rock,
　And the night it was dismal and wild;
And the Abbot of Hatton, by Binger Loch,
　Looked over the whirlpool and smiled ;—

The winds they did howl, and the trees they did rock,
　And the Baron of Lorch he said,
Now who is the fool that so loud doth knock ?
　May the thunderbolt fall on his head !

And the Baron he look'd through the wicket gate,
　And he thought to have seen a Knight;
But a little old man on the ground there sate,
　With a beard both long and white ;—

And the little white man he moan'd and he wept,
　And his face it was wrinkled and old ;
And the wind, as it whistled and over him swept,
　Made him shiver and shake with the cold.

" Now open, now open, my Baron, so good,"
　The poor old man then said,
" And give me some warmth, and some kindly food,
　Or ere morning I shall be dead."

But the Baron was vex'd that his sleep was broke,
　　And thus in wrath he cried :
" You may sleep in your beard, it will serve for a cloak,
　　And many, your betters, have died."

Then the little old man he grinn'd and he frown'd,
　　And his eyes they grew terribly bright,
And he mutter'd, as slowly he rose from the ground,
　　" You shall pay for your insolent spite!"

The vines they are fresh in the morning air,
　　And the birds they do sing so sweet,
And the board is spread with the scanty fare,
　　And the Baron hath taken his seat.

But his daughter, and eke his only child,
　　Obeys not the castle-bell's peal ;
And the Baron in mirth and in mockery smiled,
　　As he finish'd the whole of the meal.

But the day wears on, and the sun is high,
　　And Imogen still delays,
And her father begins to wonder why
　　In her chamber so long she stays.

H 5

And loudly he calls, " Come, linger no more !"
   As he stands on the castle-stair;
And quickly he mounts to her chamber door,
   But Imogen is not there.

And the day wears on, and the sun is set,
   And the mountains are blue and still,
But Imogen's step delayeth yet—
   And long delay it will.

For the peasants have told to the Baron their tale :
   How, as day began to break,
They had seen what had made their cheeks turn pale
   And their limbs with dread to quake :—

In his wither'd arms, a little old man
   A fair young girl did bear;
And up the Kedrick's cliff he ran,
   As if it had been a stair.

Then the Baron his forehead in terror cross'd,
   And thus, appall'd, he said,
" Now Christ be good, or my daughter's lost !
   'Twas the Spirit of Kedrick's head."

And many a weary day and night
  Did the desolate father pass ;
And his altar with many a lamp was bright,
  And his priests said many a mass.

The song was so long, continued my friend
that I only wrote down the most material parts
Ruthelm, the Knight, returns from battle
hears of the disappearance of the Baron's daughter, and hastens to her rescue. In this he is assisted by the old Fairy, *who* sends him to the
carpenter, her relation, for a ladder as high a:
the mountain where the damsel is detained.

Then his horn the little old carpenter blew,
  That echoed the woods among,
And straight a wild and a dwarfish crew
  Around began to throng.

And each little Imp had a saw and an axe,
  Such as carpenters use, but much less ;
And they look'd, as they straighten'd and set up their
    backs,
  Like mice in a masquerade dress.

Then the carpenter master he said to the knight,
  "Hie away to your home and your bed !
But be sure that you come by the first day-light
  To the foot of old Kedrick Head."

And Ruthelm is sitting his castle within,
  But he watches till morning appears ;
For his heart is awake, and the hammering din
  Of the carpenters rings in his ears.

But soon as the stars began to go out,
  And the rooks began to caw,
He heard no more of the carpenter rout,
  And still was every saw.

And quick to old Kedrick's Head he hath leapt,
  And there stood a ladder as tall
As the ladder which Jacob saw when he slept,
  That is painted on our church-wall.

Then up young Ruthelm nimbly did creep,
  And soon the top did reach,
And there amid flowers and silk did sleep
  A maid, like a Dresden peach.

And Ruthelm bends down to her cheek, and sighs,
    And his breath it was burning, sure,
For the maiden hath open'd her deep-blue eyes,
    And their beams he could scarce endure.

But a little old man on a sudden appear'd,
    And he frown'd upon the knight,
And he mutter'd, " Who is it that thus hath dared
    To scale my castle's height ? "

Then Ruthelm low to the earth did bend,
    And the story he faithfully told,
How the little old dwarf to the wood did him send,
    And made his hands so bold.

Then the little old man he laugh'd, with a wink,
    And he said, with a cunning grin,
" Ho ! ho ! my fine Sir, you are modest, I think,—
    You must labour before you can win.

" Go back, my young spark, since your love is so fast,
    By the way you so nimbly have come ;
" And ere the last steps of the ladder you 've past
    Your bride shall be safe in her home."

And the little old man his promise hath kept,
  For safe in her home is the bride ;
And the Baron, that long in his hopelessness wept,
  Hath forgot all his sorrow and pride.

And the old castle rings with the shouts of the cooks,
  And there 's plenty of Bacharach wine ;
And the dainty young bride, in her white veil, looks
  As soft and as *stattlich* as mine.

Now there is my story, now there is my song,
  And our bark hath gone merrily down,—
'Tis as well I have done, as 'twas passably long,
  For we anchor at Bacharach town.

Bacharach, where we stopped to dine, is a remarkable town. Its name would seem to denote a place peculiar for its excellent wines, if it be indeed a corruption, as some assert, of Arra Bacchi ; but that reputation is much past by, and it must be content with being one of the most beautifully situated of the Rhenish bourgs. Its ancient walls spread along the banks of the river, high mountains rise up behind it, and upon one of the lower heights, stand the ruins of the fief of Staleck. Close to it are those of the old church of Saint Werner, which was consecrated to an infant martyr, whom the Jews murdered, and cast into the Rhine, but who floated upon its surface against the current as far as Bacharach.

The view from Staleck is noble: the river seems to have just escaped from its defile, and spreads itself wider and slower, before forming another of those magic bends which suddenly display to the delighted eye fresh beauties of rock and vine, and frequent feudal towers, where " ruin greenly dwells." A small island lay in the middle, a short distance below Bacharach, with its little church, and a huge dark cliff projected itself into the water just opposite. After enjoying this prospect for some time, I descended : our boat was ready, and we proceeded on our course. But why should I fatigue you with a long detail of places which you never saw, and the beauty of which, it is impossible for you to conceive from my description? Echoing rocks with their Siren legends, white whirlpools, majestic vine-covered heights, monasteries and towers, and old towns and cathedrals, crowning the wild and wooded banks; the castled crag of Drackenfels looking out upon the wide ocean-like plains of the low countries, and the shattered Ehrenbreitstein emulating its baronial and decaying neighbours in untimely ruin.

" But peace destroy'd what war could never blight."

The river, after Bonn, becomes stale, flat, and unprofitable, like some poet, who, in his younger and more romantic days, teems with noble and sublime images, but gradually subsides into tameness and sluggishness. I followed its course, however, as far as Cologne, where I saw the famous picture of the Crucifixion of St. Peter, with the head downwards. It is one that made me shudder, and almost feel giddy. The intense torture that such a death must produce, is starting and swelling in every vein of the countenance.

I had always thought, till, from the inquiries I made upon the subject, I found my mistake, that Cologne had been under the dominion formerly of the Elector of that name; but it would appear that his authority was as much contemned and resisted by its inhabitants, as that of the Bishop of Liege was by the fierce Liegois. The Elector's palace and residence was at Bonn, about six leagues from Cologne; and, in spite of his struggles to obtain political influence within the city, I believe he never succeeded.

Cologne is a large ancient place, and is well known by its legend of the Eleven Thousand Virgins. I quitted it the same day I arrived there, and continued my route by Juliers and Aix-la-Chapelle, and the huge city of Liege, where I was surprised to see vines.

I directed my course towards Brussels; but my old failing began now to beset me,—my funds tottered, and my shoes signified their fatigue to me by sundry gapings and yawns. I had expected that they would both have lasted me out to Brussels; but, like faithless friends, they were now evidently become less warm and bountiful. I wrote, therefore, to Boulogne, where I had a credit, and requested that some money might be sent to me to Brussels. I then furnished myself with a pair of shoes, quitting the others with as much regret as ever afflicted any antiquary at the loss of his most precious relique; and continued my journey in tranquillity, till within a short distance of Brussels. Then, recollecting the old maxim,—when you have no money never seem to have none, but assume a rich and important air,—I determined upon putting myself into the diligence, and entering Brussels in state; because my finances were in that condition, that as some days must elapse before

my remittance could arrive, I should be obliged
to live at an inn, without thinking of the bill
I therefore, Machiavel like, concluded that, by
seeming to arrive in the diligence, I should
blind every body as to the real condition of my
purse, and be a *gentilhomme qui voyageoit pour
son plaisir*, and wished to pass a few days in
the city where he had friends.

When I arrived at Brussels, I proceeded directly to a neighbouring inn, and though my
appearance was not very splendid, and my baggage slight, yet I hoped, as coming by the diligence, that the people of the house would not
suspect the state of my finances.

I was received very well; and after depositing
my effects in my room, I descended to my dinner, which I had ordered. I finished it and the
best part of a bottle of wine, and strolled afterwards about the town: I had been there before,
so, as there was nothing particularly interesting
to me in it, I returned and went to bed. Next

morning, after breakfast, as I was lounging out of the court-yard of the inn, the waiter presented himself civilly enough, and presented the bill, stating that it was customary for persons who had little baggage, to pay daily for what they had eaten. I felt myself turn pale ; but, determined to put as good a face upon the matter as I could, I marched into the house, and summoned the landlord. When he appeared, I expressed my surprise at this extraordinary mode of treating persons in his house. But the man was not to be daunted : he replied, " that he had lost a great deal of money lately by my countrymen,— *proh pudor !* and that he had determined to be more cautious in future." There was now no parrying the adventure :—so, taking out all the silver that I had left, and which did not quite meet the amount of the bill, I said, " the money I had expected to find here awaiting me has not arrived, consequently I am unable to discharge your account entirely." " Ho ! ho !"

said the innkeeper, as if all his worst suspicions were at once confirmed, " it 's just as I thought ; —this comes of your pedestrian travellers ;" for he had some how discovered my diligence plot. " John," speaking to the waiter, " go up stairs and bring down the gentleman's baggage," laying a particular and sarcastic stress upon the latter word. John departed, and returned bearing my two shirts, my guide-book, my razors, my journal, and two or three other trifles. The innkeeper laid his hand upon them, and said, " These I shall keep as pledges, for the payment of the rest of your account." I made him no reply, but immediately quitted the house, with nothing in my pocket except a collection of Views in Switzerland, that I had luckily put there before.

My situation was singular : I was a perfect stranger in a foreign city, without the only useful passport, money. I wandered about the whole of the day, and towards evening contrived

to dispose of my Swiss Views to a print-seller,
for a small sum, with which I hoped to hold out
till my money arrived.　I passed the night in a
small inn, and the next day breakfasted there.
The people of the house were, notwithstanding
the indifference of my toilet, extremely respect-
ful to me; and the woman, I recollect, would
insist that I had only come there by way of a
frolic, and that I was *somebody*.　She did not,
however, give me any *credit* for my quality, as
I was obliged punctually to pay for all I had,
before quitting the house.

Three days more passed in this way.　I was
obliged to give up my breakfasts of coffee, as
the delay about my money was so extraordinary,
that I began to fear it had miscarried, and that
the term of my perplexities would be indefinite :
and at last, the night preceding its arrival, I was
obliged to give up my bed, and I passed the
night in roaming about the city, and, when it
came on to rain, sheltered myself beneath the

porch of the church, in the Place Royale, from whence I could see the windows of the Hotel Bellevue, where a year before I had lodged *comme un Seigneur*. Yet amidst the cold and rain that were about me, I thought of Waterloo, and murmured not. I thought of the night when so many of my brave and useful country-men were " mounting in hot haste," and called away from beauty and music to slaughter and hardship! Was I then to complain of my paltry inconveniences, when the rich and titled soldier had suffered far worse? To be sure, I had not the rich banks of the *Saône* to sleep among, nor the nightingale's song to while away the night ; but I was young and healthy, and the next morning was myself, that is to say, *le Gentil-homme* again.

I proceeded on directly to Boulogne, where I arrived on the second day. I had friends there, having stayed a few days in that town before ; so I proceeded to my old quarters, the house of a very respectable and worthy Bourgeois, where I boarded. They were all happy to see me, and the recital of my past miseries made them smile. I then set forth to search for a friend who I knew resided in the town; and making inquiry of a Frenchman who was standing near the custom-house, he civilly informed me that my friend was at the *Hôtel d'Angleterre.* Straightway I proceeded into the *Rue de l'Ecu,* which is the longest street, leading down to the harbour; and entering the court-yard of the *Hôtel d'Angleterre, tenue par veuve Parker*, I asked for my friend. He was not there, and never had been. What could this mean? I quitted the house, and seeing the same Frenchman again, I repeated to him my question, but he still persisted in his account. It was very strange that this man should be so positive; and I was going back to the *Veuve Parker*, when an Englishman passed me accompanied by two men, that I concluded to be commissioners, conducting him to his hotel. As they passed, I saw two or three Frenchmen smile, and heard them say, " *Ma foi! l'autre Hôtel d'Angleterre va bien mainte nant, voilà une nouvelle arrivée.*" Ho! ho! said I to myself, we are quite safe. The *Veuve* Parker, it seems, has an opponent, there's the secret; and I followed the three persons. The new arrival I concluded to be an arrival of consequence, for every body, as he passed, turned round to look at him. It was, perhaps, our Ambassador, who wished to patronize the new hotel. Its situation however seemed inconvenient, as we were ascending to the higher town, which stands upon a steep eminence, and is surrounded with ramparts. But as the noblesse and better families were supposed to reside there, the new hotel, probably, was under their protection. We continued to ascend; and after passing through the old gate and across some streets, we stopped at a long wall, and close to a wooden door. It was a singular position for an inn, but as the noblesse like to live in houses shut in by walls, I concluded that the inn had been built upon the same plan. A sentinel stood near the door, out of respect, perhaps, to the distinguished individual I was following. One of the men knocked at the door, which was immediately opened by a little dark man that somehow looked very unlike a waiter, and the three persons entered. I was proceeding to follow them, when I was stopped by the little dark waiter, as still he must be, I thought, and asked whom I wanted. I mentioned my friend's name, and was directly admitted into a little court, on one side of which was the porter's lodge, and straight before me a large solid door. I had not time to speculate much upon the strange appearance of the hotel, for the little dark waiter opened the huge door that was locked, too, and admitted me into a court-yard. The scene that suddenly met my eyes there completely confounded me. Instead of a collection of persons of distinction, assembled probably in the gardens of the new *Hôtel d'Angleterre*, I beheld a square yard, along the right side of which ran a low building, looking very like a parcel of cow-sheds. In one corner of the court sat upon the ground two wretched-looking men, half naked, at least with nothing but trowsers, and torn shirts like sacks; and they were devouring with avidity some worse than Spartan bread, and looked even more degraded than Helots. Some persons, whom I immediately recognized as Englishmen, were walking backwards and forwards, seeming as restless and unquiet as mice in their revolving cages. Looking to my left, I perceived a kind of garden surrounding an arbour, through the trees of which I saw a small table and two or three men sitting round it. I began now to conjecture where I was. My friend had been doing like so many others—living at other people's expense, and was now paying the necessary penalty. He had observed me from the arbour where he was sitting, and came out in considerable confusion. We shook hands, and he explained to me the circumstances which had led to his arrest; but they were nothing but what every body may guess. He did not ask me to stay, nor did I feel very anxious to do so; I therefore quitted the *Hôtel d'Angleterre*, struck with mortification, and even grief, to find that my countrymen had, by their undignified and dissolute conduct, brought this disgraceful stigma upon the English name, and caused such a significant title to be given to the *prison civile* of Boulogne.

I continued to reside for some time at Boulogne. The family with whom I boarded was extremely kind to me, and lived in the most patriarchal and simple way. I was present at all their *fêtes*; I partook of all their dainties, not omitting the famous *gateau de Mazarine*, which may have derived its title from the beautiful duchess of that name, who was niece to

Cardinal Mazarin. I had accompanied a young man, the son of my host, one day to the church of Saint Nicholas, in the market-place, to see the ceremony of the annual service for the unfortunate Louis the Sixteenth. When we were returning, we met a lady whom the young man knew, and to whom he introduced me. I formed an intimacy with that lady; and some time after I happened to advert to the funeral service at which I had been present, and to say that I considered its celebration as impolitic and dangerous; since it might be considered as a sort of perpetual reproof to the nation. "I am rather of your opinion," replied the lady, "and think that it would be better for all the crimes and horrors of the terrible Revolution to be, if possible, forgotten. I am sure I try to forget all in which I was myself particularly concerned; and though I see daily some of the actors in those dreadful scenes, I endeavour to avoid betraying any signs of disgust or recollection."

I felt anxious to know to what circumstances my friend alluded, and told her so.

" If you will come and take your coffee with me to-morrow morning," said she, " I will relate to you the share which I had in the sufferings which we all, I believe, more or less, underwent."

The next day, accordingly, I was punctual to my engagement ; and as we sat near the window of her house, which commanded a view of the market-place in the high town, my friend commenced her story.

"You see," said she, "that priest passing across the market-place with the holy sacrament ; mark now some of those fishwomen rise as he passes, and cross themselves. I can remember the time when the sight of such a man would have been enough to make some of these very women howl and rage like furies. That market-place, too, which now looks so cheerful, filled as it is with your countrymen, who now live here unmolested, was once the scene of blood and horror! and I myself, that am pointing it out to you, wonder that I am alive to do so. The circumstances which you have expressed a desire to hear, I last night put down upon paper, and I will now read them to you."

CHAPTER XXI.

" I was still almost a child, when our dreadful Revolution commenced.   The first event which I can recollect as having particularly impressed itself upon my memory, is this:—Boulogne had become, at the time to which I allude, a prey to the wildest and most desperate of its inhabitants; and all religion and order were at an end.   I was then about sixteen, and at a school in a street not far from where we are now.   One day there was a loud knocking at the gate of the house, and presently one of the men that I had been told was particularly active in the revolutionary Committee, which was established in Boulogne, came into the school-room, where we all were.   He was a shoemaker, and had been employed by my father.   He walked directly up to the schoolmistress, and said, " Citoyenne, the Committee of Public Safety has sent me to signify to you their commands, that your school be all present to-morrow at the burning of those Aristocratic Saints, and at the *fête* of Reason. We are going to make a glorious bonfire of the old puppets ; and I hope the smell of them will reach as far as the Austrians' prison;—that's what I call odour of sanctity ;" and he burst into a loud laugh. We were all too much alarmed at the bold appearance of the man to betray any signs of attention to what he was saying ; but he came straight up to me, and took the book which I had in my hands from me. " *Ah! c'est bien, ma petite,*" said he, pointing to the page of the history that we happened to be reading. " Read it attentively, and you will see how the people can take off a king's head as well as his crown, when both are troublesome." I saw the schoolmistress turn pale ; and as the man returned me the book, I glanced over it, and per-

ceived that we happened just to have reached
the reign of your King Charles the First.   " I
have become a very learned citizen lately," continued the man ; " I have left my shop to my son.
Ma foi ! politics are the best trade : I had rather
make a constitution than a shoe any day.   But
I must be off.   Don't forget, citizen, to-morrow,
mark !" and away he went humming

> A ça ira, ça ira, tous les Aristocrats à la lanterne,
> A ça ira, ça ira, les Aristocrats on les pendra !

As soon as the last echoes of his voice had died
away, our mistress rose, and coming to each of us
separately, explained what the man meant, and
told us to pray all that night that our presence
at the wicked sacrilege might not make us sinful. In those days, you know, Sir, we had much
more respect for such things than now ;—a
great deal of nonsense was swept away with the
good and real ceremonies of our church ; and we
have recovered the latter without being anxious

about the former. We all obeyed our mistress's directions, however; and I remember now that it was a curious sight to me, to see us all kneeling, with our books, in the little chapel that was close to the school, and which was just lighted by a single lamp. There was something even awful to me in this unusual circumstance; and it seemed as if we were all endeavouring to avert some terrible calamity by our entreaties.

As soon as it was light, we heard the drums of the National Guard rolling through the gates of the town, and the bell of the *Hôtel de Ville*, which is supposed to be prodigiously old, and certainly, old as it was, never had tolled for such a sight as was preparing. Presently the terrible *à ça ira* echoed under our windows, and two or three of the fishwomen came screaming by, and bawling out, " *Allons ! allons ! citoyennes ! citoyennes !* the devil's mass is going to begin; and the Virgin will soon be a little warmer than she was when stuck up in the old cathedral; *allons! allons!*" and they beat with their fists against the shutters. We dared not delay any longer; so dressed in white frocks and tri-coloured sashes, and preceded by our mistress, we directed our steps towards that very *place* which you are now looking upon. When we reached it, Guche, the shoemaker, was standing close to the door of the *Hôtel de Ville*, which we passed as we came upon the *place*, surrounded by a mob of the most desperate rabble of the town.

" Stand back!" said one of the wretches, that seemed from his red cap and bare arms to be a butcher ; " stand back there ! and let the aristocratic lambs pass. There, my pretty one," said the man to my companion, " you shall give me a kiss for picking up your glove," and the dreadful wretch actually put his lips to her cheek. My friend almost fainted, and the butcher, as he perceived her disgust, growled out " *Diable !* what a mighty fuss about nothing; what will

you do if I choose you for my wife?" Guche
however, who still considered himself under
some obligations to my father, seeing that my
friend and myself were thus molested, called
from the steps on which he was standing, "Come,
come, Constant, let them alone now; they are
not ready yet; I will not forget you when we
divide the flock. But to business, to business!
move on, move on there! and take your seats,
girls." We passed on, and were conducted to a
large gallery, that was erected on one side of
the *Hôtel de Ville*, where we found all the other
schools of the town collected. In the middle of
the *place* was a great pile of wood, surrounded
by a railing, and encircled by a few of the National Guard. Some of the firemen were stationed at a short distance, with their little engine;
and upon the top of the pile of wood was fastened a pole, surmounted by the tri-coloured flag
and the red cap. A great crowd of persons was
assembled all over the *place*, and extended down

hrough the gate as far as the Esplanade, which
'ou probably well know. We remained look-
ng at their preparations a short time, till our
attention was called to the approach of some
heavily-laden cart or carriage. The sound of
ts creaking wheels gradually came nearer; and
presently, amidst the shouts and yells of the
nob, a waggon slowly made its appearance,
Irawn by four horses, decorated with tri-
coloured ribands, and escorted by a party of
he National Guard. We all hastily looked to-
vards our mistress as it turned the corner and
Irew up near the pile, who made us a sign of
caution. And it was necessary, for, young and
nnocent as we were then, the sight that met
our eyes was enough to have made children
ike us weep! Piled up in vast heaps, like
useless lumber, were all the pictures and images
und reliques that we had so long been accus-
omed to reverence; while upon the very top
of all was that famous effigy of the Virgin Mary,

that is said to have worked so many miracles
What would her friend Louis the Eleventl
have said (he that dedicated our whole county
to her) if he had seen her in that desperate si
tuation? But really, at that time, I myself wa
much distressed; and when I saw the whole wag
gon-load thrown upon the pile, I felt a kind o
terrible presentiment of evil. The yells increasec
as the wooden boxes and pieces of bone and bot
tles and beads and pictures clattered down upoı
the logs, and many of the mob commenced
dance round the pile, as it began to send uƥ
its smoke, and spread a strong smell around
arising from the pitch, with which the saint
were covered, shouting, "There's odour of sanc
tity for you!" and singing that parody upon ou
national air of Henri Quatre, which begins thus

Aristocrats,
Vous voilà bien fichus,
Les Démocrats
Vous mettent le pied au c—l
Aristocrats.

I could have wished my friend to continue the song, but she had forgotten the rest; and, indeed, from the nature of its commencement, I suspected that she had chosen to do so; as, though Frenchwomen are not very particular about the songs they sing, yet this was probably something that was too much even for them.

Guche, who appeared to take the lead in the ceremony, (she continued,) now mounted upon a scaffolding that was raised at a little distance from the flaming pile, accompanied by a priest, upon whose head was the red cap. He made signals for silence, and having at last succeeded in obtaining it, called out, " *Ecoutez, citoyens : voici un bon prêtre*, and a man that knows as well how to patch souls as I shoes; he will give you a little bit of a sermon, and I warrant he knows how to do it as he ought, else his new wife won't save him from Madame la Guillotine."

I will not offend you by repeating the impious ribaldry that this apostate uttered. I

am no bigot, but cannot regard the man who
acts in direct opposition to the principles o
his religion, without contempt. This man wa:
one who had thus acted:—terrified by the
threats of the Committee, he had abjured hi:
former celibacy, had married, and continued to
preach, but in derision and insult of his pre
vious doctrines.

When he had finished his speech, he was sa
luted with loud cries of "*Bravo! bravo! Mon*
sieur le Curé; encore! encore! Monsieur l
Prédicateur! your sermon is worth fifty speeche
of the quack doctor that 's standing down on the
place of Saint Nicholas ; haven't you got some
boxes of salve too for a sore conscience?'
" Who's that talks of sore consciences?" bel
lowed the butcher Constant. "Where are the
aristocratic rascals that think of such things a
that? Sore consciences indeed ! such ones de
serve to have sore necks !"

The confusion and tumult of the scene wa

terrible, and seemed not likely to subside; for we suddenly heard, as the mob beneath us had paused for an instant to breathe, other and still more outrageous clamours, that seemed to come from the direction of the Grande Rue; and, as they came nearer, we could distinctly hear the words, "*Vive la belle Déesse! O le beau Apollon! A bas les Prêtres! Vive la Raison!*"

My schoolfellows and myself sat trembling, and anxiously wondering what this fresh uproar could announce; and we would gladly have had the most difficult embroidery to finish before dinner, rather than stay where we were.

But our curiosity, however, counterbalanced in some degree our terror; and the spectacle which we saw advancing through the dark gate, was sufficient to make us forget both that and the hunger which had for some time annoyed us. The crowd, too, beneath us seemed to be as much struck by the approaching sight as ourselves, for they all stood gazing in silence ; and Guche, clapping the priest on the shoulder, who was quietly retreating down the steps of the scaffolding, said in a loud fierce voice, " Come, come, my friend, none of your blinking ! we 'll see which can make the best use of their tongues, you, or our worthy Apollo there. You still pretend to be a bit of a Saint ; so let 's try if you can work a miracle, and teach that Goddess yonder to say her paternoster."

In the mean time the God and Goddess alluded to, were fast coming on ; and we, who had never heard of, or seen such things, except in our histories, were almost frightened when we saw the strange figures which presented themselves.

First came a party of fishermen, in their large sea-boots and check shirts, bearing the heads of some of those immense conger eels, which you may have seen lying in the fish-market, fastened upon long poles. After them came a man, dressed in a large black robe, painted all over with devils, and his face covered with a mask of the same colour, carrying a wooden representation of the guillotine. Next marched seven or eight persons, some in the habit of friars, and others grotesquely dizened out in faded laced coats, with large cocked hats, which contrasted oddly with the miserable appearance of the rest of their dress. These men continued to sing a couplet of the revolutionary air *Cadet Roussel*:

> " Cadet Roussel a un habit
> Tout doublé de papier gris ;
> Il ne le met que quand il gêle.
> Que direz vous de Cadet Roussel ?
> Ha ! ha ! ha ! oui vraiment
> Cadet Roussel est un bon enfant."

Then succeeded some extraordinary-looking personages, attired in the most singular costume. One of them had a quantity of artificial vine-leaves sewed about his body, mixed with some black-looking lumps that were probably meant for grapes; and as he passed yelled out—

> " Le bon Bourgeois, le dos au feu,
>   Le devant à la table,
>   Caressant sa bouteille,
>   Et puis sa démoiselle."

Ten or eleven others followed in pairs, just as strangely dressed, one like a huge bear in shaggy skins, another covered with an old piece of flowered tapestry, a third as white with flour as a miller, and another in a dingy cloak with some holes in it, through which some glittering pieces of tin were occasionally seen.

Immediately after these followed half a dozen men in the habit of friars, bearing upon their shoulders an arm-chair, in which sat a woman. Round her head was twined a garland of artificial roses: she was dressed in a white robe covered with silver spangles; in one hand she held the branch of a tree; in the other, what, from its appearance at that distance, seemed to be the mass-book.   Round the chair jumped and danced the fishwomen with their children, screaming, *Vive la Déesse ! Oh ! la belle Déesse !"* which applause the woman appeared to receive with much satisfaction.

Close behind this last personage, and mounted on a small horse, that had a sort of wings fastened to his sides, rode another comic figure, dressed in fiery-coloured clothes, with a large gilded sun fastened upon his breast, and holding in his hands a guitar, from which he occasionally attempted to draw some sounds.   His head was encircled by leaves, and he smiled and bowed to the rabble that threw up their caps about him, shouting, *Voyez douce le superbe Apollon ! Voyez douce son joli cheval aux ailles.*

As this extraordinary procession slowly came through the arched gate, and mounted the little ascent that leads upon the *place*, a party of drummers that were stationed just below our gal-

lery, began to beat as they were used to do at
the appearance of the Holy Sacrament; and the
unanimous crowd burst into the—to us unintelligible, cry of *Vive la Raison ! à bas les Eglises !
Vive notre bon prêtre Apollon !*

The pile was still blazing and crackling, and
as it rose above the motley assemblage, I recollect that it put me in mind of the sacrifices that
we used to read of in our Ancient History.
Guche, who had remained with the priest
standing upon the scaffolding, now held up his
hand ; and the procession, which had continued
to advance and had come as near as it could to
his post, stopped. *Silence ! silence !* was roared
by a host of voices ; and at length was procured.
Guche then, taking off his cap, and making a low
bow towards the spot where the goddess sat,
called in a loud tone, " Most high and mighty
Princess, great Goddess of Reason ! we thy true
and loyal subjects are hither met to do thee
homage, and to ask of thee if thou wilt suffer us

o eat our own bread and wear our own shoes. Thy trusty Priests and Barons there, we see, ook hungry, and their feet as if they had run nany a mile; but, great Princess, we trust that hou wilt not take from us our goods to give to hem, when thou hast so many good things in hine own shop." And as he concluded, he urst into a hearty laugh, which was echoed by ne crowd, and certainly by the Butcher Con-:ant, for I saw him grinning and rubbing his are arms with pleasure.

But the business was not yet finished; for the gure that was mounted upon the little winged orse now rode forward, and made his way nrough the crowd up to the scaffolding.— Great Prince of Poets!" cried Guche to m, "thou art doubtless come to claim thy :stined victim; but ere we yield him to thy)wer, he must be heard;" and turning to the riest, who now stood trembling by his side, Come, most holy man," said he, "confound

the wicked God and Goddess with thy heavenly
words ; tell them that a good fat priest is worth
an Apollo any day in the year, except Sunday,
and then he 's worth more, for he drinks and
sings more than any Apollo ever did in his life."
The trembling Priest began to mutter something
which we could not hear ; but he was interrupted by the mob, who shouted " A song! a song!
let 's have a song from the *Cardinal de l'igno-
minie.* Guche, make him sing the *Reveille ;*"
and the terrified man was compelled to sing that
military air, while the crowd accompanied him,
and Apollo made a show of touching his guitar.
We were all obliged to join in the chorus of
Aux armes, Citoyens! and as the people threw
up their caps, and the butcher brandished his
instrument of slaughter, the blazing pile sank
in with a crash, and, throwing its sparks and
glare over their hard features, made them look
like some of the figures that we had seen represented as suffering in purgatory.

Presently the drums began to roll, and the rest of the Committee of Safety came to the windows of the *Hôtel de Ville*, with the red caps upon their heads, and were saluted with cries of *Vive le Comité! Vive le règne de la Raison! à bas la Cathedrale!*

The flames now began to die away and expire, and thick volumes of black smoke spread themselves over the *place*, almost blinding and choking the persons there collected. The crowd seemed about to disperse, and the procession was thrown into complete disorder. The grotesque figures that composed it, were mixed among the rest of the people; and the white man that was intended to represent the month *Nivose* of our new calendar, got many a curse from those upon whom his snow fell. Guche came up to the gallery and called out to us, "Now you may go and learn your catechisms, my pretty virgins; you'll say them all the better after hearing such a capital sermon from our good *Curé* here," giving the Priest, whom he held by the arms, a push—" Eh ! my holy one, what do you think of those sweet little birds there ? Would not you like to have one of them to serve the mass for you ?" The man tried to laugh ; but terror was evidently struggling with the smile that he assumed, and he seemed to be entreating his tormentor to let him depart.

We, as you may suppose, lost no time in making use of Guche's permission ; and, after suffering some more insults and annoyance, we reached our house.

The noise and tumult still continued till late in the night ; and next morning we were told that our beautiful cathedral had been pulled to pieces by a desperate set of the worst of our inhabitants, whom the sight of the burning images had, no doubt, instigated to the act. It was a great loss to the town, since our present churches are but very indifferent ones. Many of our

Kings had made vows of golden hearts within it upon their accession ; and some of our bigots here, asserted that the unhappy Louis the Sixteenth had perhaps suffered for his neglect of that duty. Well, Boulogne seemed tranquil for a few days after the scene I have just been describing to you, except that now and then we heard the execrations of the people as the carriages that were conveying some suspected individuals to Arras passed across the *place*.

One day, however, about a week afterwards we heard cries of Bravo ! bravo ! in the street, and listening we could distinguish the words

> " La Louve Autrichienne
> La Louve de Vienne
> La Louve Autrichienne
> Est morte et enterré,"

sung to our old air of Marlbrook. Our mistress told us to lay down our work and follow her ; and we went into the chapel ; there she told us that our innocent Queen had been wickedly put to death, and that we must all pray for her soul.

When we came back from the chapel, a servant of my father arrived, who had attended him to Paris, whither he had gone to the Convention, of which he was member, but a very unwilling one, I may say. Still, by being so, he was enabled to be of use to many of our friends, and he had hitherto escaped any suspicions of aristocratic tendency. He was a very good kind of man, and acted so evidently from the best motives, that even in those bloody days he was much respected. The servant informed me (my father had not ventured to write) that Paris was in a dreadful state, that the Queen had just been executed, and that he was endeavouring to arrange matters so that he might come down to Boulogne without rendering himself obnoxious. He succeeded, poor man ! and about a week after I had the delight to embrace him.

We had a house at Outreau, a village which you may have remarked standing upon the hills above the port, and commanding an extensive view over the sea and country. We retired hither; and under the protection of Guche, whom my father had once saved from going to prison, we were allowed to live undisturbed. Our only society was the excellent *Curé* of the village, who was much beloved by the country people, and who had been still allowed to remain in his house. But the love of the simple villagers could avail him nothing; he was too near the horrible place in which nothing but suspicion and cruelty prevailed.

After we had lived quietly for about six months, we were one evening alarmed by the heavy sound of the bell from the *Hôtel de Ville*, that was never rung at that hour, and portended consequently some fresh scene of confusion. We went out upon a rising ground, a little way from the village, whence we could see the

quays and the town ; it was growing dark, bu
there was still light enough for us to distin
guish a crowd of persons collected near the old
custom-house. Presently we heard the drum:
of the national guard beating to arms, and, a:
the darkness increased, we saw lights moving
about on the quay, some of which seemed to
descend down the ladders which were fastened
to its sides as the means of communication witl
the boats at low tide. They rapidly passed
across the now dry bed of the harbour, and w
then lost sight of them.

My father and myself proceeded to the re
spectable *Curé*, whom we found in considerabl
agitation. We mentioned what we had seen
but his manner was unusually hurried and ab
rupt, as he asked how long it was since w
had seen the lights pass across the port. " Abou
half an hour," replied my father : " we merel
returned to our house to conclude our collation
and then came here."

The old man turned pale ; and so did we, for we suddenly heard the well-known threatening cry of "*Ah ! le scélérat ! ah ! le traitre !* We 'll show him how to write to the *Emigrés* ;—we 'll give him ink, plenty of red ink." And a mob of horrid-looking wretches rushed up to the *Curé's* house, and into the room where we were, leaded by Guche and the butcher Constant. ' Good night, citizens," said Guche to us ; " we have a little business with the worthy priest here, and perhaps (but I should be sorry for that) with you too. Eh ! my clever clerk, do you know this bit of paper ?" and he held up to the *Curé* a torn scrap of a letter. The excellent Butiaux, perceiving that it was useless to deny what spoke but too strongly against him, calmly replied, " Yes, I wrote it."— "That 's right," said the butcher grinning, " nothing can get him off now ; this will be glorious work for me ;" and he began with his hands to imitate the descent of the guillotining axe.

"*Allons! allons!*" shouted all the rest of the party, "don't let us stop here: let's have them all away to the committee—ay, this young wolf and all," seizing me by the arm. My father appealed to Guche for his protection, that we might not be carried off that night; but the man was incapable of preventing the gang from following their own bent, even if he had wished. "It is impossible, citizen," said Guche; " the committee would have my head off if I left you here after finding you with this traitor; so, come along; and as for you, *M. Ecrivain,* you may just say good-b'ye to your hens and your servant there, that we ought to have made you marry, for you'll sleep somewhere else very shortly." We were all accordingly hurried down to Boulogne, and confined in the prison.

The next morning Guche came to conduct us to the town-hall, where the committee were sitting. Our trial was short, and the unfortunate Butiaux was condemned to die; as it appeared hat a person whom he had intrusted with a letter for one of his brother *Curés*, who had emigrated, had been apprehended as he was making his way from the port, having just returned rom Outreau. The president of the committee, when he sentenced him to the guillotine, said o him with a sneer, "This room is a little altered now from what it was when your noble friends the Seneschals used to sit and drain he poor peasants of their money." "Yes," answered the venerable man, "this is the place where innocence formerly sat in judgment on rime, but where criminals now condemn the innocent." I thought the wretches that filled the hall would have torn him to pieces; but Constant, the butcher, darted forward, and laying his bare arms upon the unshrinking *Curé*, bellowed out, "Let my ox alone, I say; what! would you pretend to know how to kill him better than myself?" And the people with a loud laugh shouted, "Well done, my boy! we hope you'll never want such fat Easter oxen to slaughter, as long as you live."

In the midst of this frightful uproar, Guche had succeeded in obtaining our liberty, as nothing had appeared to implicate us in the unhappy Butiaux' proceedings; and we were, towards evening, allowed to return to Outreau.

Four or five days passed on, and as the town had been tolerably quiet every day, we hoped that the execution would not take place, for we knew very well that we should be compelled to attend it. But one morning the dreaded bell from the *Hôtel de Ville* began to toll, the drums echoed over the harbour, and up to our village, and we could see from the rising ground, to which we had hastened, the quays covered with people hurrying into the streets. When we returned to our house, we found Guche waiting for us. He told us that the *Curé* was to be guillotined immediately; that the guillotine, which had been purposely sent from Arras, had arrived

the preceding night; and that we must follow
him down to the town. " I have some gratitude
in me," said the man, " and if I could, I'd let
you stay, for it's an awkward sight after all ; but
my own safety is the first thing,—so come along."

When we got to the *Place Saint Nicholas*, we
found it covered with the furious people, who
had been dragging their victim about the streets,
and displaying him to the town, preparatory to
his being sacrificed. They had tied up the few
white hairs that were scattered upon his forehead into a knot, with a piece of tri-coloured
riband, and were singing another couplet of the
same air, *Cadet Roussel*, that I alluded to before.
It was this :

> " Cadet Roussel a trois cheveux,
> Deux pour la tête et une pour la queue,
> Et quand il va voir sa maîtresse
> Il les met tous les trois en tresse.
> Ha ! ha ! ha ! oui vraiment
> Cadet Roussel est un bon enfant."

And they danced around him. His beard had been suffered to grow, for, poor man ! he had probably passed the last few days in prayer and preparation for his death ; and one of the mob pointing to it, said with a wide grin, " *Monsieur le Curé* has not shaved himself this morning for the mass, but the national razor will do it nicely for him !" This was an allusion to the guillotine, which had acquired that name. The butcher was of course there ; but he had assumed an air of mock gravity, and stood near poor Butiaux, who seemed quite unmoved amid the horrors that surrounded him. The butcher had a large tricoloured scarf round his body, and shouted, " Gently, gently, citizens ! don't you see I 'm one of the committee?" pointing to his scarf ; " the good gentleman is under my protection. I 'm appointed inspector of public works ; and if he will do me the honour of accompanying me, I will shew him a very pretty one I have just finished in the *place* up in the high town," bowing to the *Curé*.

The crowd began to ascend up the high street ; but I was luckily spared the rest of the miserable spectacle, for I was so shocked and terrified by the screams and yells of the mob, that I fainted.   When I recovered, I found myself with my father at a house upon the *Place Saint Nicholas;* and as soon as I was able, we returned to Outreau.

" *Mais apropos,*" said the French lady, " I am obliged to go out to Ostrohove this afternoon ; so we will postpone the rest of my story till to-morrow, if you will do me the honour of dining with me."

I passed the afternoon in wandering about the country round Boulogne, and proceeded as far as the column, which was commenced when the grand army were encamped in the neighbourhood.   Its erection was for some time discontinued ; but Louis the Eighteenth has

ordered that it should proceed. The following
account of its foundation may, perhaps, not be
uninteresting to you.

Upon the day appointed for this ceremony
Marshal Soult, accompanied by all the superio
officers of the army, proceeded to the elevated
ground where the column was to be placed
Then, after distributing several crosses of the
legion of honour, the Marshal, assisted by a
grenadier of each of the regiments which were
drawn up around, placed in the foundation a
block of granite brought from Marquise, a
small town between Calais and Boulogne, where
there are quarries. Upon this block of stone
was the following inscription :—

" Première pierre
Du monument decerné
Par l'Armée expéditionaire de Boulogne
Et la Flotille
A l'Empereur NAPOLEON
Posée par le Maréchal Soult, Commandant en chef,
18 Brumaire An 13 (9 Novembre 1804)
Anniversaire de la regénération de la France."

This column was intended to commemorate the triumph of the army of *England*. But it is now to serve a very different purpose, namely, that of celebrating the restoration of the Bourbon family. A statue of the great man was to have been placed upon the top of it; but it is now to be surmounted by the *fleur de lis*.

Continuing my walk as far as Wimille, a pretty village buried in a valley about two miles from Boulogne, I visited the monument of the unfortunate *Pilatre de Rosier*, who was killed in endeavouring to cross from Calais to England in a balloon. His balloon took fire, and he fell like another Phaëton.

On my return I walked upon the ramparts, from which a very pretty view presents itself. The small river Liane, which forms the harbour, is remarkably picturesque when full, winding away with its serpentine bends as mysteriously as more important rivers. The country is irregular, with a few villages scattered along the tops of the downs; and in the distance the brown sands of Etaples overtopping the hills about them. Outreau, the village where my friend had lived, was opposite to me, and the bell of its church was ringing. The high street, which is remarkably steep, and may be seen in its whole length from the ramparts, was crowded with persons coming to the fair, which covered the Esplanade, an open space before the prefecture and beneath the ramparts. Vast numbers of English were lounging among the booths, and making purchases at the *boutiques à dix sous et à vingt.* Some of the fishwomen, with their red petticoats and long golden ear-rings, were clattering about the crowd; and just beneath me was a man with a sort of shed, in which he was making *gauffres,* or thin cakes of flour, milk, and sugar baked and eaten hot. " *Voyez! voyez! Messieurs et Dames, toutes chaudes, toutes chaudes,*" was the cry, mixed with the drums of the shows, and the proclamation of " *Tout à dix — la boutique à cinq.*"

While I was looking down upon this scene, an old white-headed man upon crutches placed himself near me. He did not beg; but there was no doubt of his profession. I spoke to him and said, it was a pity that so old and infirm a man should be obliged to ask charity. " *Ah! Monsieur,*" said he, " *que voulez vous?* I cannot work, I am obliged to pay high for my little room, and I have nothing but what I get from the goodness of a few kind persons. There is one family here that give me a glass of wine every Sunday from their windows which look upon the ramparts, and the young ladies are all very good to me, — *mais c'est une pauvre affaire.*" I gave the old man something, who, as I departed, uncovered his white head, and made me a low bow.

" But," said my friend the pedestrian, " as it grows late, I will defer the rest I have to tell you till to-morrow."

CHAPTER XXII.

THIS morning, according to agreement, my friend and I met again after breakfast, and he thus continued his narrative.

"The day following I proceeded to my friend the lady's house. I met there a Frenchman, who amused me much. He was a pompous sounding man, looking uncommonly like a shoulder of mutton, the lower part of his body was so much broader than the upper, and tapered up to his neck, which was long and slender. He was a great epicure; for though he was not in his own house, I heard him particularly instructing the servant as to the dinner; and he ended his suggestions with this earnest admonition, " *Surtout, que le café soit chaud.*" He went away soon after we had dined, and my friend mentioned to me a little anecdote of him which establishes his reputation as an ingenious *gourmand*. He has two houses belonging to him, which he lets, the one to a pastrycook, the other to a butcher. From these he derives a considerable rent in money ; but he has also established the system of feudal service or relief within them, receiving from his pastrycook and butcher vassals, every Sunday, the homage of three *petits pâtes* and *un gigot de mouton.*

When we had concluded our dessert, my friend said to me, " Let us walk up to the ramparts, we shall find seats there, and while we enjoy this fine evening, I will conclude my story." We accordingly ascended by a flight of steps at the side of a fountain, representing a Cupid, and called *Puits d'Amour ;* and after walking a little, we sat down upon a stone bench that commanded a view of the country and the sea.

" It was on a fine evening like this," she began,

" and some time after the events I have before read to you, I was walking upon the heights which you see extending towards the sea. The town had continued tranquil since the execution of poor Butiaux, and we had remained unmolested. I had reached the brink of the rock which hangs over the beach, and was amusing myself with looking upon the view, which is much more extensive than what we now enjoy. The whole line of coast, as far as the point of land called Grinez on one side, is discovered; and the white cliffs of your country are distinctly seen, with the castle of Dover. Our fishing-boats were waiting for the flowing of the tide to come into the harbour; and a large party of the women you may have observed gathering muscles among the rocks, were returning along the shore, and singing some of their favourite songs. The tide now began to murmur towards the wide range of sands at the harbour's mouth, and soon came swelling into the port. The fishing-boats one after the other swept in, and were hailed by their wives, who ran along the quay with their baskets to receive the fish.

It grew dark, and I was turning to go home, when I observed a small boat come cautiously round a point of land at some distance, and steal in towards the shore. There were two persons in it, and, as soon as it had grounded upon the beach, one of them, after looking carefully in every direction, stepped out, and walking hastily on, disappeared from my sight. He had apparently turned into a road which leads up from that part of the sands towards the town. The other man remained with the boat, and sat humming the *ça ira*.

The manner in which these persons had approached struck me as singular; but, as it was now late, I did not think it proper to satisfy my curiosity by staying any longer. I returned home; but my father was not in the room where we usually sat, and I heard voices in low con-

versation in the apartment above. I was alarmed, as any thing unusual in those times was
enough to agitate me; and I remained in an
uncomfortable state of suspense for some time.
I was, however, presently relieved from this,
for my father came into the room accompanied
by a stranger, whose appearance struck me as
very like that of the person I had seen leave
the boat.

" You must procure us some supper, Marguerite," said my father to me; " I have sent
our maid down to the town ; and as she has got
some of her friends there from Neufchâtel, she
said, I told her she might remain all night."

I was surprised at this, as my father was generally very strict about the servant, and would
scarcely ever allow her to go to Boulogne. I
could not help connecting this circumstance with
the arrival of the stranger ; but I immediately
went out and got the supper ready. When we
were seated, my father, pouring out a large

glass of wine for the stranger, and another for me, said, " Come, let us drink success to our cause! and you, girl, drink with us. We have been too long slaves to that bloody convention ; any mild form of government will be better than its terrible reign. Come ;" and we all, (I perplexed and frightened,) drank success to the patriots.

The stranger then said, "*Mais, Monsieur*, we have much to do in Paris ; we are scarcely organized yet, and the money which we expected from Coblentz is not arrived. Things go on but badly in La Vendée. Charette has separated himself from the rest ; and the Republican Rousillon has beaten part of our friends at Doué. We must hasten our measures."

My heart now began to sink. I foresaw some of those dreadful scenes I had only heard of at Boulogne ; and my father, it seemed, was to be engaged in them. I looked attentively at the speaker, whom I had not before closely examined, and perceived that he was evidently in a disguise, and wore a dress somewhat resembling that of the fishermen of Normandy.

He continued, " I have had great difficulty in getting here; we are too well known to have ventured upon coming through the provinces, where every body is now stopped and examined; and I therefore, with one of our party, have crept along the coast protected by this dress. We procured our boat at the mouth of the Seine at Havre, where we have friends, and have succeeded in our commission. But we must not delay; the tide will be falling, and I had rather keep clear of the other fishing-boats when they go to sea. We may depend, then, upon your joining us ?"

" Certainly," said my father; " in a very few days you will see me in Paris, unless the people here refuse to allow me to depart."

" And that, I fear, is very likely," said the stranger, " in the present state of affairs."

"*Attendez*," said my father; " this girl here hall aid us in our just conspiracy. Marguerite, my dear, you have seen to what wretches our ountry is a prey ; you have seen our unforunate friend the *Curé* Butiaux dragged away to death by them; will you not assist us, then, in ridding France of such pests ?"

I was perplexed, and looked at him without replying.

"*Ce n'est pas grand chose*," continued my father, smiling ; " but you must turn cheat, and feign yourself afflicted with some severe illness, and I will persuade Guche to let us go to Paris to consult Choppart. That man is not so bad as he is obliged to appear ; and I think he will do what he can for us. What do you think of our plan ?" concluded he, turning to the stranger.

" Possible enough," replied he, " and if you can get away from this place, you may make pretty sure of reaching Paris, for they let every body in ; but, when once in, it is not quite so easy to get out. But I dare not delay : I shall then tell the general that he may immediately expect you."

"Certainly," said my father. The stranger then grasped his hand, and bowing to me, after looking out, hastily disappeared.

My father then explained to me that Paris was at present upon the eve of insurrection, that the Convention had become so obnoxious to many of the people as to have made them resolve upon rising against their tyrants, and that a general who had commanded in La Vendée was to head them. "You know, my child," said my father, "that I sat in that Convention; but when its career became so bloody, I was fortunate enough to be able to retire and live tranquilly with you. But the moment is now come for action ; and as I have many friends in Paris, my influence may do some good. We must therefore go thither. I grieve to carry thee to

L 2

that dangerous place ; but where could I leave thee ?"

" *Oh mon Père !*" I replied, " let me share all your dangers ; I should be miserable if you were to be again absent from me, and exposed to all the horrors I have heard of."

" Well," said my father, " we have now about a month before us. You must gradually fall sick and complain of lameness and debility, and leave the rest to me."

Accordingly, a few days after the event I have related to you, I did so ; and, being naturally pale and delicate, I succeeded, by remaining in the house and eating little, in giving myself the appearance of an invalid.   My father distressed himself perpetually at the penance he was inflicting upon me ; but I told him that I was as anxious for the happiness of France as himself, and that I had read of Roman women who had undergone greater hardships than mine for the benefit of their country.   My father embraced me ; and in about a week afterwards procured permission for us to set out ; but not till we had received a visit from Guche, who called me *pauvre petite*, and said, that I had better stay in the fresh sea-air, than go to that gloomy capital.

We quitted Boulogne about the middle of September. I had never travelled before, and, in spite of the dangerous business we were going upon, the novelty of all I saw delighted me.

We passed Beauvais, which was once saved from a siege, you recollect, by a woman. My father mentioned to me a singular custom, a privilege as they then thought it, attached to the butchers of that town. Upon some particular day, I think *Mardi Gras*, they used to present to the King at Paris a sheep decorated with flowers and ribands ; but I do not know if his present Majesty keeps up the ceremony.*

* This resembles the old custom which formerly existed in Yorkshire, and which gave the name to the

Upon quitting Beauvais, I saw for the first time the vines which are scattered about it: the grapes were all ripening, and our postilion dismounting went and gathered a bunch, which he brought to us. I had never tasted grapes fresh plucked from a vineyard before, and they seemed the better to me;—but I was young, and disposed to find pleasure in every thing. The rich country we passed before reaching Paris made me anticipate seeing a magnificent city; and I continued to look impatiently from the windows of our chaise. But I was disappointed, for it grew dark as we passed through St. Denis, and I saw nothing of the city from a distance.

When we reached the barrier we were stopped; our chaise was closely searched, but, as I counterfeited extreme indisposition, we were not

estival of Lammas. The tenants who held of York Minster or Monastery, were obliged upon a certain day to resent to their priestly lords a lamb, decorated with owers, as a feudal homage.

detained any longer, as our passports were in
proper form. But now commenced our difficulties; for had the Convention known, which
they certainly would in the course of the following day from our passports which had been
left at the gate, that my father was in Paris, he
would have been immediately arrested. We
drove to the hotel which we had given as our
address at the barrier; and terribly disappointed
I was at the dark narrow-looking streets we
passed through. The Boulevards, however,
which we crossed, struck me much; the *Cafés*
were filled with people whom I could see in
violent debate; and vast crowds were walking
under the trees. Several ragged desperate-look-
ing men and women came close up to the chaise-
window and looked in, calling *Vive la Convention!* but they did not offer us any farther mo-
lestation; and we reached the hotel.

But my father had no sooner discharged the
chaise, than taking me under his arm and un

perceived by the people of the house, who were
engaged in attending to a diligence which had
arrived at the same time as ourselves, he hurried
me along from the Rue Saint Honoré, where
we had stopped, down upon a quay, and across
a long bridge, from whence I saw the river covered with barges, and dark high houses and
towers rising all round me. We hastened on,
and turning to the right after we had crossed the
bridge, presently reached a gateway, at which my
father knocked. A voice from within called out,
" *Eh bien, citoyen, que veux-tu ?*"—" *Le Monsieur de numero cinq, est il là ?*" said my father.
" *Oui! oui! il est là,*" replied the same voice,
and we heard the heavy bolts of the gate drawn
back to admit us.

When we entered the court, a man stood
there, who immediately shut and bolted the gate
behind us. He then, after looking steadily at
my father, said to him, " *Ils sont en haut :*"
and pointed to a staircase a little way from the

place where we were. My father and myself as
cended that staircase, and on the first *étage* found
a person standing with a gun upon his shoulder
and who instantly called out, "*Qui va là?*"
"*Numero cinq,*" said my father. "*Passez,*" replied the sentinel, pointing to a door behind him
through which we passed into a large room.

At the upper end of the apartment we had
just entered sat three or four persons in the national uniform, with apparently a large map before them. One of them seeing us enter, immediately rose and came forward. "Welcome
to Paris," said he to my father; "I wish I
could give you and this young lady," bowing to
me, "a better reception; but I trust that ere a
few days be past, we shall have turned those
rogues out of the Tuileries, and then I think I
can promise you both a more commodious lodg-
ing than you will have now."

"Oh general," said my father to him, "as to
this girl, she does not deserve to be better treated

L 5

than the Convention ;—she has been making a
false constitution too ;" and he laughingly explained the circumstance of our departure from
Boulogne.

The rest of the persons, who were at the other
end of the room, now came up, and were introduced to us, " *A propos, Général,*" said one
of them (whom I recognised as the person I had
seen at Boulogne) to our first acquaintance, " I
see by the plan, that if we can get possession of
the quays, and secure the gate of the Tuileries,
where the Convention now assemble, we shall
spread such a panic among our enemies, that
our success will be assured."

" Are the Sections disposed to rise which you
have visited ?" said the person who had been addressed as General ; "can we depend upon the
Fauxbourg Saint Germain, and the quarter of
Le Peletier ?"

" I think we may," replied the other ; " we
have even secured the assistance of Hebert and

the Cordeliers; bad companions to be sure, but if we succeed, we shall soon be able to rid ourselves of them."

" But we must be breaking up," interrupted the General, " and I fear," turning to my father, "that you cannot remain here with your daughter. This house has been lately watched and suspected, and it may possibly be searched. But the young lady will be perfectly safe, since it belongs to a concealed patriot, and the old woman that takes care of it, will pay her every attention."

My father acquiesced, though reluctantly; and when they all left the house, we both felt our separation deeply. " But cheer up, my daughter!" said my father, " in a very few days I trust that we shall meet again at the Tuileries."

Several days passed away in suspense and agitation. From the window of my room I could see the whole length of the quay, with the dis-

tant Pont Neuf,· and the river covered with its
galleries of washerwomen below.   They went on
rubbing and beating their linen, as industri-
ously and careless to what was passing about
them, as if they were washing the shirts of the
gardes du corps in the king's time. But the rest
of the populace of Paris seemed to act very differently ; for I could perceive frequently parties
of women and men standing in various quarters
of the quay, and appearing in violent dispute,
while many shouted, *Vive la Nation !* and *A bas
Pitt !* round some man who was addressing them
from a bench.   And other sights, too, at times
presented themselves, which made me shudder
and fly from the window.

I saw the virtuous Malesherbes pass along the
opposite side of the river to his execution ; and
the old woman who was standing by me at the
time, and who had told me who he was, said,
" *Voilà ! Mademoiselle, voilà !* that is the great
lawyer that spoke up for the king when he was at

his trial, as they called it——the murderers! Look, he is going to the same fate as the poor Louis! But we shall see, we shall see presently, whether that Satan Robespierre can sit upon the tumbrel as calmly as that good man does now? Shame! shame! upon those wicked women that are howl_ing and hooting at him;" pointing to a number of the *Poissardes*, who were among the crowd which covered the quay.

Well, as I told you, some days passed on, and I was beginning to feel great alarm and perplexity, when one night, I think the 5th of October, I was suddenly awakened by a great noise. I instantly got up and went to the win- dow. I heard the tocsin ringing, and the drums rolling; and opening the window, I saw the opposite bank covered with people extending away towards the Pont Neuf, and their shouts of *A bas le tyran!* echoed over the river. Many of them had torches, which they waved about, and occasionally shewed me several offi-

ers in the national uniform among the crowd.
They all seemed to be pouring towards the gate
f the Tuileries; but at that moment I saw a
ody of cavalry, with two or three pieces of
rtillery, and some infantry, advance from with-
n the palace. The insurgents, as I now con-
luded them to be, appeared surprised and
larmed at this event, and stopped. But soon
resh cries rose of " *Aux armes! aux armes!*
Citoyens!" and they rushed on. The tumult
nd confusion then became dreadful; I heard
he cannon and musquetry rolling along the
iver, and at intervals the shouts, and the quick
inging of the tocsin. A party of cavalry gal-
oped past beneath my window, pursuing a
umber of the people, who fled, crying " Trea-
on! treason!" And when I bent forwards
rom my window, to look at something in the
iver which had attracted my attention, I per-
eived several persons struggling among the
arges, and grappling with one another. This

alarming uproar continued for some time. But I soon heard the discharges of artillery grow fainter; and when the smoke cleared away a little, I saw the cavalry in full possession of the opposite quay.

The old woman, who had been looking on with me, now cried out, " *Mon Dieu! ils sont perdus!* Those bloody wretches have got the upper hand." Her exclamation made me tremble; and good reason I had to do so. For the next morning when she went out she brought me back the intelligence that the insurrection had entirely failed, and that some of its leaders had been discovered, and would be that day sent to the guillotine. I was struck with horror; my father might be among them. But the old woman again told me, that he certainly was not one of the arrested persons, but that they were in search of him.

I waited in dreadful anxiety for some days, in complete ignorance of his fate, when I received a letter from a friend at Boulogne, stating that my father had been detected there endeavouring to escape to England, and imprisoned. I immediately went out, disguised as a peasant, in some clothes furnished me by the old woman, and hastened to the barrier Saint Denis; then, telling the sentinel a lamentable story of my being shut in from my home and my sick mother, he allowed me to pass for a kiss,. which I was compelled to grant him. *Mais vraiment,* if he were to see me now, I am afraid he would have little pity for me.

I made my way as well as I could down to Boulogne, and went directly to the prison. I found my father in terrible alarm about me. " Thank God ! my daughter," said he, when he saw me, " you are safe. I had trusted to our friend, to whom the house where you were belongs, that he would protect you, till I was safe in England; but he, too, has been thrown into prison in the department of l'Isère. But you are with me again, and I am relieved from a great weight."

The next day Guche came to inform us that my father was to be conveyed to Arras, with another gentleman, there to be tried. " I am sorry," said he to my father, " for your sake and the Citoyenne here ; but all the others would have it so, *et je tiens à la vie, moi comme de la cire.*"

Accordingly, the same afternoon we left Boulogne ; Guche having obtained permission for me to accompany my father. With us was another inhabitant of Boulogne, who seemed terribly affected by his situation. The next afternoon we arrived at Arras, and, as we came upon the *Grande Place*, the guillotine stood there surrounded by a crowd, and just performing its terrible office. Our companion looked once at it, and then, uttering a loud exclamation of affright, sunk back upon the seat of the conveyance we were in. We thought he had ainted, but to our astonishment and dismay, we found that he was dead !——terror having antici- pated what the axe would have performed.

This circumstance added to the confusion and misery of my mind, and I had well nigh faint- ed myself; but I endeavoured to hold up for the sake of my father, and succeeded. We were lodged that night in the prison, amidst a vast collection of prisoners of all descriptions ; and a dreadful night we passed.

The next morning we were carried before the Revolutionary Commission, which was then pre- sided by the execrable Joseph le Bon. When we were led up to the table at which they sat, the monster called out to the guard who was retiring, " Hollo there! you may have your prisoner again in a moment ; I see guillotine marked on his neck. And you, citoyenne," look- ing at me, " do you want to save useless ex- pense in head dresses? Come, come! you have not been long enough in a situation to wish for

death ; but we will make you see how we shav
your father here ; the barber at Boulogne coul
not do it neater."

One or two of the other persons who were a
the table said something about trial ; but Le Bon
bursting into a laugh, said, " Tried ! let th
Bourreau try him : he 'll see plenty of witnesse
from the little window," which was another nam
for the guillotine.   Then calling to the guard
" Here 's a head to be chopped off withou
mercy ; and be sure you shew this citoyenn
here how nicely our Arras cooks can mak
aristocratic sauce."*

* An anecdote is related of this Joseph le Bo
which shews his character fully.   He was one nigh
returning home through the streets of Arras, when h
heard a female voice singing and the tones of a guita
He had not proceeded far from the house from whenc
these sounds had issued, when he received the intelli
gence of a defeat which the republican army had sus
tained.   " What !" cried Joseph, " music ! singing

We were both immediately hurried away to the *Grand Place*. I had no time to think or speak or communicate with my father. The whole scene had been so horrible and instantaneous, that I was bewildered, and did not recover any sort of capability to see what was passing, till I found myself upon the scaffolding near my father. But, my God! what a moment that was! I saw an immense crowd yelling and shaking their fists at us, the dark arcades of the place shutting them in all round; my father with his neck bare close to me, and a horrid-looking man all bloody at his side. I fell at his feet, I screamed with agony; I saw them drag him away; I heard a heavy blow, and remember nothing more till I found myself in the house of a friend we had at Arras.

and the enemy at our gates!" And the next morning the young lady, who had been singing and playing, perished on the scaffold with her mother.

Some time after, I was allowed to return to Boulogne, where I have lived ever since. But that dreadful sight never entirely leaves me; and every time I hear Arras named, my blood runs cold, and a shuddering ague comes over me.

I expressed my thanks to my friend for the trouble she had given herself to relate her story to me, and took my leave. And, added my friend the pedestrian, I must now do the same, for I have an appointment with my German master, as I am endeavouring to guarantee myself against any future unlucky ignorance of that language. We accordingly separated.

CHAPTER XXIII.

I HAD not seen my friend for some days, but this morning, as I was strolling towards the village of St. Canat, I met him returning from an excursion he had been making among the mountains. He seemed fatigued, and we proceeded together to my house, where he refreshed himself with some grapes. He was then preparing to go away, when I said to him, " You afforded me so much amusement the last time you were here, that I should be much gratified if you would endeavour to recollect any other circumstances which may have occurred to you."

" I am very happy," replied he, " that I have been able to entertain you, as it was entirely for that reason that I ventured to tell you so much about myself. I have little else, however, to mention, except the following short anecdote :

A few days after I had heard the story I last related to you, I happened to find myself in company with an officer of a French regiment which had been disbanded. I was mentioning to him my having gone to visit the column, and could not help insinuating that our preparations to resist the threatened invasion by the Army of *England* had been such as to have rendered its success impossible. Like a true Frenchman and soldier, he vehemently maintained the contrary.

" If you had seen our superb army," said he, " you would have said otherwise. *Ma foi!* I think we should have eaten many a beef-steak in London." He then added in a lower tone " If we had such a general now as we had then, *parbleu!* you would see."

I did not choose to pursue our argument further, as it would either have ended in nothing,

or a duel, so I turned the conversation upon
the sudden departure of the army for Germany.
"That was a very unexpected circumstance,"
said I.

"*Oui, oui!* I believe we may thank England
for it," replied the Officer. "However, that
campaign made me an officer out of a serjeant-
major."

"Then you have no reason to regret it," said
I ; "but pray, might I ask what the circumstance was to which you allude?"

"Certainly," replied the Officer, "you seem
un Monsieur bien honnête, and I will relate them
to you. Let us adjourn to the *Café Veyez,* and
take some refreshment."

We did so, and as we sipped our *petit verre,* my
new acquaintance said, "It appears very strange
to me to see so many English residing here.
Some years ago, we should as soon have thought
of seeing the devil as an Englishman in Boulogne,
except when our privateers had taken some pri-

soners. But at the period to which more parti
cularly I allude, certainly an Englishman would
have been in no easy situation among our troops
We were all encamped on the heights above th
town, and in daily expectation of crossing L
Manche. We used to see your cruisers com
dodging about; and we often pointed out to
each other the Castle of Dover, and longed to
be garrisoning it. The Emperor was with us
and I have often seen him standing upon a bat
tery that was to the right of the harbour on th
cliff, and watching the motions of your frigates
and when your admiral Sir Sidney Smith at
tacked our flotilla, the Emperor was himself in
a little boat at the mouth of the harbour, encou
raging the sailors.

" But what I have to tell you about myself is
this. We had just proclaimed Napoleon Emperor, and we were all ordered to assemble in
grand parade on the heights, at the right
camp, to take the oath of fidelity.——*Ma foi!* we

had no occasion to take an oath for that," (this was said in a lower tone); " so on the morning of the twenty-eighth of August, while the cannon of all the forts were announcing the *fête Saint Napoleon* to the surrounding country, the whole army formed themselves into brigades, in a semicircle round the Emperor's throne, which was raised upon a platform and decorated with trophies and flags. Our generals placed themselves at the head of their respective divisions; and to the right and left of the throne stood all the bands of the different regiments. We waited under arms till about twelve o'clock, and then we heard the cannon begin to roll again; and shortly after the Emperor, attended by all his staff and ministers and great officers of state, came upon the ground. He advanced slowly up to the throne, while the music struck up, *Où peut-on être mieux?* one of our national songs that is a little out of fashion now. When the Emperor had reached his throne, he sat down for an instant, while all the Marshals and Princes ranged themselves round. I was a youngster then, and as I looked at them all, I said to myself,—Why should not I be a Marshal and a Duke one of these days?—the Emperor himself was not much more than I am, once. So while the Emperor was sitting down, the Grand Chancellor pronounced a discourse to us, which none of us heard or cared about; we wanted to hear Napoleon. As soon as the Chancellor had finished, the drums and trumpets struck up, and the Emperor rose. We were all as silent as mice; the ensigns stood a little in advance of the line, and the whole army presented arms. Napoleon then deliberately pronounced these words: ' Soldiers, swear that you will always be faithful and obedient to your Country and your Emperor.' Instantly, *Nous le jurons!* was shouted by thousands of voices; the music again burst out, and the whole flotilla and artillery along the coast fired an unanimous salute. I was thinking then that if the gentlemen of the Thames, *pardon, Monsieur,*" (I smiled) "could hear us, they would be locking up their shops and hiding their guineas. As soon as the oath had been taken, we all marched by the throne, and the Emperor spoke to some of us. I looked, I remember, very hard at him, and he called out, ' *Attention ! attention !*' and advancing a little, he said, ' *Comment donc, tu es Serjeant Major ? tu es bien jeune de l'être.*'—' *Et tu es bien plus jeune d'être Empereur,*' I suddenly replied, without hesitation or reflection. I did not know that I had said any thing singular, but I saw the Princes glance at one another and turn pale. Napoleon looked hastily round, and then said smiling, ' *Ma foi, Messieurs, il m'a bien payé : qu'en pensez-vous ?*' They all smiled too, and bowed. ' *Tiens, Monsieur avec la risposte en main,*' said he to me ; ' here is the cross for you, and let me see you as sharp in the field, as you have just now been in reply.—' *Marchez !*' he then called out to our company, which had halted, and on we passed. My comrades all shook hands with me after the parade, and said I was a lucky young dog ; and proud enough I was of my cross.

" But I wanted to be moving, and we were all wondering why we were not embarked on board the flat-bottomed boats which were ready for us. One morning, however, about three o'clock in September, the *generale* beat to arms, the whole army was in motion, and by eight o'clock we were all on board. The Emperor came down and inspected us, and we were in high spirits, and thinking we should in a day or two be at Cantorberi ; when the very same afternoon down came an express from Paris, and in two days we were on our march for Germany. We were sorry to leave Boulogne: we had been very happy there, and had had our little garden about our tents, where we used to work and look down upon the port, and amuse ourselve

with keeping rabbits and poultry; and one of
our officers made a song about our going, which,
as there is no one now in the *café*, I will sing to
you." The officer then sung, or rather murmured, the following verses :—

> " Le tambour bat, il faut partir,
>   Ailleurs on nous appelle ;
> Oui, de lauriers il va s'ouvrir
>   Une moisson nouvelle.
> Si là-bas ils sont assez fous
>   Pour troubler l'Allemagne,
> Tant pis pour eux, tant mieux pour nous,
>   Allons vite en campagne.
>
> Là par ses exploits éclatans
>   On connoit notre armée,
> C'est là qu'elle est depuis long temps
>   A vaincre accoutumée ;
> C'est là que nos braves guerriers
>   Vont triompher ;
> C'est là que pour nous les lauriers
>   Sont en coupe réglée.

OF AN EXILE.

Il faut quitter ce camp charmant,
    De bons enfans l'asile,
Dont nous avions fait si gaiement
    Une petite ville ;
Si des murs, malgré nos soins,
    La forme est peu correcte,
Nous n'avons pas été du moins
    Trompés par l'Architecte.

Adieu, mon cher petit jardin,
    Ma baraque jolie,
Toi que j'ai planté de ma main
    Et toi que j'ai bâtie :
Puisqu'il faut prendre mon mousquet
    Et laisse ma chaumière,
Je m'en vais planter le piquet
    Par de la Frontière.

Adieu, poules, pigeons, lapins,
    Et ma chatte gentille,
Autour de moi tous les matins
    Rassemblés en famille.
Toi, mon chien, ne me quitte pas,
    Compagnon de ma gloire ;
Partout tu dois suivre mes pas,
    Ton nom est la Victoire.

Adieu, peniches et plats bateaux,
   Prâmes et cannonières ;
Qui deviez porter sur les eaux
   Nos vaillans militaires.
Vous ne soyez pas si contens,
   Messieurs de la Tamise,
Seulement pour quelques instans
   La partie est remise.

Nous aurons souvenir de vous,
   Habitans de Bolougne,
Mais, pour le retour gardez-nous
   Du Bordeaux, du Bourgogne :
Nous songerons à vos appas,
   Gentilles Boulognaises,
Les Allemandes ne font pas
   Oublier les Françaises."

The song amused me, and I requested that
my acquaintance would have the goodness to
favour me with a copy. "Certainly," he replied, and a day or two afterwards, when I met
him, presented me with one. The rest of his

story was simply, that he had subsequently been taken considerable notice of by Bonaparte, and, having distinguished himself at the battle of Austerlitz, had been raised from the ranks.

When we left the *café* we strolled up together to the High Town, upon the *place* of which stood what is called in France *Le Carcan.*—This is a species of pillory, in which criminals are exposed when their sentence includes this preliminary proceeding. The man who was then standing in this instrument had been found guilty of a robbery, and was to be imprisoned for five years. A few persons were standing round, but did not appear particularly interested by the spectacle.

" These are no new sights to you," said my companion to me: " I have been in London myself, and I am well acquainted with the English taste for sights of this kind ; *ma foi !* even your women seemed to me to be as fond of them as the men."

I endeavoured as well as I could to parry this attack, by assuring him that as to the latter part of what he had said, he must have been misinformed.

" *Parbleu, non!*" he replied ; " why, I saw it with my own eyes. I was one morning going to what you call the city, I suppose because it is an island.   When I was arrived at the corner of a little street which turns out of your *Rue de Flotte*, I perceived a great crowd of persons all down the *rue*, and raised above them a scaffolding. Several ladies, *très comme il faut*, pressed by me; and one said, ' We shall be too late, how unfortunate !' As I wish to see the spectacles of the countries I visit, I went into the street, where I expected to see, perhaps, *les Jongleurs Indiens faire des tours.   Mais je fus frappé.*   A man was just struggling upon the *potence* in the agonies of death, while the windows of the houses all round were filled with women.   *C'est tout-à-fait unique*, I said to myself, and hastened away; but the rest of all that day I was much surprised to see men running about through the streets with a paper fastened to their hats, representing the hanging man and uttering loud cries, who, I concluded, were his accomplices, that had thus been branded, and were compelled to make a public confession of their guilt."

I was silenced and mortified: but, in order to have my blow too, I said; " At all events, I doubt if such instances of credulity and folly would be found in England as this very town lately exhibited. A friend told me that he happened to be at a banker's one day, about the period that Thistlewood"—' *C'est lui-même,*' cried my companion, ' *que j'ai vu.*' I continued—"that Thistlewood was condemned to die. Some wag had spread a report that the convicted person had offered a reward of twenty thousand pounds each to three persons who would consent to draw lots to take his place, and an additional ten thousand to him upon whom the performance of the condition might fall; and several peasants positively came into the banker's, requesting to know if he were not the person employed to pay the money, saying, *C'est une triste chose que la mort, mais, diable! je pourrais gagner deux cent mille francs.*"

" *C'est possible que cela,*" said the officer when I concluded, "*mais des dames se plaire à voir pendre!* You must avow that such a taste is *parfaitement* English." I had nothing to reply, and we parted rather upon bad terms.

" And now," said my friend the pedestrian, " I am afraid I must take my leave of you. I propose setting out to-morrow for Nice, on my way to Venice, where I am going."

This communication was unexpected and unwelcome to me, as I felt that I should probably relapse into my former depression and misery. It is great weakness for a man to yield utterly to these in common cases; and even in my singular and melancholy one, I have struggled

hard, but the labour is with me so hopeless as
to this world—it is so like that of the slave com
pelled to work in order to save a sinking vessel
that when I have no companion, and such I find
it difficult to find, my heart sinks, and I give
up the contest. I requested my friend to favour
me with his correspondence, which he promised
and we parted towards evening in mutual regret

CHAPTER XXIV.

APRIL 10th.—I have written nothing here for some time past. I became indolent and indifferent after my friend's departure, and have not once entered the city. The spring has rapidly advanced, the heat of the sun is becoming intense, the vines begin to freshen, and the almond-trees are all in blossom. I may exclaim with Surrey,

" And thus I see, among these pleasant things,
    Each care decays, and yet my sorrow springs ;"

every thing feels the reviving approach of the new life of nature but myself. Once I could welcome it with all the pure joy and transport which it communicates to the artless and happy : the green springing corn, the opening bud, the triumphant skylark floating and singing at Heaven's gates above me, used to make my blood flow faster, and my heart beat with the anticipation of warmth, and perfumed gardens, and dark woods and shining rivers, where I might ramble and roam " one long summer's day of indolence and ease." I thought not of the world as a struggle and temptation; I saw not, knew not the real world. While others sought for employments and ambitious distinctions, while they fluttered and danced and trifled in promenades and balls, my pleasure was to wander away among shady lanes and meadows and babbling streams. I remember I used to fly from the bustle and gaieties of Leamington, where I once was, and hasten to the decayed turrets of Kenilworth, which lay near; and there my imagination peopled the grass-grown halls and chambers with many a knightly form. But my humour was misunderstood: when I was only shy, I was considered sullen; and when my heart was full of affection and disposition to do well, I was believed selfish, unfeeling, and cold. I was wilful, because I loved what was natural in preference to the artificial enjoyments amidst which I was placed, and sighed for the ties of affection and social life. But enough of this, and let me walk forth.

*   *   *
*   *   *

I returned much fatigued from my morning's expedition. I ascended the rock which lies at the mouth of the harbour, and visited the chapel and fort of Notre Dame. The path to it was steep and stony; and had not one of those mists which sometimes hang about the sun shaded me, I should have found the ascent at mid-day impossible. The fort is small, and without any cannon. Upon its gate is painted a sentinel, and the importance of the post has been thus described by a French poet:

Gouvernement commode et beau,
A qui suffit pour toute garde
Un Suisse avec sa hallebarde
Peint à la porte du Château.

The chapel which I entered is small, and hun
round with numerous votive offerings and pain
ings,—models of ships, whose originals had bee
preserved from wreck by the assistance of th
Virgin ; pictures of persons dying and console
by angels ; of a man delivered from some in
minent danger, while the Saviour or saint ap
pears in a cloud above.

Some of the Catalans were kneeling there, an
perhaps making some vow. These Catalans
whom I have mentioned before, are a distinc
and peculiar race. They are the fishermen o
Marseilles. They live on the outside of the
walls upon the coast, in a long collection o
houses enclosed within a gate, and entirely separated from the other inhabitants of the neigh.

bourhood. They have courts of their own, in which one of the most respectable of the patrons or master fishermen presides, and is called *Prud'-homme* (an abridgement of *Prudent homme.*) This court is only, however, for the trial of disputes among themselves, and its decision is announced in these simple words by the *Prud' homme*, " *La ley vous coundano.*" It is usually upon Sunday afternoon, and a fee of two *sous* is paid by the plaintiff and defendant.

Coming out of the chapel, I stood gazing upon the various objects which there present themselves:—The harbour, the old black town, the graceful and fair modern city looking down with refined contempt and superciliousness upon her unpolished neighbour, the scorched smoking mountains in the distance shutting in the myriads of bastides, with their endless walls, and their scattered fig-trees, and closed shutters. Then spreading before me, the wide Mediterranean, with the Quarantine Islands, whose

anchored ships looked like some of those dark
and fatal vessels which used to convey devoted
victims to the monster, or the fire, while the
white and sparkling sails of those which contained no sin flitted along the horizon like
summer insects.

Upon the quays beneath, six or seven of the
Atlantæan porters of Marseilles were nodding
along with their huge burthen,—a vast trunk of
a tree. These men are peculiar to Provence, and
I never saw any who might compete with them,
except perhaps the Titan draymen of London.
Yet their nourishment is very slight,—a bunch
of grapes, some bread, and a little wine, being
sufficient to recruit the strength of their enormous limbs. As they bear along their load,
slung by ropes between them, divided in two
lines, each man lays his hand upon the shoulder
of him on the other side of the trunk, who places
his in the same manner. Then the wild cries
of the sailors as they were heaving the merchan-

ise from their vessels, echoed up to the rock, nd brought to my recollection the time when I ad heard them in the midst of tempest and the ark Biscay.

It was an animated varied scene. Stern ocks, white bastides, freshening gardens, a oble city, a crowded harbour, fishermen, sol- iers, priests, merchants, mingled together; hile as the noon came on, shouts of *pére, pére, utte caude, tutte caude,—poires, poires, toutes haudes,* proceeding from the true Provençale omen that were issuing out of the narrow efiles of the old town. And on the other side ie silent sea, waiting in deceitful and crouching illness for some of its destined prey: for iat smooth polished surface, that looked as if could bear the trusting foot, might ere long e broken into yawning abysses, and swallowing p whole navies.

The gradual approach of a storm is indeed n awful and mysterious sight. We behold the

effect produced by an unseen agent, we see innocence and tranquillity transformed into de-
structiveness and fury. Let the materialist,
the man who says he has no soul, but that
his thoughts, words, and deeds, are the mere
effects of mechanism and matter,—let him stand
upon the lofty mountain, and from thence let
him look out upon the world of waters; let him
see them sleeping quietly and placidly, harmless
and beautiful: then let him behold them rearing
themselves in dark and gloomy ridges, whitening and roaring, crashing together, and leaping
up against the cliff upon which he stands, and
scattering their foam and spray along the sandy
shore. Then ask him what it is that has caused
this mighty change; if it be merely the opera-
tion of chance and necessary change from one
extreme to the other, or if there be not " a wind
that bloweth where it listeth, though no man
can tell whence it cometh and whither it goeth :"
and if he acknowledge that there is, but looks

upon the scene before him as a simile *to*, and not an illustration of himself, then leave him to enjoy his mechanism as he may.

12th.—I have this morning received a letter from my friend, dated from Turin. He seems in high spirits, and speaks in raptures of his journey. " I set out from Chambery," he says, " on foot. I had gone thither in the public carriage; but as you know that my funds require management and that I prefer at all times walking, I determined upon going as far as this city in that way. I had a delicious ramble along the rich winding valley of La Maurienne, living chiefly upon milk which I procured in the cabins of the poor *goitreuse* Savoyards. Shut up within their narrow defiles, with no noise or tumult to disturb them, but the rushing of the Arque or mountain torrent which rolls through the valley, or the blowing of the wintry wind, they pass their lives in innocence and ignorance, with no riches but their goats, and no ambition but that of having the best milk.

" You will be induced to think from my passionate description of this mountain life, that my date is a false one, and that I am imitating your friend the hermit. But I am afraid that though in speculation I may admire the simple life of these Savoyards, from comparing it with my own restless and wandering one, yet were I to practise it, I much fear that its charms would vanish away; for I am just as delighted with this gay bustling city, as I was with the valley of La Maurienne.

" I arrived here.four days ago. I crossed the Mount Cenis on foot, but ascended by a wild rugged path with a muleteer, who was driving his mules to Susa. By the by, I must tell you that I was wonderfully amused to find a little English woman in the Inn at Lanslebourg, which is a village at the base of the Alps, where formerly asses were employed to transport the baggage of travellers, and thence it derives its name *Les ordes anes le Bourg.* The English woman is married to the master of the inn, and is just as active and landlady like, as if she were upon the Great North Road.

To return to my muleteer.——Giving his mules two or three smart lashes with his whip, they scrambled and stumbled up the stony rock like goats, while we followed them a little more cautiously. The man told me that he had been employed once to *ramasser* Bonaparte; and I asked him how he felt while they were gliding down. "I felt," said the man, "as if I were the *plus grand homme de mon pays, car j'avais le plus grand homme du monde sous ma garde.*" And indeed, it was certain, that any false manœuvre of this *ramasseur* might have precipitated the second Hannibal from his Alpine chariot, and preserved the world from fields of carnage, and himself from future moral ruin, and headlong descent. The road across the mountain which he made, is a glorious memorial of him. Indeed, all who travel on the Continent may exclaim with the Scotch inscription,

" Had you seen these roads before they were made,
  You'd lift up your hands, and bless General Wade,"
—or Buonaparte. For he has done wonders; the Alps, the Mountains of Tarar, in the Lyonnois, the beautiful road along the banks of the Rhine, and the unfinished and magnificent one over the Genoese Alps, from Nice to Genoa, all attest his vast and enterprising genius. But the particular work which I have just passed is perfect. Avalanches checked, precipices avoided or guarded against, a road as wide as any moderate-sized one in the plains beneath, regulations established by him, and kept up by the King of Sardinia, for its safety and that of the traveller, —such are the benefits which he who crosses the Mont Cenis must acknowledge. There are about twenty-five huts in different stations along

the road, which may afford refuge during the snow-storms. There is likewise a company of Cantonniers, commanded by an officer, who are constantly employed during the winter in clearing away the snow ; and strong tall posts are fixed at intervals all along, to mark the direction of the road, when concealed by a recent heavy fall of it. There are two small inns upon the summit : I dined at one of them, upon some of the trout of the lake, which was still frozen over. The road proceeds along the *plateau* of the mountain. At the hamlet of La Grande Croix, it begins to descend, and winds down sometimes upon the brink of the most terrific precipices, which are furnished with a stone parapet.

Just before entering Piedmont, one catches the first glimpse of Italy. To the left of the descent, the Valley of the Cenise is seen as far as Susa. I could have shouted with the Trojans, " *Italia, Italia !*" When I first looked to-

wards the distant Paradise, the afternoon was
still and warm ; and as I slowly dropped down
the mountain, I indulged in those luxurious
visions. I was then, at last, upon the point of
setting my feet upon the birth-place of Cato, of
Cicero, of Camillus ; and I exclaimed, as the
plain opened itself upon me, and I could see as
far as the *Superga*, which stands above the Po.

" Salve, magna parens frugum, Saturnia tellus,
Magna virûm :"

I reached Susa about five in the evening ; and
after visiting a Roman arch, which is in excellent preservation, strolled into the church : it
was the eve of Good Friday, and I entered just
as a procession which had been making the tour
of the town had returned. The Virgin, whom
they had been carrying about, was in grand costume, all flowers and beads and gilding, as fine
as a tragedy queen at a fair ; but there was
something intoxicating in the warm glow of the
sky which fell upon the group within the church.

as with their veils and hoods thrown back they chaunted some hymn, and glanced occasionally with their black Italian eyes upon the English strangers, of whom there were several looking upon the ceremony besides myself.

There are, perhaps, no two contrasts so strong as those which France and England present, the moment one has passed the sea, and Savoy and Italy, when the traveller descends into the valley of Susa. The two barriers which are the causes of this striking difference, are alike seldom passed by the peasantry ; there is no gradual mingling and blending of the manners of one country into another; all is abrupt and isolated. This sudden change more particularly struck me while I was within the church of Susa, and afterwards, as I paced along its streets, surrounded by painted walls, rich Madonna faces, green and flowery gardens, a softer dialect, a more graceful air ; in fine, the characteristics of the land of poets and painters. But a few hours before, I was among rude wooden huts, squalid people, bleak mountains overhanging dark and barren defiles, a French *patois*, coarse food, and all the marks of a poor and unfavoured country.

" I dined in the evening at the *table d'hôte* of the Inn, where I found the other English travellers. Some of them had arrived in their travelling carriages, and some by the diligence. Diligence! I think I hear you exclaim,—diligence among the Alps! Even so, my friend ; and the old blunder of the schoolboy could now be verified, for Hannibal certainly might pass these *montes præruptæ summâ diligentiâ*—upon the top of the diligence.

Our dinner was amusing, as it afforded me an opportunity of observing the different characters present. The real *Milords*, who had condescended to dine at the same table with the stage-coach people, sat retired apart, and whispered together in the most *gentlemanly* manner. They had their *Cotty Rotty*, as one of them called it, that is *Côte Rotie*, and looked round with as much contempt upon us and our inferior wines, as a man does at a tavern when he is beginning his dinner with salmon, while his neighbour evidently intends to allow himself nothing but a beef-steak.

" There was near me, however, one Englishman who had come in the diligence, and who assumed that sort of air which a person who considers himself a considerable traveller often does. He shook his head at the soup, slowly savoured the wine, earnestly recommended some pigeons à *la Crapaudine* which stood near him, and instituted a comparison between the long pipes of bread which one finds upon entering Piedmont, and the *petits pains au lait* of Paris. He then commenced a political argument with a dark whiskered Frenchman opposite to him, and, intending to pay the compliment of a citizen of the world to his opponent, he said, " *Mais tout corps faut doute moins dire que la Angleterre et la France sont les deux plus grandes Potences de la Europe.*" There was a general tendency to break out into a roar of laughter among those who heard him; and the explosion took place with stunning violence, when the Frenchman gravely replied, that "*En vérité, la potence d'Angleterre allait toujours bien, mais celle de France* was a little less flourishing since the unhappy days of the guillotine." The poor discomfited Englishman, who had by this time discovered his mistake, said no more, and took the first opportunity of retreating from the room.

"I passed the night at the Inn, during which I heard some of the *tourmentes* rumbling and rushing in the mountains above; and the next morning continued my route towards Turin, passing by two or three villages with ruined chateaux above them, and Rivoli, the castle of which once served as a prison of an abdicated king of Sardinia, Amadeus the Second, who was confined there by his son. Abdication seems to

ıe very fashionable among these princes ; I think
iistory mentions three or four who have descended
rom their thrones, besides the late instance.

" From Rivoli the road runs in a straight
ine to Turin, the baby capital of the Sardinian
lominions. I entered it as a procession was
passing along ; and besides the priests, and tapers, and canopies, there was a train of young
girls with long white veils, who were educated
by the Government, each carrying a white wax
cierge, and looking like fair nuns performing
their noviciate.

" I was too much fatigued to roam about the
city that evening, so I remained at the *Buona
Fama*, as the Italians call the *Bonne Femme*, one
of the inns of Turin.

" The next morning I strolled about, and
from the Piazza del Castello enjoyed the singular appearance which the rectangular correctness
of the streets presents, and the tall bastions of Italy, standing sternly at the end of the long view

from the gate of the Doria. There is another noble *place* here, that of Saint Charles, and a beautiful chapel dedicated to Saint Seraine. The theatre is one of the finest in Italy : I believe indeed, it is the third ; *La Scala* at Milan and that of *San Carlos* at Naples ranking the two first. It is unfortunately closed ; but I have been at a little theatre called *del Principe Carignano* where some of Goldoni's pieces are very well represented. There is another house where Operas are now performed—I was there last night. We had an *Opera Buffa* called *La Foresta di Hermanstad*, the music of which is by Coccia. It was prettily done, and seemed well attended ; but the Court is at Genoa now.

"I have been likewise to see the Church of the Superga, which stands upon a high hill on the right bank of the river Po. There is a light elegant bridge over this river, built by the indefatigable Buonaparte. The Superga is a very beautiful structure, and contains the tombs

N 5

of the Kings of Piedmont, who seem to wish to take heaven by storm, so high are their bones laid.   The man who attended me through them pointed out to my attention the chamber of the family Carignano; and this made me say,— ' But where is the Prince now ?' as you will recollect that he was implicated in the late Revolution.   ' *Si dice*,' replied the man, '*che fa viaggio per la sua sanità*;' and I thought the answer could not have been more appropriate to his situation, if my guide had intended to say something sharp.   The Prince is, I believe, endeavouring to restore his *health* at Florence; he is married to a daughter of the Grand Duke of Tuscany.

" I was much pleased with the Superga, but infinitely more so with the beautiful prospect from its terrace : the rich plains of Lombardy, with the *Fluviorum Rex Eridanus*, and the Alpine Doria, the green-wooded banks, the city with its cupolas and surrounding chateaux, and

the white villages scattered away even to the
Alps, which spread themselves along the boun-
dary of the plain like giant sentinels suddenly
petrified into snow and stillness. And, indeed,
they have but ill kept the watch which Nature
would seem to have assigned to them. First,
Hannibal passed them, while the avalanches
and *tourmentes* spared the bold Africans, of
whom it might have been said, as of the fallen
Angels, that they

" Raised impious war in Heaven, and battle proud
    With vain attempt."

But the attempt was not always to be vain;
Transalpine armies, one after the other, have
scaled the once impregnable fortress; and the
very church upon whose terrace I stood, had
been erected to commemorate a defeat which
the French or Gauls had sustained under the
walls of Turin. Poor Italy!—nothing now remains of thy boasted Republics, but

" Towns unmann'd and lords without a slave !"

Emigration, oppression, and a foreign yoke, have
defaced and degraded " this most replenished
sweet work of Nature" into petty principali-
ies and subject provinces.   But, concludes my
friend, I fear you will find my letter already too
long,—so, till my next, adieu."

CHAPTER XXV.

APRIL 30th.— I made a little excursion as far as Aix the other day. This city lies at about fifteen miles distance from Marseilles, in the centre of a valley, through which a small river called the Arc runs. I was curious to visit it, as its name has been often mentioned in the accounts of the Troubadours which I have occasionally met with.

I arrived there about the middle of the day; and, having taken a slight dinner, rambled over the town. The first object which strikes the stranger, is the magnificent entrance into the city. A rich screen of iron railing and gateway separates the *Orbitelle*, or *Cours*, which the traveller first meets with as he comes from the North, from the high road. Upon the outside

of this gateway, at some distance, and in a conspicuous position, is placed a tall crucifix, with an
image of the suffering Saviour nailed upon it,
and an inscription is placed beneath it, comme-
morating the pious care of the missionaries under
whose superintendence it was erected. The
more devout and humble peasants, as they pass
it on their way to the market, uncover themselves,
and, making the usual sign of the cross, murmur
a short prayer.

Passing through the railing, four avenues of
the *Orbitelle* present themselves. This noble
promenade derives its name from the following
circumstance :——A Cardinal Mazarin, brother to
the cardinal of that name, was archbishop of the
diocese of Aix, at a time when the houses which
line each side of the *Cours* were being con-
structed. One day, as he was going in solemn
procession, attended by his priests, to lay the
first stone of one of the gates of the city, near the
new buildings, the sudden springing of a mine

burst open and rent the rocks which were near the holy train, who fled probably in superstitious alarm. The populace, who, however bigoted and subservient they may be to their spiritual guides, never let any occasion of sarcasm and merriment pass unnoticed, immediately exclaimed, that the archbishop's enterprise had failed like his father's at Orbitello, a town in Italy, the siege of which he had been obliged to raise. Since that period, its present name of *Orbitelle* has always been attached to it and the surrounding quarter.

This anecdote brings to my recollection another of the same description, which is related to have happened at Marseilles. During the siege of that city by the Constable of Bourbon, who, like Coriolanus, commanded the armies of the enemies of his country, the Imperial troops were encouraged in their tedious blockade by Bourbon, who openly boasted that the Consuls of the city would presently bring him the keys. No.

hing of the sort, however, seemed likely to happen; and the Constable's promises became the
subject of ridicule in the camp. Pescara, who
commanded jointly with Bourbon, was engaged
in examining the works of the besieged place at
a distance, when a battery, which he had not
observed, opened its fire upon him and his at-
endants, and killed one of them. Upon which
the Spanish general ordered some of his train
to collect two of the balls, and, having covered
them with a cloth, to present them with great
solemnity and state to Bourbon, informing him
at the same time, that they were the keys of
Marseilles, which the Consuls humbly desired
his acceptance of. The siege was shortly after
raised.

The *Cours* is planted with four rows of noble
elms, and lined on either side by some of the
finest houses in the town. About the centre of
it stands a fountain of warm water, which rises
probably from the same source as that which

supplies the baths, which were formerly very famous, and, having been particularly attended to
by a Roman governor called Sextius, gave the
name of Aquæ Sextiæ to the city, which is now
modernised into Aix. Some years ago, the proprietor of some ground near this fountain sunk
a well in his soil, which produced cold water,
but the warm spring immediately failed. The
inhabitants, to whom its waters were a great
convenience and even saving, were much annoyed
by this circumstance, and agreed to pay this
inconvenient neighbour a sum of money to fil
up his well ; and, upon this being done, the good
Bourgeoises of Aix had the pleasure of seeing
their buckets full of smoking water again.

The *Orbitelle* is the great mall of fashion,
several *cafés* are among the houses at the side,
from whence on a Sunday evening pour out
troops of idlers. But, as a person remarked to
me, whom I happened to speak to, I should have
seen this promenade before the Revolution, when

Aix had its own parliament. More than a hundred splendid equipages used to parade slowly along the stately avenues, filled with the descendants of all the most illustrious families of Provence. Madame de Grignon, too, was among them, the immortalized daughter of Madame de Sévigné; for Monsieur de Grignon was governor of Provence. But Aix suffered like the rest of the fair cities of France in the great moral earthquake; her parliament disappeared, her nobles and princes perished upon the scaffold or wandered over foreign countries, her monuments of poetry and beauty were defaced and destroyed, and nothing now graces the *Orbitelle* on the *Dimanche*, but a few old Counts on foot, the rumbling chest of a coach of some ancient dame who has contrived to retain a part of her demesnes, a number of English characters *en pension* in the families of the *noblesse*, and a host of students belonging to the University of Law, there being one there.

I happened to have arrived on Sunday, and

continuing my walk through the town, I entered
the cathedral church of St. Sauveur. Mass was
being performed, and the Archbishop sat en-
throned in archiepiscopal state at the upper end
of the choir, on the right end of the altar. At
certain periods of the service he rose and made
some low bows to the altar, upon which the
priests bowed, and the little assistants bowed,
and the Pontiff's footmen who stood close to the
throne bowed, and the tall moustachioed *hallebarde* man, and the people;—in short, it was
something like the Court of the Chinese Emperor Ching. Now, in Paris, this mummery
would have excited ridicule among the great
mass of the congregation; for it occurred so
often that it became quite ludicrous to me, who
am generally disposed to look upon all the ceremonies of religion with respect. But among
the Provençals the spirit of devotion is much
stronger than that of the northern parts of
France ; their Saints are more numerous, their

fêtes more splendid, and they have, in spite of the purifying fan of the Revolution, retained or recovered all their ancient veneration for reliques and holy things. Indeed it is in general found that the people of warm countries are more wedded to the mysterious superstitions of their religion than those of northern regions.

All religion is intimately connected with poetry, at least in its origin. The first prayers were songs either of thanksgiving or lamentation; and the glowing imagination, and " Souls made of fire of the Children of the Sun," prompted them to pour out their penitence or joy in all the imagery and imaginative language of the East. Now, since the Muses were cradled and nourished in Greece, and since from thence is derived the system of Pagan Mythology, which abounds in Gods, and temples, and hymns, and all the pomp of sacrifice; and as the people of Provence are descended from Greeks, and were the first poets of France,—it is not surprising to

find among them so many legends which partake
partly of a Pagan and partly of a Christian character, and which assist in keeping alive the
flame which their own burning skies never cease
to feed. All their passions, all their feelings, are
stronger than those of colder people; the very
simple circumstance of taking off the hat and
repeating a prayer as the southern peasant
passes the Christ crucified, is a striking instance
of this imaginative devotion.

The church of St. Sauveur is, like all other
cathedrals, cold, solemn, and abounding in
traces of the Republican hostility, during the
reign of reason, to statues and tombs. But
much of this devastation is gradually disappear-
ing under the pious care of the Archbishop, and
the attention of some of the respectable inhabitants of Aix. It contains a monument which
has lately been put up to Peiresc, who was born
in Provence and died at Aix. He was a liberal
and enlightened patron of the arts, and his ca

binet of medals was reckoned one of the finest in the world. Peiresc was buried in the church of the Dominicans; but the unsparing hand of anarchy overthrew the white marble tomb which had been erected above his ashes. At his death the Academy of Rome caused a funeral oration in his praise to be pronounced, and his memory will be ever honoured by the antiquary.

As I was returning from the cathedral, the Archbishop passed me in his carriage. He was going out to visit a college which he has established near the city, or at least which he principally supports with his revenues. These amount to about two thousand pounds; but little for so high an ecclesiastical dignity, when compared with the incomes of the English bishops. But indeed the French clergy of the present day are by no means rich: the days when bishops were courtiers, and paraded through the streets of Paris in splendid equipages, are past; both they and the *Curés* are now lessened, as well in importance as in wealth, and are obliged to live cautiously and correctly, in order to stem the general tendency in France to despise them.

I passed the night at a small inn kept by an old woman, who, seeing that I was in bad health, treated me as if I were her own son. I had my fire of olive-wood, as the evening had become cold; an old book written by Nostradamus, which she brought forth from a dark chest; and even some tea. My old hostess had lived through the Revolution; and mournfully did she talk of the former splendour of Aix. She showed me two dragon-footed chairs covered with rich faded tapestry, that she said had formerly belonged to Monsieur de la Tour du Pin, one of the noblest families of Dauphiné. "I remember well," said she, "that the poor lady was concealed in my house after the destruction of the chateau; and when the Marseillois used to come in and drink death to all the aristocrats, I used to tremble so; for if they had known there was one in the house, they would have hanged us all up by the lamp among the trees."—" And was she preserved?" said I.

"O yes, God be praised!" replied the old woman; " she disguised herself as a servant, and, as her person was not known at Marseilles, she went and lived there; and some time after, when matters came round again, she recovered some of her property, and now resides in Paris."

I began to be rather tired, however, of the garrulous old lady, which she, no doubt, perceived, for she soon left me to myself. I turned over the pages of the book, which contained some curious old prophecies. Nostradamus was a great favourite with Henry the Second, who sent for him to Paris, and gave him two hundred golden crowns for his pay. Stephen Jodelle, a contemporary poet with the prophet, made this satirical distich upon him,—

Nostra damus, cum falsa damus, nam fallere nostrum est,
Et cum falsa damus, nil nisi nostra damus.

Nostradamus was born at Salon in Provence, and buried there. He was supposed to have predicted the fate of *Cinq Mars*, in the reign of Louis the Thirteenth, in these lines:—

" Quand robe rouge aura passé fenêtre
    Fort malingreux, mais non pas de la tousse,
    A quarante onces on tranchera la tête,
    Et de trop près le suivra de Thou."

The Cardinal Richelieu was, at the time of the conspiracy of Cinq Mars, ill, and carried in a litter in the King's suite : his bed was introduced into the hotels through the window. Forty ounces make five marks, or Cinq Mars, and De Thou was beheaded shortly after Cinq Mars. This De Thou was the son of the famous President De Thou ; and it was said that the true reason which made Cardinal Richelieu bring him to the block, was not because he had concealed Cinq Mars's conspiracy, which had been com-

municated to him, but because the president, in
his account of the plot of Amboise, speaking of
a great uncle of the Cardinal, had thus charac-
terized him. "*Antonius Plessiacus Richelius,
vulgò dictus monachus, quòd eam vitam pro-
fessus fuisset, dein voto ejurato, omni licentiæ
ac libidinis genere contaminâsset.*" And that
Richelieu, like the wolf in the fable, made the
son suffer for the father's offence.

I retired to bed early, and was amused to observe a black crucifix, with a little *benetier* for
holy water, fastened above my pillow against
the wall. The next morning, after breakfasting
upon coffee and some of the nice bread of Aix,
I strolled toward the Public Library.

I was anxious to discover something about the
Troubadours ; and, upon entering, proceeded
up to the Librarian, and asked him some questions respecting their poetry. He seemed a
great enthusiast in all which related to the old
Provençal language ; and showed me a poem

which he had written in praise of silk-worms, or *Magnans,* as they are called in Provençal. These precious insects appear to have furnished frequent occasion to the poets of these warm provinces for description: among others, Anto nios Alena, a native of the country round Tou lon, has composed a sort of Georgic upon them, giving directions how they should be treated, and relating their manners, as Virgil did those of the bees.

The Librarian shewed me a collection of old Troubadour songs, and annals relating to the courts of love, which used to be held at Aix. The courts were presided by the Princess or Countess of Provence; and among others, Beatrix of Savoy, the wife of Raymond Beren ger the Fifth, the last Count of Provence, is particularly handed down as a patroness of song, and a poetess. They were attended by all the brightest and noblest ladies of the principality, who sat as judges upon all disputes concerning

o 2

love and beauty :——as, for instance, if two knights were at issue respecting the comparative brightness of the eyes or richness of the complexion of their respective mistresses, they both came into the court, and in alternate verses, as the shepherds of Virgil, contended each for the superiority. The decisions of the fair and learned judges were always given according to the common law of gallantry and chivalry ; and they have been *reported*, in a poem entitled *Les Arrêts d'Amour*, by Martial of Paris, or Auvergne, as he is indifferently styled. In examining the collection which the Librarian had put into my hand, I met with the following curious *suit at love.*

Savari de Manleau, a noble of Poitou, loved a fair dame of Gascony. Savari imagined that the lady was as fond as himself ; but the fraudulent Viscountess had wilfully and maliciously inspired hopes into two other Knights ; and upon one occasion, when they were all three present

before her, coquetted with every one. They
as the report states, did not perceive this, til
upon quitting the coquette's apartment, two o
them boasted of the kind words and glance
which had just been bestowed upon them. Th
third, (Savari,) astonished and displeased at thi
unexpected language, proceeded directly to con
sult his two professional men, Hugo of Bache
leri and Gaucelin Faidet; and laid before then
his case in the following manner :

> Gaucelin très jocz enamoratz
> Partix à vos et à d'Ugo
> E quascus prendetz lo plus bo,
> E laysatz me qual que us vulhatz ;
> Qu' una dame a très preyadors,
> E destrenh la tan los amors.
> Que, quan tug trey li son denan,
> A quascun fai d'amor sembian ;
> L'un es grand amorosamen,
> L' autr' estrenh la man doussamen.
> Al tertz caussing à 'l pe rizen,
> Diguatz al qual pus aissies
> Fai maior amor de tug tres.

Which may be thus translated :

Gaucelin, three youths whom love doth grieve,
Of learned Hugo ask, and thee,
To name the fairest of the three,
And as ye will the others leave.
We all to one bright Princess kneel,
But she her choice doth so conceal—
Smiling on all—accepting none—
She seems to love us every one.
The first's a Saint, and talks of masses ;
The next her hand so softly presses ;
The third with sonnets her addresses.
Now, gentle Gaucelin, prythee say,
Whose skill should bear the prize away ?

The two poets, Hugo and Gaucelin, accordingly, having been thus retained, conducted the case with great ingenuity ; but I do not find judgment thereon reported. It was perhaps delayed, and leave given to *imparl*.

These singular contests were called *tourney-amens*, and probably gave their name to the chivalrous onset in the list. For the Provençal

Troubadours were certainly the founders of that spirit of romance and enterprising devotion to the fair sex, which was the great characteristic of the Knightly Creed; or rather, they first spread its influence through Europe. For it appears that we derive that species of poetry and imagination from the Arabs.

It would seem indeed that the two great fountains of song sprang up in the North and the East. The ancient Scandinavians, as they quaffed their dark juice of the pine in the Hall of Skulls, chanted the praises of the warlike God Odin; and their descendants, among whom we may reckon the English, have retained the peculiar tone of composition which distinguished the northern nations;—for it was not till considerably after the Norman conquest, that our poets became acquainted with the lyrical and gentle style of the Troubadours, who had been first introduced into Provence upon the marriage of Raymond Berenger, Count of Barcelona

with Douce, one of the two daughters of Gilli-
bert, Count of Provence, who died without
male heirs. Raymond introduced into his new
dominions the arts and sciences which the Arabs
had spread through Spain ; and the warm skies
and fiery blood of Provence easily adopted the
glowing language and imagery of the East. But
the compositions of the new minstrels were
chiefly amatory ; they had neither taste nor inclination for epic poetry : and while, in England
and the northern nations, the monks, amidst the
gloom of the cloister, wrote annals in verse,
while the early English poets sung the praises of
rude kings and their banquets, who " women ne
kept of" the Troubadour thought only of love
and ladies, and celebrated the feats of gallantry
which he himself had performed, and the yield-
ing tenderness of some bright beauty. But
Chaucer first, by translating much of the old
French poetry into English, introduced, or en-
grafted upon the northern plant, the sweet blos-

som of the east ; and thus is it that while
France has continued, as it were, to feel the influence of her ancient prevailing taste for light
and amatory song, that being her chief poetic
excellence, England has produced poems both
epic and lyric, both stately and tender, which
place her upon the highest pinnacle of Parnassus.

I have been unexpectedly led into these
thoughts concerning the origin of modern poetry
which have often presented themselves to my
mind, but which I had never before followed up
Let me return to what my memory may yet retain of Aix.

When I quitted the library, I walked out be
yond the city into the country. There was a
mist about the sun, and its heat was thus soft
ened. The olive-trees were putting out their
leaves but slowly, for they were much injured
last winter ; numbers of them were killed by a
frost severer than had been known to have visited
these countries for years.

As I strolled along, a peasant passed me driving an ass, and he frequently called out " *Anda, Ambron, anda* ;" and thus brought to my recollection the defeat which the Ambrónes and Cimbri are said to have sustained in the neighbourhood of Aix.   They were routed by Marius, and so great was the slaughter, that the district where the battle is supposed to have taken place is still called *Maloosse*, which is probably a corruption of *Mala ossa*.   Upon the summit of a lofty mountain, which looks down upon Aix, was erected a temple, that, in its object like the Superga, mentioned in my friend's letter, was destined to commemorate this remarkable victory.   It was the Temple of Victory, and was seen at a great distance at sea by mariners, who, the moment they espied it, saluted it with shouts of " *Lou deloubrou de la victoire !*" *deloubrou*, in the old language of Provence, meaning temple.

The country about Aix is rich and agreeable, and there are a few really pretty *châteaux*, not bar-

ren and bare as those about Marseilles, but sur
rounded by verdure, and frequently water. Th
river Arc, which runs through the valley, and i
wild and overhung by steep rugged banks, flow
into the Durance ; which latter river is at a ver
inconsiderable distance from the city. From th
heights around, Aix presents a very interestin
appearance: the tower of the church of Saint Joh
is a beautiful object, shooting up into the calm
clear sky, dark and Gothic, above the white
streets and the trees of the *Cours*.

René, who was Count of Provence, in th
fifteenth century, resided at Aix; and institute
that extraordinary procession which takes plac
upon the *Fête Dieu*, or rather *la fête du Sain*
Sacrement. This *fête* was originally established
on account of the following circumstance. In the
thirteenth century, about 1208, a pious sister
of the Order of Saint John of Mount Cornillon,
at Liege, beheld, in a dream, the moon with a
large chasm, or rent in it, during two successive

years ; and much did it perplex her.   At last, however, she discovered that the Holy Sacrament was typified by the moon, and that the rent signified the sad deficiency in the ritua which prescribed no express festival for its public celebration.   She however, as we are told kept this secret for twenty years, and never dis covered it till she was sure that her superior pe netration could not impede her advancement namely, till she became Lady Prioress of th Convent of Mount Cornillon.   Then indeed sh made it known ; and a Bishop of Liege, in 124€ established a *fête du Saint Sacrement,* whic was not, however, introduced into France ti 1318.

The procession to which I allude was esta blished by René, as a religious and instructiv lesson to the people.   It consists of a long trai of heathen Gods and Goddesses, and the Dev is also introduced, who parade through th streets upon the evening preceding the *fête,* bu

who are all supposed to be put to flight by the
approach of the following holy day ; upon which
the same individuals appear again in solemn show,
but dressed as Saints and Apostles. This ceremony bears some resemblance to the *Fête des
Anes*, which was established at Sens, and to
those which took place in Scotland even, during
the dominion of the Roman Catholic religion
They were first invented by the Priests, to dis-
countenance theatrical shows and amusements
and it is singular that these very ceremonies o
their own establishment should have tended
eventually to throw additional ridicule and con
tempt upon themselves,—since they were fre
quently the vehicles of Presbyterian triumph
And as to the hymns which were sung at them
their music was afterwards applied to songs of
very different description. But it is curious tha
during the wars of the League, the amorou
adventures of the Duke d'Epernon were chant
ed in the cathedral church of Saint Sauveur a

Aix ; and during that period, and considerabl
after, subjects of the most profane kind wer
introduced into sermons. One of the most sin
gular discourses which I ever remember to hav
heard or read is the following, in which a Pries
announced the death of Pic de la Mirandola :

" Io vi voglio rivelare un secreto, che a qu
non ho voluto dirlo, perche non ho avuto tant
certezza come ho avuto da diece hora in quà
Ciascuno di voi credo che conoscete il Cont
Giovanni- della Mirandola, che stava quì i
Fiorenze, ed è morto pochi giorni sono. Dicov
che l' anima sua per le orazioni dei Frati, ed anch
per alcune sue buone opere che fece in quest
vita e per altre_cagioni, è nel purgatorio. Orat
pro eo !"

CHAPTER XXVI.

Upon my return from Aix, I found a lette
awaiting me from my friend the pedestrian
dated Venice. After enquiring kindly after m
health and spirits, he thus continues :—

I think that the old proverb of " *Fede Napo*
e poi mori" might be just as correctly applie
to the city from whence I now write : there i
no other like it; and, when others hurry to Rome
Naples, and Florence, as the only objects of in
terest, they neglect the most singular and beau
tiful city which Italy contains. Let me give yo
a short account of my journey hither.

I quitted Turin about a week ago with on
of the *Vetturini* : our party consisted of a
officer of the royal regiment of Savoy, who wa

going to Novara; a ditto of the Austrian *Sani*
tary troops stationed at Vercelli; a youn
Frenchman; a ditto Frenchwoman, and m
humble self. The Savoyard and the Austria
curled their whiskers at each other frequently
and seemed very unlikely to form any hol
alliance together. But I was a good deal sur
prised when I heard the former speak. He ha
a strong English accent, and made as many tru
English blunders as if he had been born on th
other side of the French Sleeve.

I took an opportunity, some time after, o
hinting to him that I thought he had been i
England; and added, that I was a native of tha
country, as my good French had made ever
body take me for a Frenchman. Upon whic
he instantly shook me heartily by the hand, an
exclaimed in good English, " Why we are hal
countrymen; for I was carried when a child b
my father, who emigrated, into England, and
served as a midshipman in the English navy.'

We became very good friends consequently
and he was of some use to me upon the road.

Another singular occurrence took place. W
had stopped at Cigliano, a small town, about si
posts from Turin, to dinner ; another carriag
like our own had likewise arrived, and the tw
parties met in the same room. We sat down t
our *risotto*, a thick soup of rice, for which
have the greatest veneration, on account of it
connexion, as they say, with one of the mos
beautiful airs Rossini ever composed. Whil
we were discussing this, an old blind man wa
led in, who immediately struck up a very cu
rious song, in which all the peculiarities of dia
lect and habits of the different people of Ital
were characterised. It finished with a descrip
tion of the Frenchman, who has endeavoured t
establish himself in every country, in thes
words :

> " Salta fori un Franchese,
> Ben conûto in queste contese,

Qu' un Tarquino più amoroso,

E qu' un Orlando più furioso ;

E la puo cantar dolcemente—

E qui gridà terribilmente,

Halte la Monsieur ! que faites vous ?

Restez tranquille ou je vous coupe le cou."

There was of course a general laugh at this conclusion ; and the young Frenchman, who was of our party, seemed rather nettled ; but one of the travellers in the other carriage, who, it appeared, was also a Frenchman, called out to the old blind man to get out of the room, or else to sing something against the English *hulks. les pontons,* as he called them. " *Mon Dieu !*" vociferated our Frenchman, "I ought to know that voice ;" and jumping up, he hastened towards his compatriot. Their recognition was then complete and mutual ; but a long time had elapsed since they had met, for they had never seen one another since they had both been prisoners together at Chatham on board the detested *pontons,* a period of seven years. They had both

served on board privateers, and had been take
prisoners about the same time.

After dinner we continued our route throug
the rich plains of Piedmont, and slept at Vercell
or, as the French call it, Verceil, and whicl
place an Englishman once mistook for Versaille
near Paris.   In the treasury of the cathedra
of this town is a manuscript of the fourth cen
tury, which contains the Gospel of Saint Marl
in Latin ; and some zealots pretend that it i
written with the Apostle's own hand.

The next morning we proceeded through wid
fields of rice to Novara.   This is an old towr
with a few fine palaces, and is remarkable a
having been the place where the Swiss defeate
Louis de la Tremouille, who commanded th
French army in the time of Louis the Twelfth
and drove him out of the Milanese.   It is als
since known, as having witnessed the breakin
up of the Piedmontese revolution, an engage
ment having taken place beneath its walls, be

tween the Austrian troops and those of the new constitutionalists, which was a second *journée des Eperons.*

We arrived at Milan on Sunday evening, and the streets were all filled with loungers. The graceful tuft of hair, winding about the bright pin which the Lombard female peasants wear, now gave way to the black hoods of the city dames, which could not, however, conceal the bright flashing of their eyes. The Frenchman, with whom I had had some conversation, invited me to accompany him to his family, who lived in the city; which invitation I accepted. I dined with them; they were civil, decent people, and were engaged in the silk trade; my young acquaintance acting as their *Commis Voyageur.*

The next morning I received the following note from the Police.

" I. R. Direzione Generale della Milano.

" S'interessa la compiacenza del Signor———, Gentiluomo, a voler recarsi a questa I. R.

Direzione nella contrada di S. Margherita
dirigendosi al sotto scritto, in quell' ora d'uffici
che gli tornerà piu a grado, nel giorno di doman
all mezzo giorno.

MORELLI."

I was rather alarmed at this summons, as
had heard strange stories about the Austria
Police. But my acquaintance told me that h
knew Signor Morelli very well ; and that, if
had any difficulty about my passport, he coul
assist me ; which, in fact, he afterwards did.

You who have read much will not expect me t
enter into a long account of this city, its churche
and promenades. You have, of course, ofte
heard of its wondrous cathedral ; that marbl
mountain, as it has been called, which had re
mained for a long time in an unfinished state
but which Buonaparte, that indefatigable builde
up and destroyer, caused to be completed.

I have neither time to detail, nor would yo
perhaps have inclination to listen to, the variou
circumstances which occurred to me till I ar

rived here. I passed in safety the robber-haunted shores of the Lake Dezenzano, which was quite calm and bright, and prevented my exclaiming in due form and ceremony :—-

" Fluctibus et fremitu adsurgens Benace marino."

I had heard accounts of numerous assassinations and robberies having been committed upon these shores; and I confess that, as the evening drew on, I was not quite sure whether we might not suddenly hear the terrible " *Fermate Cani di viaggiatori.*" But we reached the little town safely, I and my companion, who was a Brescian, and the only person with me, *for all* the others had remained at Milan; and this man had there joined me.

But let me hasten to Venice, which, after passing through Verona, " birthplace of sweet love," Vicenza with its beautiful covered portico or arcade two miles long, which leads up to the church of La Madonna del Monte, and Padua, which once contained Petrarch and

Galileo, and near which the former lies buried, I reached in impatient anticipation.

I embarked at night upon the Brenta. The moon shone brightly, and as we gently glided down, I sat upon the deck listening to the songs of the men who guided our boat, and gazing upon the white palaces of Palladio, which line the banks of the river, and form a magnificent avenue to the Queen of the Isles. As the morning broke, we gradually came out upon the Adriatic; and then I saw the fairy domes and spires of Venice glittering in the rising sun, and looking like those of some magic city which had risen from the waters and was peopled by Tritons and Nereids, who had deserted their coral grottoes for its floating halls. Sanna zarius has thus described Venice—

Viderat Adriacis Venetam Neptunus in undis
    Stare urbem, et toto dicere jura mari.
Nunc mihi Tarpeias quantumvis Jupiter arces,
    Objice, et illa tui mœnia Martis, ait:

Si pelago Tibrim præfers, urbem aspice utramque,
Illam homines dices, hanc posuisse deos.

The black mysterious-looking gondolas soon came hovering around us; and I hired one, that conveyed me up the grand canal to my hotel, which was the *Lion Blanc,* and whose windows commanded a view of that noble watery street. I only allowed myself time to engage my room, and change my dress, and I then hurried away to the Place Saint Mark. I was not disappointed, and that is saying much, for it has frequently been my fate to be so upon these occasions.

The first object which struck me was the mosque-looking church which gives its name to the place. Immediately before it stand the three lofty bronze staves, which were first placed there in 1505, when Loredano was Doge, and from which the ancient standard of the Republic used to wave upon days of state. Then, as I advanced, the famous horses, pawing and snuffing the air, next presented themselves. They had returned from their northern wanderings; but to whom and to what?—To the Austrians, and to an enslaved and degraded city.

So much has been already said concerning these steeds, that I should only be repeating uselessly what you have probably read, did I enter into their history. But let me give you a little anecdote which was told me at Paris, concerning Buonaparte. The Venetian horses had been placed upon the triumphal arch of *Le Carousel*, and a chariot was attached to them, in which it was intended to place a figure of the great Napoleon; and the general remark was, "*Le char l'attend.*"

The rich overloaded front of the church delayed me a few minutes, and I then entered it. It is as ornamented and glittering within as without; and its Mosaic pavement has long been famous. It is full of animals, and, among others, there are two cocks bearing a fox which are supposed to represent Charles th

Eighth and Louis the Twelfth of France, who dispossessed Ludovic Sforza of the Milanese, whose cunning is characterised by the fox.

I continued to ramble over the city, and visited some of the palaces and churches; in one, the name of which I have forgotten, lies buried the poet Aretino, so well known for his impiety, and whose epitaph is sufficiently characteristic :

Quì giace l'Aretin Poeta Tosco,
Che disse mal d'ognuu fuorche il Dio,
Scusandosi dicendo no'l conobbe.

I then hired a gondola, and crossed to some of the islands ; to Murano, famous for its glassworks, and to the Isle of Saint George, with its beautiful church, the work of Palladio. Within it lies buried the Doge Ziani, during whose government Pope Alexander the Third took refuge in Venice from the Emperor Barbarossa, who had acknowledged the Antipope, Victor IV. Alexander, during his residence here, bestowed upon Venice the dominion of the sea in the following words, addressed to Ziani: giving him a ring, he said, "Receive this, O Ziani, with which thou and thy successors must annually espouse the sea, in order that posterity may know that the empire of the sea, acquired by thee of old and by right of war, is thine, and that the waters are subject to thy power as a wife to her husband."

Upon the peace which was made between the Pope and the Emperor, a splendid ceremony took place at Venice, which was represented in a painting and hung up in the Papal Palace at Rome. Urban the Eighth removed it, upon some pique against the Venetians; but it was replaced by Innocent the Tenth, which gave rise to the following remark, "Quod Urbanus inurbane deleverat, Innocentius innocente restituit."

Upon my return from the Island, I saw upon the quay an unfortunate young man exposed upon the *carcan ;* and upon his breast was attached a label containing his sentence, which was *Al prigione solitario per la vita.* Dreadful fate ! he was taking his last look of the bright sun and skies which were around him,—a sort of conscious death, such as a man that should be buried alive might undergo as the earth rattled fast upon his straining eye-balls.

There are many objects which I must omit, all equally interesting ; for I must hasten to mention a singular circumstance which happened to me.   I had been taking my coffee in one of the houses for that purpose, upon the Place Saint Mark, where I was much amused by a party of Venetians who were conversing with great animation.   Among them was a very pretty woman, with lively black eyes and white teeth, and an uncommonly soft sweet voice.   I sipped my Mocha coffee in silence.   It was excellent ; and I recollected the anecdote respecting it, which my friend the Frenchman had told me on the road.   When the news arrived of Buonaparte's death, upon the whisper which arose of his having been poisoned, it was asked how ?—By coffee, was the reply.—Was it the Mocha coffee ?—*Oh non, c'étoit du café Bourbon.*

After I had finished it, I returned to my hotel, and stood upon the steps, which were bathed by the waters of the Grand Canal. The night drew on, and I was looking upon the fast fading palaces, and the distant Rialto, and the gondolas, only discoverable by their little bright lamp, darting and shooting about the canal like winged glow-worms. The gondoliers, as they passed, were singing, as I chose to imagine, some of their favourite Tasso; and I could occasionally hear a guitar tinkling and a shout echoing along, as some of the gondolas were turning sharply round a corner, to warn others of its approach. Presently I saw one of these dark boats move towards the terrace where I stood, and come directly up to it. A man immediately stepped out, and asked me if I were not the English gentleman who had been that afternoon taking my coffee."——But I must conclude my friend's account another time, as my servant has just brought me a letter from England which I am anxious to read.

* * *

* * *

[From the unconnected and illegible papers which form almost all the remaining part of the Journal, it would appear that it must have been about this time that the change in the life and habits of the Journalist, alluded to by the peasant, must have taken place. The letter which he was anxious to read was probably the cause of this, as the following unconnected reflections would seem to indicate.]

It is enough ! I have long deceived myself : I thought I was calm, that I could have heard of this with resignation; but no, no, resignation ! My God, if I could have been spared this last blow !

*　　　　*　　　　*

*　　　　*　　　　*

Forgotten, desolate man, thy hour is come—
thy real happiness was all past long since; and
now that the being who was the idol of thy imagination—the bright star which still seemed to
go before thee, and lead thee on to other hopes,
is taken from thee, now indeed thou canst not
wish to live!

*　　　　*　　　　*

*　　　　*　　　　*

July.—I grow weaker and weaker; my visits
to the hermitage are over; but yet I would fix
my last look upon the sea which flows towards
England, where now　　*　　　　*

*　　　　*　　　　*

I have made my will; they may bury me as
they please, all places here are the same to me.
But I have begged them to lay my Prayer-book
by my side, in which are those features that I
may perhaps see again in heaven, for on earth I

now could not wish to look upon them—smiling upon others.

*　　　　*　　　　*

*　　　　*　　　　*

I saw a little infant to-day that they were burying. There it lay soft and still, as if it were asleep, with its little white fingers clasped over its breast, and its silky lashes gently closed over those eyes that had not yet learned to weep with this world's woe. Innocent, peaceful creature! when the trumpet shall sound, how many would give crowns and sceptres to be as that child! how many would give their earthly kingdoms for its heavenly inheritance!

*　　　　*　　　　*

*　　　　*　　　　*

How mysterious are the ways of Providence! I, that could have lived happily in my own country, am about to die miserably here: strange when I look back upon the past.

*　　　　*　　　　*

The mid-day sun is beating fiercely down,
The Vista's dusty length is glaring white,
The walls are hot in yon sepulchral town,
And the faint peasants pant and wish for night;
But the cool winds, that mingle with the light
Of starry skies, breathe o'er my burning brain
Unfelt and heedless, mocking as in spite,
Like to the Phrygian Chief's consuming pain,
Whose endless thirst was slaked by neither fount nor rain

It is not that the stings of gloomy guilt
Awake the pangs that through my veins do creep;
It is not that some fairy castle built
On sandy shores is swallow'd in the deep;
It is not that the lover's dreamy sleep,
When all but fancy's syren voice is hush'd,
Hath promised smoothly what it will not keep,
And left me like a ruin'd garden crush'd,
Where once the bee rejoiced and Persian roses blush'd!

It is that deep and desolating woe
Which springs from utter hopelessness of fate,
When all that we can ever feel or know
Can only come and counsel us too late,

When we behold the world we cannot hate,
Such as it seems to sober solemn truth,
And think upon our own degraded state,
When we have done, in first and foolish youth,
Some deed that gnaws our hearts with unappeased t

To know that we have never tasted life,
Such as it is to others, and to all
Who dream not of the restless bosom's strife,
And are too cold and feelingless to fall :
Better it were that plume and velvet pall
Had borne our infant bodies to the grave,
Than to be left thus reptile-like to crawl
Amid the flowers and fruits that o'er us wave,
Or as the madman waked in double torment rave.

Come, let me think and ponder o'er the past,
And see how rose this edifice of man,
And try if time will any shadow cast
To aid me in its measurement and span ;
In sooth I little thought, when once I ran
In truant childhood to escape from school,
Mocking at tasks and toil and future ban,
That thus so gravely I should talk of rule,
As erst the dreaded voice from Pedagoguic stool.

I was a wayward, strange, and timid child ;
My very sports were not as other boys' ;
And when the rest in mirth and riot wild
Made the wide playground echo with their noise,
I shrunk from all their ruder games and joys,
And wander'd lonely through the cloister'd aisle,
With some soft book or vision for my toys ;
And oft I'd sit beneath the sacred pile,
And at the jesting tomb in artless wonder smile :

But when the organ's loud tempestuous peal
Swept like the whirlwind through the Gothic choir,
Then I was happy, and could inly feel
The solitary joys those tones inspire ;
For I have worshipp'd music, as the fire
That cheer'd and warm'd my soul, and, when despair
Had left me nought to cling to or desire,
Its perfumed breath hath almost still'd my care,
As the Camelion feeds on thin and filmy air.

But years crept on, and other thoughts arose,
And the first buds of youth began to blow
E'en as the young and tender mossy rose
That knows not of the thorns which round it grow ;

And soon to statelier halls I then did go,
Where the proud boy, disfranchised from his chain,
Is cast a prey to that most deadly foe,
His own free will, and there in lawless reign
He works unto himself long lingering years of pain.

Yet was I not as other youths, who spent
Their precious hours in idleness or vice,
Who every morn to hunting parties went,
And pass'd their nights amid the deadly dice,—
Of first and tempting class I knew the price :
But all my study was a thing of nought,
Aimless and barren as some weak device ;
For I could never read the books I ought,
But only such as pleased my wandering turn of thought.

My heated brain with many a story teem'd
Of wild romance and all their desperate woes,
And the true world a blank and desert seem'd,
While all around my magic castles rose ;
And thus I lived, amid the light that throws
Its rainbow colours o'er the misty plain,
And all its fields in prismy glitter shows,
Till the bright sun, that taught the clouds to feign.
Speeds on to other worlds to smile and cheat again.

Then, I created out of dust and clay
An Idol which embodied all my dreams,
And charm'd it with the warm Promethean ray,
That from the mystic lamp of fancy streams ;
And, as the fond enthusiast madly deems
The statue he hath form'd from lifeless stone
Endued with power to love, so fair it seems,
I worshipp'd in my blindness what alone
Such restless hearts as mine could e'er have form'd or
    known.

But like the weak Sicilian, who did frame
The brazen instrument of tyrant hate,
And perish'd by his own ingenious flame,
Cursing his cunning handy-work too late—
So was I doom'd to feel the burning weight
Of grim repentance, scowling as in scorn,
While on my palsied breast it darkly sate,
E'en as the dreaded night-mare, that is born
Of feverish thoughts and blood, yet melts away by morn.

And then I wander'd forth I cared not where,
For all the world was still the same to me,
Since in the land that gave me being—there
I could not, as my nature prompted, be,

Nor the soft smiles and eyes unmoved see
Of her who knew not of my charmed days :
Like to the wretch, when I would bend the knee,
To Demons sold, who all their bonds do raise
And laugh in fiendish mirth as hopelessly he prays.

But now, the very wish for change is gone ;
The only star that still did bless my eyes
Hath left me with my darkness all alone,
And never, as it rose before, can rise :
For it hath fled its own unspotted skies,
And gone to cheer and shine on other lands,
While my sad heart in dust and ruin lies,
As the cleft arch where Thebes in silence stands,
Rearing her broken halls mid hot Egyptian sands.

And now farewell to all ! to thee farewell,
My distant Country ! though I left thee, still
I loved thee, as these burning tears can tell,
But my stern fate was stronger than my will.
I *did* cling to thy parent bosom, till
Thou wouldst no longer hush my wild alarms,
Nor my hot mouth with syrup moisture fill,
But cast me from thy cold and careless arms,
As the young Mother Bride that fears to taint her charms.

I could have wish'd that this decaying flesh
Had slept beneath *that* village church-yard ground,
Where I beheld *that* vision sweet and fresh
Spreading its holy influence around ;
And that its evening bells, with pensive sound,
Had flung their music o'er my quiet grave,
Where I at last a resting-place had found :
But this, as other things, I cannot have—
Of disappointed hopes the ever baffled slave.

And now, my thoughts to other regions turn,
Where the parch'd tongue of grief forgets its thirst,
Where the hot temples cease to throb and burn,
And on the wakening ear Hosannahs burst.
Oh ! that my longing soul could rise, as erst
The Tishbite Prophet in his fiery car ;
Or as the flattering tale of him the first
Imperial Cæsar, mount my chariot star,
Speed through the Milky Way, and dwell where Spirits are

But I have finish'd : all my race is run ;
I feel my heart beat feebler, and the voice
Of coming Death its sighing hath begun,
As the soft breeze that bids the night rejoice :

For between sleep and pain is now my choice.
And thus my wilful course is told, and I
Have shewn in song of unblest deeds the price,
E'en as the pining swan, that ere he die
Pours out his latest breath in funeral melody."

THE END.

LONDON:
PRINTED BY S. AND R. BENTLEY, DORSET STREET.

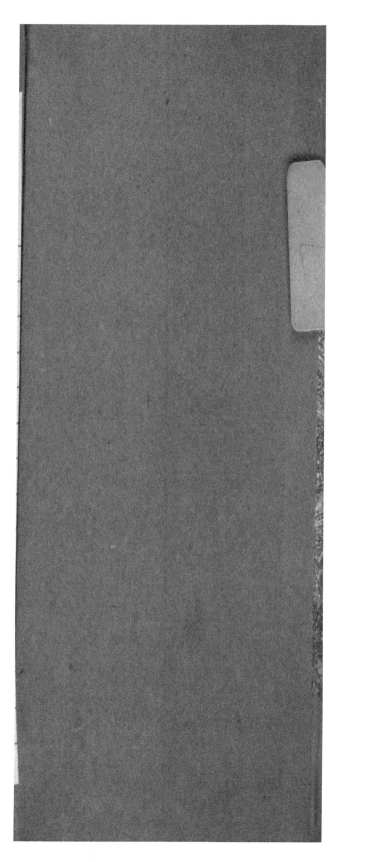

Check Out More Titles From HardPress Classics Series In this collection we are offering thousands of classic and hard to find books. This series spans a vast array of subjects – so you are bound to find something of interest to enjoy reading and learning about.

Subjects:
Architecture
Art
Biography & Autobiography
Body, Mind &Spirit
Children & Young Adult
Dramas
Education
Fiction
History
Language Arts & Disciplines
Law
Literary Collections
Music
Poetry
Psychology
Science
…and many more.

Visit us at www.hardpress.net

Im The Story
personalised classic books

JANE IN WONDERLAND

LEWIS CARROLL

"Beautiful gift.. lovely finish.
My Niece loves it, so precious!"

Helen R Brumfieldon

★★★★★

UNIQUE GIFT

FOR KIDS, PARTNERS
AND FRIENDS

Timeless books such as:

Kids

Alice in Wonderland · The Jungle Book · The Wonderful Wizard of Oz
Peter and Wendy · Robin Hood · The Prince and The Pauper
The Railway Children · Treasure Island · A Christmas Carol

Adults

Romeo and Juliet · Dracula

Highly Customizable

Change Books Title

Replace Characters Names with yours

Upload Photo (for inside page)

Add Inscriptions

Visit
Im The Story .com
and order yours today!

CPSIA information can be obtained
at www.ICGtesting.com
Printed in the USA
BVHW082203110819
555624BV00019B/2790/P